THE SAME WIFE
IN EVERY PORT

The Same Wife
In Every Port

by

SUZANNE KYRLE-POPE

Suzanne Kyrle Pope

The Memoir Club

First published in 1998 by
The Memoir Club
The Old School
New Road
Crook Town
Durham

British Library Cataloguing in
Publication Data.
A catalogue record for this book
is available from the
British Library.

ISBN: 1 84104 002 9

Typeset by George Wishart & Associates, Whitley Bay.
Printed by Bookcraft (Bath) Ltd.

For Michael

Contents

Childhood and school years; paternal oppression. An admiral's
daughter in pre-war Malta. Meeting Michael Kyrle-Pope –
eventual 2nd husband. Marriage at 19 to John Parlby in 2nd
Battalion, the Devonshire regiment. Parents return to UK.

Italy comes into the War. Hostilities start in Malta; 2nd Devons
dispersed round coast of island on Garrison duty; wives ordered
into Barracks; permitted to move out during ineffective Italian
bombing; husbands get 24 hrs weekly leave. Living alone in
Valletta Hotel. Working in Military Intelligence as cipher officer.
Hotel hit by German parachute mine; buried in rubble; Sappers
retrieve trousseau from 2nd floor bedroom still standing. Rent flat
outside Valletta. Marmalade for 10th submarine flotilla. Escape on
motor-bike from machine-gunning. Bombed 2nd time.
Evacuation by Wellington bomber to Egypt; unexpected arrival in
desert and ensuing chaos at Army HQ. Home in troop ship.
England in wartime; cool family reception.

Naval intelligence work in Oxford – preparation for Normandy
Landings. 2nd Battalion Devons return to UK from Sicily and
Italy to train for Overlord. Husband wounded in Normandy.
Birth of daughter, Virginia. Father appointed C-in-C Portsmouth.
Return of Michael Kyrle-Pope from POW camp; final breakdown
of marriage; consequent excommunication from family and
enforced separation from Virginia; divorce. On my own working
as nanny and cook.

Chinese cookery in Chinatown. Hospital visiting with impounded cigarettes from Customs for sailors. Accompanying drug squad on opium raid. Holiday in Malacca. Second trip to Hong Kong; ferry to Macau – playing Fantan in Casino. Return to UK; James's accident on troopship and consequent deafness.

List of Illustrations

Acknowledgements

'You'd better write a book,' Doctor Winn Everett had been saying for years, and I am indebted to her for suggesting it, and for her continued support; alas, she is no longer here to see the result.

Gilbert Wheat, Frank and Beryl Jackson, Bryan Smalley and Tom Vincent have added their encouragement; David Mills has endured without complaint frequent visits to his office for the use of his photocopier.

John King has given invaluable help with the illustrations by transferring prints on to negatives for reproduction, and vice versa. Judy Ryan has hunted through archives in *The Times of Malta* offices to find the photograph of the bombing in the Second World War siege. This photograph had miraculously survived the fire in *The Times* office in 1979; I am grateful to Mr Agius for his permission to use it.

Freddie de Butts has helped immeasurably with the text and the spelling of Arab place-names, as well as ensuring that I learned all I could from his recent publishing experience, and I must thank Ann Hibbert for allowing me to include her poem 'A Summing-Up', as well as George Staempfli for permitting the inclusion of his cartoon. I am most grateful to Jim Davey of MENAS for providing the outline map of the Arabian Gulf.

To all the above I give warm thanks, but especially to Amanda Robinson, who typed out the whole text on to her computer in the evenings, once she had put her babies to bed; sadly she lost the lot when a virus attacked her machine and gobbled up everything in its memory. She dared not begin all over again, out of consideration for her long-suffering husband, so Sarah Forde took over.

I cannot thank Sarah enough for all she has done, and for the fun it has been to work with her.

When Reg Hibbert agreed he would very kindly write a foreword, I had no idea he would write so generously, and I thank him very sincerely for his support and recommendation of my book.

To my editors, Anthony Phillips, and especially Andrew Clark, who have given their time with amazing forbearance and patience, I am extremely grateful; as the publication process progressed, it all became more and more exciting, and I have enjoyed the fun of working with them enormously.

My family has maintained constant encouragement, particularly Emma, who has rescued the bits I have tripped over on my word-processor, and has given advice and much of her time to reading and editing the first draft.

Lastly, not least but most, I thank my husband Michael, for putting up with me during this long literary pregnancy; for all his help with dates and political detail; for his patience and enduring encourage-ment; without him I could not have written the book. Indeed, without him, there would have been no book to write.

S.K-P.

Author's Note

Whilst the descriptions of events, incidents and characters are correct and accurate the reader may appreciate that time has the unfortunate effect of distorting the memory somewhat.

I would like to ask the reader to accept that, on occasions, a degree of dramatic licence has been used in order to emphasise points or enhance the flow of the narrative. Nevertheless, in all fundamental aspects, this remains a true and essentially personal memoir.

Foreword
by Sir Reginald Hibbert, GCMG

Accounts of other people's lives are always fascinating, provided they are frank enough and written with zest. Sue Kyrle-Pope evokes a vanished past in a characteristically lively way. The world she describes has disappeared. Britain no longer has military bases supporting active fleets and armies and air forces in every continent and ocean. British representatives and commanders no longer carry imperial, nor even power-backed, authority into remote countries. My own profession, the British Diplomatic Service, still extends world-wide, in fact in many more posts than in the past; but its voice is much diminished. Sue Kyrle-Pope's way of life is a nostalgic memory for members of my, the wartime, generation. It must seem a fantasy to those born after the war, unless they happen to have been children of families in service overseas in the 50s and 60s. The back-packers, businessmen and mass tourists who are Britain's present-day travellers abroad start from a wholly different viewpoint and have a totally different experience.

Life abroad in the armed services and the foreign, commonwealth and colonial services has always been good for the men, difficult for their wives and unsettling for their children. Women with the spirit and style of Sue Kyrle-Pope approached it with verve and turned it into a coruscating experience. Underneath the bright surface, however, there was the hard work of frequent moves, separation, settling in, constant adjustment to new personalities above and below, the juggling of household accounts to fit the concertina effects of exchange rate fluctuations, inflation and budget cuts, and above all the inexorable demand for long-range staff-work to cope with the swiftly changing needs and moves of distant (or near) children and ageing relatives. Sue Kyrle-Pope's lucid style makes it possible to glimpse the rocky bottom of the stream through the sunny reflections at the top of the current.

Before the war, at school or university, it was common for men to think of careers overseas in the various services of the Crown – the armed services, the Colonial service, the Indian Civil Service, the Burma service, the Malayan service, the Consular services in China and Japan, the Diplomatic Service and service in the old Dominions and eventually in the new Commonwealth. Most women did not have careers in those days. They married their men before postings or during leaves, almost as in wartime, although not quite so hurriedly. They followed their husbands abroad to whatever destinations the great departments of state decreed, and there they put together a British way of life with exotic adaptations, sometimes crabbed and uncomfortable, sometimes luxurious by UK standards, but always with a window opened wide on world affairs and never with an inward-looking, insular attitude. Sue Kyrle-Pope gives the flavour of all of this. The young men of more recent times, for whom careers in the City or the media or academia have seemed the natural choice, will have to turn to books such as this to know what life was like, every now and then, to discover the pearl. The young women whom they marry, who now have their own careers, will probably find it difficult to believe that either the brilliance or the hardships of imperial life were real. They should read this book.

The Royal Navy was the foundation element of Britain's power in the world. By the very nature of naval service, with men absent for long periods on ships at sea, it confronted the wives and families of its officers, petty officers and ratings with the problems of overseas service in concentrated form. Naval bases formed tightly organised, even enclosed, societies, where long-established habits of mutual help and support bred strong and worldly-wise characters. It was always a pleasure for someone like myself, coming from the less tightly disciplined, looser, more individual background of the Diplomatic Service, to be invited into their circle. It was a salutary reminder of the importance of being British. It was also a lesson in restraint as well as power. The Navy viewed events from offshore and was therefore less interventionist in small matters than the other armed services sometimes felt obliged to be. It was also a pleasure when naval officers and their wives and families broke out of their own circle and joined us in the chequered society outside.

Sue Kyrle-Pope had a great capacity for breaking out, as these pages show. She brought enjoyment with her, and she has distilled much of it here.

I had the happy experience of being a close colleague of Michael

Kyrle-Pope at Singapore on the staff of the Commander-in-Chief, Far East and South-east Asia, in the final years of Britain's military presence there. My job, like his, took me all over the Far East and South-east Asia and Australasia and on occasion far into the Pacific. It was the usual case of the men having the best of things while our wives had to spend more time at base. Our wives made occasional excursions with us, but on the whole they became more closely acquainted with Singapore and Malaysia. Sue Kyrle-Pope made up in intensity there for the advantages which we, the men, had in our more extensive wanderings. For me, she has illuminated my memories of Singapore in unexpected ways, and she has drawn pictures of places and people in the Middle East which are entirely new to me and very enjoyably vivid. They will give pleasure to old hands and young blood alike.

Sue Kyrle-Pope followed her husband's career, endured it and enjoyed it, and lets us follow it and her through its high points, its routine and its vicissitudes. She makes those years come alive for us. That is a generous and precious act for those of us who shared them and an entertaining memorial for younger people who want to know, and ought to know, what we did during and after the war. I am grateful for the invitation to me, a non-naval person, to write these few words of introduction and commendation. Like the book, it has given me great pleasure.

CHAPTER 1

1920s and 1930s

I WAS SUPPOSED TO have been a boy. I was to be called Timothy, and my future was mapped out even to the exact date that I would be entered for Dartmouth, and a naval career in my father's footsteps.

When a third daughter arrived, eight years after the family had been considered complete, my father, I think, lost all interest and, on being asked by my mother what name he would suggest I was called, he is reputed to have replied:

'Call her what you like!'

My initial failing to come up to expectations must have been a disappointment to my mother as well, but she never let me see that, and in fact my elder sisters have always told me how much she spoilt me in my early childhood. However, she too was at a loss to decide on a name for me, and casting wildly about, she lit on the Wimbledon women's singles champion of the previous year, and I was christened Suzanne, after Suzanne Lenglen. We were not even a tennis-playing family to any great extent, although my father had aspirations in that direction in later years, nor had we any particular interest in any other sport. Poor Mother, she must have been pretty desperate.

My elder sister, Winifred, senior to me by eleven years, has recently told me that I was a 'celebration baby'.

'Celebrating what?' I asked.

'Father's promotion to captain. The night he was told of it, he and Mother had a celebration dinner, and you were the unexpected result!'

In those years just after the First World War, the Navy was being drastically cut back, and there was not only the 'Geddes Axe' to fear, that is involuntary retirement with little, if any warning, under a policy introduced by Lord Geddes, a politician appointed by the government to review and reduce the size of the armed forces, but also the threat of half-pay for those naval officers lucky enough to be retained in the service but awaiting a new appointment, or even for some of those holding certain forms of appointment. This could be very worrying indeed for men with wives and families, possibly with children being privately educated, which most of us were in those days, when state schools were of a low academic standard, and in any case when school age ended at fourteen. My father was extremely fortunate that he was never put on half-pay, and that he escaped the Geddes Axe.

Both my grandfathers were solicitors. My mother's father, Frederick Langley, headed the family firm in Wolverhampton, where I was born in 1921; my paternal grandfather was in the Layton family firm in Liverpool until he died when my father was a young boy. Father, born in 1884, was one of nine children; he ran away to sea at the age of eleven or twelve, but was brought home to his matriarchal mother, who said:

'If you want to go to sea, why didn't you say so? Now you had better do it properly and join the Royal Navy!' and she arranged for him to join HMS *Britannia* officers' training ship.

The Laytons and Langleys were distantly connected, and my mother used to be regularly invited to go to stay with the Laytons in Liverpool. My father courted her assiduously whenever he was home on leave; Geoffrey Layton was adored by his mother, brothers and sisters, but my mother, Eleanor Langley, found him 'noisy and bumptious', and fended him off for two years. They were married in 1908, soon after Father had volunteered to serve in submarines.

Submarines were in the early stages of development, and it was never certain that, once submerged, a boat would successfully surface again. A strong bond grew between all who served in the submarine service, officers and men alike, which pertains to this day.

My father commanded several boats during the First World War, including *E13*, which ran aground in Danish neutral waters in the entrance to the Baltic in 1915; she was torpedoed and fired on by a German destroyer, which entered neutral waters to make the attack. This was one of the first German atrocities contravening International Law, and the resulting shock and horror reverberated world-wide. My father and the other survivors were interned in Copenhagen, and a few weeks later my father successfully escaped and got back to England.

His upwardly mobile career continued through the 1920s and 30s, and in 1940, as Vice-Admiral, he was appointed C-in-C China Station, based in Singapore. Mother accompanied him, but he sent her home shortly before Singapore fell; he had predicted this, but was not listened to in London. However, when proved right, he was asked to

The author's mother – Eleanor Layton in 1962.

go to Ceylon as Governor and C-in-C, to prepare that island for the next expected Japanese assault.

His last appointment in the Navy was as Admiral and C-in-C Portsmouth in 1945, from which he retired in 1947.

Discipline was strict in our family. Instant obedience was demanded: 'At the double!' my father would shout, when I was instructed to go and fetch something for him. No questioning was expected, no explanations given as to why things must be done immediately, if at all, and I was a compliant and probably rather a dull child, who accepted the regime as a secure milieu from which I never had the thought of venturing.

It was a happy and uneventful childhood. Only later in life when I had children of my own did I realise what I had missed. Money was very short; my father had only his naval pay to support the family and educate us three girls, and my mother had no income until her father, a country solicitor, died in 1926, leaving her a few hundred pounds.

We lived in Alverstoke, then a sprawling village on the shore of the Solent, largely inhabited by naval families whose men were in ships or shore establishments in the Portsmouth and Gosport area. There were therefore plenty of children of all ages, who mixed and formed groups according to their friendships and interests. My parents never took us away on holidays, for we lived within two miles of the beach, so we had no need to be taken to the sea-side, and it would have cost too much to go away for a country holiday. No-one in our circles dreamed of holidays abroad, and when the ships were sent overseas, for periods of up to two and a half years, there were no fares or facilities provided for wives and families to follow. Separations were long and harsh, although I was rather glad that Father was away so much, for to me he was a frightening parent, for whom I could do nothing right.

We were not taken to a circus or pantomime throughout our early years, nor even to a visiting fair; we had no Christmas trees, nor birthday parties, all of which we tacitly understood to be beyond the limit of the family budget. I used to have friends to tea occasionally, but seldom was invited to their parties, presumably because their parents knew no return invitation would be forthcoming. It is true to say that what you've never had you don't miss, and during those years it never entered my head to resent or even notice what I was missing.

On the other hand, as a naval daughter, I was always invited to the wonderful annual Christmas and summer parties at each of the naval establishments. HMS *Vernon* (the Torpedo School) held the best and most exciting ones, where the naval ratings dressed up as fearsome pirates, and there was a terrifying Pirate's Cave to negotiate, and a gruesome Ghost Train to travel on, as well as the usual 30ft high chutes, down which one shot on doormats to avoid having one's knickers scorched on the precipitous slide; there were as well other thrilling entertainments of the fairground type: marvellous! HMS *Dolphin* (Submarine Base), the RN Barracks, HMS *Excellent* at Whale Island (the Gunnery School) were others that gave memorable parties, longed for throughout the year, a great deal of the fun being in crossing the harbour in ship's boats and tenders to reach each establishment, and the wonder of returning after dark, with the lights of ships and shore reflected in the harbour.

I must have been about four years old when Father acquired an Airedale which was called Conquest, after the ship he then commanded; it was a huge dog, called Conk for short. One summer afternoon we were all in the garden, Father beavering away in the vegetable garden at the end of the lawn (he kept us entirely self-supporting in all vegetables and summer soft and tree fruit). It was too hot to have tea outside, so it was laid in the nursery, which opened on to the garden. I was sent in to wash my hands for tea, and I noticed a large dish with half a pound of butter on it on the table near the crusty loaf. I loved butter, and the temptation was too much, so curving my fingers, I scooped up a fat palm-full as I passed, and ran to the cloakroom, locked myself in, and sat on the lavatory while I licked off the butter in great slurps . . . Oh Bliss! In due course the family (and I) moved in to tea.

'Good Heavens!' exclaimed Mother, 'Whatever has been at the butter?' Other cries of surprise and dismay followed; eventually, and quite coolly, without a blush, I said:

'It must have been Conk; look, you can see his paw and claw marks,' (which about matched my own in size). To my amazement this suggestion was accepted, and poor Conk was severely chastised, while I got away with it, without even a moment's queasiness to punish me for my greed!

Mother kept a cook, and a house-parlourmaid in those days. The cook was paid £40 a year, the maid £25. They lived in, of course, sharing a bedroom, and were given their uniforms: the maid wore a striped cotton dress and white starched cap and apron in the mornings, and a black dress with a fetching diminutive frilly white organdie cap and apron in the afternoons. It didn't much matter what the cook wore, as no-one ever saw her. I was never allowed in the kitchen in case I disturbed her concentration, but occasionally I'd be given the delicious hard crescent of sugar from the segments of crystallised citrus peel when a fruit cake was being made; these were handed to me through the kitchen window, whither I'd be summoned by a low call while I played in the garden in the morning. There was no pre-chopped mixed peel sold in plastic jars in those days, dry and flavourless as it is today.

In 1926, when I was five, my father was appointed to the Admiralty for two years, so our house in Alverstoke was let to another naval family. Alverstoke had a constantly moving population, as most naval appointments were for a two-year duration. We moved to Epsom, from where Father commuted each day to London. We rented a double-fronted bay-windowed Victorian house with a large garden, in which there was a grass tennis-court, and I suppose it was from this time that Father began to take up tennis, and expected his family to do so as well. Mother developed a low, fast under-arm serve, which was lethal, and earned many envious cries of:

'Well served!' from her mortified opponents, and:

'Oh Bad LUCK, Partner!'

I was lucky to be too young to take part in these family battles, which often became rather acrimonious. (Father hated to lose!)

I began school at Epsom, going to a dame school called the Orchard School, where I was given a good grounding in the three R's by Miss Winifred, one of the two sisters who ran the school. She was plain and thin, with a sweet smile of infinite patience, and wore, term in, term out, a green skirt and long grey cardigan, both drooping at different levels in sad loops and waves. I loved her dearly, and also loved the rows of pot-hooks and hangers I traced for her in my copy-book, and the elementary sums she set. I was fetched home for lunch, and after my hour's rest on my bed (no books allowed) I was taken out for a walk by a horrid woman who came in the afternoons to look after me, give me tea in the nursery (the others had it in the drawing room), and put me to bed. She was vindictive and sly, and would pinch and bully me, but her reign did not last long, mercifully, as my father started to flirt with her (she was very pretty), so she was dismissed, not a day too soon for my liking, and a dear, kind woman called Daisy took her place.

Daisy taught me to ride my first fairy cycle, and we would make toast by the nursery gas-fire for tea, eating it with dripping running down our chins.

On winter afternoons the muffin-man would pass our house, ringing his bell, and I might be sent out to stop him and buy some crumpets for tea, which cost four a penny. He would wear a long white coat and a flat white cap, and on his head he'd carry a huge board piled high with muffins and crumpets under a white cloth. He'd ring his bell with one hand, and steady the board with the other. One day I was sent out with 6d. to get some crumpets, and when I returned with twenty-four crumpets and no change, my mother was horrified, and my sister Diana was sent off to return sixteen crumpets and reclaim 4d. change.

The street lights were gas in those days, and at dusk the lamp-lighter would come by on his bicycle, with his long pole to open the little glass door in the lantern and light the three glass mantles inside. I used to think they were large white glass grapes, and he a magician to transform them into luscious fruit.

Mother was a very economical housewife, and nothing was ever wasted. Each morning she would don her apron, made from old curtains, and visit the cook in the kitchen, to survey the previous day's left-overs in the larder, and decide how best to use them up, and to plan the day's menus. She would then go to her store-cupboard, which was always kept firmly locked, and take out any pots of jam or bottled fruit or other provisions needed. She would not ever allow a bought cake in the house, nor commercially made marmalade or jam. Everything that could be was home-made, and she annually 'put down' dozens of eggs pickled in isinglass, which were saved during the spring glut and used when eggs became expensive in the cold months.

As many of our clothes as possible were also home-made, and I suffered from being the third daughter. Presumably Winifred, as the eldest, had new ones, but dresses and especially jerseys had become faded, worn and felted by the time I inherited them. However, Mother's sister, our Aunt Olive, had married well, and she had an only daughter, Josephine, who was two years older than me; occasionally a parcel would arrive with a pretty party-dress in it for me, but sadly there were few opportunities for wearing them, for at the naval parties

I attended, much sturdier wear was necessary than silks and muslins, to withstand slides and roundabouts and climbing in and out of ship's boats.

Winifred went off to Paris to be 'finished' and Diana, who was seven years older than me, was at boarding-school. I have no recollection of either of them at that time, nor of having any friends of my own at Epsom.

During the school holidays I played in the garden all morning, being called in for 'elevenses' of milk and a biscuit. Being a solitary child I invented many games, and spent hours making miniature doll's gardens, with trellis hedges of twigs, and rows of cabbages with the smallest chrysanthemum buds I could find. I found this a curiously fulfilling occupation, and would lie in bed before falling asleep, planning tomorrow's garden.

Father always had a boiled egg before whatever was the daily cooked breakfast dish, and I would be given the top of it, lifted off with his spoon; I remember being rather put out when Diana came home from boarding-school for the holidays and reclaimed her previous right to be given it on alternate days. We were all going up to Suffolk for Easter one year, driving in the new, and first, family car, a smart entirely square red Vauxhall. There were boiled eggs for breakfast before the journey (which was expected to take six hours or so); the yolk of my egg looked funny to me, being a glorious technicolor blend of green, blue and yellow. We children were never allowed to complain about our food, and had to eat up what was on our plates, and leave them clean, so I ate up my egg, in spite of its peculiar smell and unpleasant taste. Disaster struck about an hour into the journey, when I was violently sick. Diana and I were sitting in the back of the car, and she was wearing her fur gauntlet gloves which she had been given for Christmas.

'Drat the child!' cried Father, crashing the gears while trying to draw into the side of the road, 'Catch it in your hands, Diana, don't let her mess up the car seats!'. . . end of poor Diana's gloves, and the rug over our knees (no heating in cars in those early motoring days), and my teddy-bear did not escape either. The drive that followed was not a pleasant one, and Father's temper did nothing to relieve it. He had only just learnt to drive, with a few rudimentary lessons from friends; there were no synchro-mesh gears in those days, and if he could not engage the gear he wanted, he crashed and ground until he succeeded.

His greatest dread was being stopped on the High Street in Guildford, which was then the main Portsmouth – London road, and having to start again on the extremely steep gradient. We all came to dread driving through Guildford on this account.

I had a strong aversion to rice pudding, and was usually given a small helping, but was then expected to eat that up. One weekend Father gave me more than I thought fair, so I said so, greatly daring, and he replied:

'Eat what you can, and rub the rest in your face!' which was his idea of humour. He was in a good mood that day, so I did exactly what he had told me, to the horror of Mother and my sisters, who waited in consternation for the expected explosion, but all he did was roar with laughter, and I was led away to have my face washed, rather surprised at my own nerve, and that I had got away with it.

My pocket-money in the 1920s was a penny a week, which could buy quite a lot. Transfer-painted tin toys from Germany cost a penny, pencils two or four a penny, a packet of four coloured chalks a penny, and you could buy a roll of liquorice bootlace half an inch wide with a coloured gob-stopper in the middle, which changed colour as you sucked it, necessitating its frequent inspection during consumption, for two a penny. Many other strips of toffee or nougat, sticks of barley-sugar, triangular bags of sherbet with a liquorice 'straw' were each only four a penny. Father would encourage me to supplement my income by earning a penny a hundred for slugs which I would catch and put into a jam-jar of salt water. I didn't fancy this little money-earner though, as I had to pick up the slugs in my fingers. Father never checked the number that I told him I had caught, but I would not have had the courage to cheat!

When we returned to Alverstoke from Epsom, I was sent to Holt Corner School, all day now, and I walked the one and a half miles there and back unescorted, rather dreading having to pass the state school in Anglesey Road each morning, when rough boys in the playground would sometimes pelt me with stones: I suppose I was fair game, and I never thought of throwing any back. Family photographs showed me as being small for my age, fair, with curly hair and a pink and white complexion, all to change sadly, as I progressed through a mousy and podgy adolescence.

I learned nothing at Holt Corner. I remember being scared stiff of the mistresses there, who obviously saw nothing promising in me, and few brains. My end of term exam marks were never more than 20 per cent in any subject, and once I even achieved 6 per cent in scripture, and 0 per cent in history. When my school reports arrived my father would rant and rave, how I dreaded those days! I was threatened with being sent away to a convent school, which was made to sound like a fate worse than death, but where I think now I might have been happy, and would certainly have learned something. As my lack of progress became more and more abysmal, the threat of being sent to the state school down the road loomed over me, and this really did scare me. I simply did not understand the page after page we were made to read aloud in class, it presumably being assumed we absorbed the printed words like sponges; questions were discouraged, we just droned on and on, one page at a time being read by each girl in turn through each half-hour period. The only thing I was any good at was spelling and dictation.

There were few books for children produced then, and very few of what there were could be found in our house. Reading was not encouraged by our parents, who read little themselves. I never read a newspaper until I grew up. *The Times* remained by Father's chair, and the *Daily Mail* by Mother's. Current affairs were not discussed with us three daughters, and there was no wireless in the house until the early 30s. I used to hide a story book and a torch under my mattress so as to read during my afternoon rest, and after I had my light turned out at night, but if I was caught I was smacked on my bottom, which was administered in an almost ritualistic way, with me being made to pull my knickers down and bend over, standing with my feet apart; it had the effect of causing me to urinate involuntarily, so Mother soon learned to put a pot on the floor between my legs to save the carpet!

In the spring each year Mother would organise a family primrosing picnic. A day would be chosen when Father would be at home, and sandwiches and thermoses prepared. Mother had had made a special bicycle basket, deep and wide, tall enough to conceal Father's quart bottle of beer, with which she was ashamed of being seen. We would set off on our bicycles, Father leading on his heavy black machine, the others strung out behind him, and me pedalling furiously on my fairy-cycle along the pavement. We would always go to Swanwick, six miles away, where in those days there were woods carpeted with primroses, wood anemones and violets. One of us would take a ball of wool in our basket, and we would return after tea with bunches swinging from our handle-bars. They were happy occasions, which we all looked forward to, and enjoyed each year.

It was decided that my tonsils should be removed. My afternoon 'minder', Miss Gregory, whom I called 'Gregs', took me on foot to a small private nursing home about a mile from our house after tea one March day. A motherly bustling woman called Mrs Heather owned and ran the home; she must have been a trained nurse for she wore a huge enveloping white nurse's veil above her starched dress and apron. I was put into a pleasant light single room by myself, and as far as I remember, slept like a top. The next morning two men in white coats, caps and masks came in, one of them holding a tray and a black rubber mask and pad, which without warning or explanation, was held over my mouth and nose. As I kicked and struggled and screamed for Mother, I was told to be quiet and breathe deeply. I yelled and fought, but was eventually forcibly held down by the second man until I lost consciousness and knew no more until I woke up after the operation. I have never forgotten the nightmare of that terrible panic, and often relive the terror of it in my dreams even now. I have had to undergo surgery many times in my life, but I always tell the anaesthetist this story, and make him swear not to put a mask over my face until the initial injection has rendered me unconscious.

My parents were regular churchgoers, and I was quite young when I was first included in the family party, walking to church on Sundays to attend the 11.00 am Matins service. Our church in Alverstoke was St Mary's, which always attracted a congregation of one to two hundred for Matins; there were also services of Holy Communion at 7.00 am and 8.00 am, and a children's service at 3.00 pm and Evensong (sung) at 6.00 pm. The family attended what was known as Early Service at 8.00 am, once monthly.

Our family pew was at the back of the big church, facing directly on to the north to south aisle, and so all the congregation had to pass immediately in front of our pew, before turning right into the main aisle to reach their places. This was very satisfactory for us all, and many assignations were arranged, invitations given, and probably gossip exchanged, as friends stopped for a whispered conversation with either of my parents. My sisters, too, enjoyed seeing the world pass by, and indulging in some whispered comments regarding friends' new hats, etc. midst suppressed giggles, and I also would smile at my friends among the younger members of attending families, greatly envying those little girls who had wreaths of flowers round their summer Sunday hats. Diana used to take me out before the sermon, the duration of which it was thought would be too testing for either me or my bladder. She would see me across the road, from where I was considered sensible enough to walk home alone.

In early 1931 my father was appointed Chief-of-Staff to the Commander-in-Chief China Station, so he departed to travel by P&O liner out to Hong Kong. There was no air transport then, and all service personnel were sent to foreign postings by sea, usually in P&O or British India line ships. The voyage to Hong Kong took between four and five weeks, with calls at Port Said, Aden, Bombay, Colombo, Penang and Singapore.

My parents had been saving hard to enable Mother, Winifred and Diana to follow Father to Hong Kong in January 1932. Children over the age of seven did not accompany their parents to foreign postings, for there were no schools available, and the hot climates were considered unsuitable for them. Mother therefore had to make arrangements to leave me behind, and looked for a boarding school and a guardian to look after me in the holidays.

Before I was born, the family had lived for a time in Elstree, and there Mother had become close friends with the Everett family, who now offered to act *in loco parentis*. Sir Percy, a publisher, was Deputy Chief of the Boy Scout movement, under Sir Robert Baden-Powell, and Lady Everett was one of the first Girl Guiders, and was the Hertfordshire County Commissioner when I went to make my home with them. Their daughter, Winn, had been one of the early women doctors to qualify, and she had her own practice as GP in Elstree, and was already much loved and respected there.

One cold January day we went by train up to Elstree, where the family stayed overnight before embarking in their ship at Tilbury the next day, leaving me with the Everetts. The next morning there was a thick fog, one of the old London pea-soupers. A taxi came to pick up Mother and my two sisters, and Lady Everett (whom I had been instructed to call Aunt Rita), Winn and I waved them off into the

The author's father – Admiral Sir Geoffrey Layton KCMG, KCB, DSO, when he was Commander-in-Chief at Portsmouth, 1945-47.

murk. I was ten years old, and I remember that day well; I knew the family were going to China, that it was a very long way away, and that they would not be coming back for a very long time. I was quite convinced that they were abandoning me, and that I would not see them again. I remember feeling sick and utterly hopeless, but Mother had prepared me to wave them good-bye without crying, and I was able to do so dry-eyed.

And so ended my early childhood at home.

Winn was wonderfully kind to me during that period at Elstree, and during the holidays would take me out with her on her rounds. I would read a book in the car while she visited a patient, and we would resume our companionable conversations while driving on to the next.

Aunt Rita was not a cosy or loveable person to a lonely eleven year old. She was an intellectual, of very strong character and opinions, with a razor-sharp wit which could be extremely sarcastic. As I grew older, I appreciated this more and more, and was devoted to her in her later years, particularly enjoying her pithy humour. But those eighteen months were not very happy, although she came to my rescue without hesitation or question, when I sent a desperate SOS during the Easter holidays.

Winifred's current, and most persistent admirer at that time (she always had a string of them) was Bill de Courcey Ireland, a young Royal Marine officer, whose parents lived in Hertfordshire, not far from Elstree. His father was the vicar of Abingdon Piggotts. For some unknown reason they invited me to stay with them in their vicarage over Easter, and I was driven over by Parkins, the Everetts' chauffeur. Bill was abroad, and I had not met his parents before. Mrs de Courcey Ireland greeted me at the door looking exactly like a witch. She was tall and thin, dressed in black from head to foot, which she always wore, and her thin grey hair was drawn tightly back into a small bun. Mr de Courcey Ireland was small and grey, both in physique and in personality: I never heard either of them laugh. There was no-one else there.

On Good Friday we spent most of the day in church on our knees, and when released, we returned to the vicarage, where the atmosphere was gloomy, and the food sparse and bleak.

On Easter Sunday I was made to attend Holy Communion at

8.00 am; Mother had not then told me about the Holy Sacrament and Holy Communion, leaving it until nearer the time when I would be confirmed, so I was totally unprepared for the rite of eating and drinking the body of Jesus. I was horrified and frightened, and thought I was in a house occupied by cannibals. I wrote a postcard to Aunt Rita, and posted it secretly, saying:

'The people here are horrid; please, please come and get me before they eat me too!'

Bless Aunt Rita! She did; so I only spent a week with those well-meaning people, from whom I could not escape quickly enough, instead of the fortnight planned.

Lady Everett had said that I must be sent to a boarding school as near to Elstree as possible, and a few days later she took me over to Abbots Hill, near Hemel Hempstead, a school for about fifty or sixty girls.

The main school building was, and still is, an imposing white stone house, with a green copper dome at one end of the slate roofs. There have been many additions to it since those days, of course. The school stands high in extensive grounds, and looks down across fields and woodland to the valley below. There was a swimming-pool, as well as tennis-courts and lacrosse fields; in the summer term, girls were allowed to hang their own hammocks between any of the trees in the garden, and there was keen competition for the best places.

Abbots Hill did not shine academically, but then it did not need to, for the girls who attended it were from wealthy families and would never have to earn their own livings. Most had ponies at home, and in the season would hunt on two or three days of the week with their parents. It was an expensive school, the fees were £60 per term, but because of my father's naval background, a special concession was made for me, and he only paid £40. I did not know that at the time, but was very conscious of being out of my social milieu; I was the only naval daughter there until Diana James arrived two or three years later, the daughter of Admiral Sir William James, or 'Bubbles' as he was known, after the well-known painting of him as a small boy, by Millais.

Few girls took the School Certificate exam, and fewer passed it, even at the most modest level. I don't think I learned much at Abbots Hill, except how to speak French fairly well. Mademoiselle Eva Delpierre was a very strict mentor, and we were never allowed to speak to her in anything but faultless French; if we made any mistake, however trivial, she would look at us fiercely over her rimless half-glasses, and say:

'*Non, non, Suzanne, je ne vous comprends pas!*' and there one would stand, trying again and again to get the sentence right, until at last she would look up and smile, and say:

'*Aaaah! Maintenant je vous comprends!*'

She was a small woman, with grey, nearly white hair, and a face to match; she would suffer no shoddy or lazy work, and forced the head-mistress to allow every form to have four French lessons each week, even more than maths; at the start of each lesson, we were made to chant:

'A.E.I.O.U; Ba, Be, Bi, Bo, Bu!' and so on through the alphabet, while she walked between the rows of desks, her head inclined to ours, so as to make sure we were using correct pronunciation. Woe betide any girl who had difficulty with her French U's.

'*Non, Non*, Patricia! *Pas SOO! Su! Su! Su! Encore! Vous seule! Cinq fois! Repetez!*' It was daunting, but we learned to speak with marvellous French accents.

As one rose through the school, Mademoiselle became less harsh, and we came to love her. She worked very hard, and I think she ruled not only us, but also the headmistress and teaching staff, all of whom feared her, and many of whom actively disliked her. There was a staff common-room, but Mademoiselle seldom entered it, for she had demanded, and got, a small study of her own, and our hearts would sink when summoned there.

In the dining room there were tables for eight to ten in rows; a mistress would preside at one end, and sometimes one at the other. Mademoiselle's table was always full and no other mistress was permitted to sit at it; at that table we had to speak French all the time. Half-way through each meal, Mademoiselle would call for silence, and then pick a girl at random at the table, and ask her to say what she had been talking about. The subject had to be topical, or of general interest, or we were in trouble!

She produced French plays, and taught us French literature and history; we learned French songs, and the whole school had to sing the *Marsellaise* each Quatorze Juillet. It was a wonderful French education, but I learned little else, except how to introduce a Duke to a Bishop, which I have not found very useful, and how to make a court curtsey.

Nearly all Abbots Hill girls went on to 'do a season' in London, and be presented at court to the reigning monarch. I knew I would not be among them, although I might have been presented, as my sisters had been, but presentations were stopped in 1938 because of the political situation. My 'coming-out' that year was to attend a royal garden-party at Buckingham Palace, at which I wore, with enormous pride, the dress I had made myself while at domestic economy school during the previous year.

It was at Abbots Hill that I first was introduced to classical music. There were two music mistresses. One was a visiting teacher who came two or three days a week from London; she was a Pole, Fräulein Lundquist, who looked not unlike portraits of Beethoven; she had wild frizzy hair, a large fleshy nose, and wide mouth; she was excitable and inclined to lose her temper often with her pupils, whose knuckles she smacked with a ruler when they played a wrong note, but she was a magnificent teacher. She used to ask me to try to persuade my parents to transfer my tuition to her, but her fees were higher than those of the resident teacher, Miss Dewar, and I knew it would be useless to ask. Hetty Dewar was a pretty, fluttering little woman, who blushed very easily, and so was often the butt of much teasing. I had piano lessons with her, and came to love her dearly; she would have gramophone concerts in the school hall after supper sometimes, which anyone could attend, but which were entirely voluntary. She also occasionally took a small group to a London concert, and I was lucky enough to be taken on three occasions, the first to hear Fritz Kreisler play, the second to an orchestral concert conducted by Sir Henry Wood in the Queen's Hall (which was destroyed by bombs during the London blitz a few years later), and the third to hear Yehudi Menuhin at one of his first London appearances as a boy: even then he was magical. Hetty (as we all affectionately called her behind her back), ran the chapel choir, which I enjoyed enormously, belting out the alto parts with great gusto. I have since loved church choral music all my life, but for many years now there have been few opportunities to sing the old canticles and psalms or even the responses in harmony, since the horrible modern innovations of liturgy; what a precious heritage we are in danger of losing forever through the obstinacy and foolishness of today's bishops and clergy.

On Fridays each week Sinclair Logan would come down by train from London to teach singing. The school was divided into seniors and juniors for his classes, which would last ninety minutes. He was totally blind, and yet would stride on foot the two miles from the station at Kings Langley, his pace never slackening, even up the long steep, and very rough school drive. One day he arrived covered with mud, with blood on his hands, and torn trousers.

'Yes,' he replied to anxious enquiries, 'wasn't it stupid of me? I fell into a hole the road menders had made in the pavement, which wasn't railed off! Very silly of me indeed!' But he had no word of blame for the negligent roadmen. His lessons were, for me, pure joy. He sat at the piano on the stage of the school hall, while we sat in rows below him, and from where he sat he could tell exactly who was singing out of tune in whatever row, and in the kindest way would ask them to desist for a moment while the rest were told to repeat a phrase, then he would say:

'Mary, will you sing this note after me?' and when the inharmonious note was repeated, he would add:

'Yes, Mary, that is very good, but can you hear that you are not quite on the note? Try again, and this time, listen to the piano very carefully and try to copy the sound you hear exactly.'

Mr Logan wanted me to go on after school to have my voice trained, which I would have loved to do, but Father said it would only be a waste of money, for I would soon be married anyway, and also it would cost too much. He had said the same when Diana's headmistress wanted her to go on to Oxford.

Sport was important at Abbots Hill, and as I increased in size during my adolescence, I became less and less athletically inclined, and indeed loathed all gym classes and the afternoons on the tennis court and lacrosse field. I was fortunate one autumn term to slip a cartilage in my knee, which excused me from games for six blessed weeks. After that, with a little practice, I learned how to put it out on purpose, and seldom played lacrosse again. It was well worth the pain. However there is one advantage to teenage adipose tissue (as a fifteen-year-old, I weighed 11$\frac{1}{2}$ stone!): it was realised that when I had a goal-keeper's protective pads on, there was little room for the ball to pass between me and the goal posts, so I was co-opted into the school team. And thereafter few opposing teams managed to score a goal, and we won most matches; all I had to do was to stand firmly, legs apart, looking as fierce as I could but with my eyes shut in terror, while the enemy, with fiendish expressions of determination, bore down on me, lax stick raised, to shoot the ball with a sickening thud into some mercifully well-padded part of my anatomy.

The only sport at which I was any good was swimming. I suppose that being more or less seal-shaped was a help. During my final year I even reached the school championship finals, and had to battle it out against my great friend, Patricia Smith, who had much the same physique as me. I don't think we minded which of us won. We had so much in common, including a similar sense of humour, and I remember those years after she came to Abbots Hill with enormous pleasure. In the event she won, and with all our contemporaries I was delighted.

My parents and sisters had returned from China in 1933, and a year later Father was appointed Commodore, Royal Naval Barracks, Portsmouth, a post which carried with it an official residence, so we left Alverstoke again and moved to Anchor Gate House in Portsmouth dockyard. It had a garden with two grass tennis-courts, which ensured many summer afternoons of misery for me during the next two years.

Winifred was by now being courted by Ian Riches, a Royal Marine Captain, whom she married at Eastney Barracks church in 1936. Diana and I were among the bridesmaids, she looking svelte and elegant in the apricot crepe dresses we wore, I bulging out of mine, and tripping often over my long skirt, which in the end I hoisted up to knee level with one hand, my enormous bouquet of roses clutched in the other, a very solid teenager, no benefit to any wedding photograph, but enjoying every minute of the day. The story is told of how, that evening, at the party for the best man, bridesmaids and ushers, in a sudden lull in conversation I said, in all innocence:

'I wonder what Ian and Winifred are doing now?'

I was amazingly innocent and ignorant, and had no knowledge whatever of the facts of life. Even on the night of my own marriage, I had no idea what to expect nor even what a man looked like with no clothes on. But that is still several years ahead.

While Father was at Portsmouth, he arranged for me to go to the naval PT School swimming-baths in Pitt Street each morning of the holidays, for swimming, diving and life-saving lessons after naval classes finished at noon. My instructors were a Royal Marine Captain, Philip Penfold, and a Commander, Mark Eveleigh; both were 'springers', i.e.

Physical Training instructors, who must have given up some of their pre-prandial leisure to teach me. Of course I fell in love with both of them, regardless of our age difference, which must have been ten or twelve years. They were unfailingly kind and patient with me, and we had a lot of horse-play and fun. I learned a lot from them, and eventually won my bronze national life-saving certificate.

One morning the C-in-C Portsmouth visited the baths during my lesson. He was Admiral Sir Joe Kelly (brother of Howard, whose chief-of-staff Father had been in China; the two brothers were not on speaking terms); the C-in-C saw me in the pool, and called to me:

'I dare you to go up on to that platform,' pointing to it about 25 ft above the pool, 'and swing out over the pool on the trapeze!'

One can hardly refuse a dare, anyway from a C-in-C, so I climbed up, and Mark came with me to give me a few whispered hints on how not to kill myself. I have never had a head for heights, and my knees were quaking; it was not a happy moment. Mark said quietly:

'Drop at the *top* of your swing out, *not* sooner, whatever you do!'

I grasped the bar, was given a push, and swung out . . . and back . . . and out again, by which time I had had enough, and not knowing if I was at the top of the swing out or not, I dropped, feet together, arms extended above my head as instructed, and learned only too soon that I had *not* been at the top of my swing, as I landed, all 11½ stone of me, in a resounding pancake belly-flop! By the time I surfaced, winded and smarting, the audience had hidden their hilarity, and even accorded me some applause. Since then I have watched circus trapeze artists with unbounded respect and admiration.

By 1936 my father knew that he was to be sent the following year to Malta, as second in command of the Mediterranean fleet, under Admiral Sir Dudley Pound, and to fly his flag in HMS *Hood*. A vice-admiral by now, he could afford for my mother, Diana and me to follow him, as soon as my education had finished. To my amazement, he gave me the choice of leaving Abbots Hill at Easter that year, then to go to Harcombe House near Lyme Regis, to do a year's domestic economy course, or to stay at school and take my School Certificate exams. As I knew I would never pass the latter, there was only one option, and I went to Harcombe in April 1937. It was a very tough training indeed, not only in cooking, dress-making, laundry, housewifery and first aid, but in such things as dietetics, changing fuses and washers on taps, re-wiring electric irons, clearing gully-traps, and even mother-craft. At the end of one's third term one took a London diploma, for which one was not entered unless deemed certain to pass, so as to maintain the proud claim of the college that only two girls had ever failed in all the forty years of its existence. Safely through that, I returned home, free of school at last, anyway as a pupil.

Having left school at Easter, I started looking for a job, so as to earn some money to buy clothes to take out to Malta in November. By chance I heard that a teacher of all subjects was required for a class of fifteen seven and eight year-olds at a private school in Alverstoke, which was only a ten-minute bicycle ride from our house. I had no qualifications, but plenty of ideas on imaginative teaching with games and competitions, which were new thinking in education in 1938, and I was taken on. (A teaching qualification was not legally required to teach in those days.)

I was paid 12s.6d. a week, for five mornings from 8.45 am to 12.30 pm which seems absurdly little today, but I was happy to be earning anything at all, and was able to buy very pretty printed cottons and voiles at 6d. per yard, which were made up by a dress-maker, who would come and work in our house for her lunch and 7s.0d. per day, during which she would make a dress and a half, or a dress and a blouse.

In September 1938 we were on the brink of war with Germany, and Neville Chamberlain flew to Munich to reason with Hitler, and returned bearing the absurd piece of paper promising 'Peace in our time'. My mother believed this, mainly from wishful thinking, I am sure, and after the previous few days of agonised anxiety, she resumed the planning for our move to Malta. She had sold our house, and she, Diana and I went to London for the final week before sailing in the P&O ship *Corfu*. During that week we had a real fling, for which Mother had been saving up; we went to two theatres every day, queuing on hired camp-stools outside the theatres for cheap seats in the pit, which cost about 2s.0d. each.

The voyage to Malta was wonderful. It was the first time I had been out of England, and I can still remember the thrill of stepping ashore at Marseilles, our only port of call on the way, and thinking: 'I'm ABROAD!' To this day, although I am now in my seventies, that excitement is just as fresh, every time I step on foreign soil. Mother bought me a long evening dress in the Rue Cannebière in Marseilles; it was to be my best dress for grand occasions, and was made of puce marocain; it was not only quite hideous, but wholly unsuited to my still plump adolescent figure.

There were plenty of young men among the passengers in the ship, as well as the younger ship's officers, and we used to be invited to meet some of them on deck before lunch or dinner most days to have drinks, when we competed to see who could blow their olive stones furthest out over the side.

The ship anchored in Valletta harbour, and we went ashore in Father's naval barge, landing at the Customs House jetty, and being met there by Kerslake, Father's able seaman driver. Little did I know then that it would be three and a half years before I would leave the island. Kerslake taught me to drive in Malta; poor man, he must have had many anxious moments while I learned to start on the steep cobbled hill leading up from the Customs House to Floriana, which was like an ice-rink when wet.

Father had rented a glorious house called Casa Messina, at the top of Guadamangia, in Pieta, just outside Valletta. Violets, anemones, and freesias grew in profusion in the garden, their scent wafting into the house in early spring, and bougainvillaea, plumbago and jasmine climbed to the first floor terrace which opened off the landing, where we sat and sewed and had tea on warm days.

The Mediterranean fleet was huge in those pre-Second World War days. The Grand Harbour would be full of battleships and cruisers when the fleet was in, and round St Elmo point in Sliema harbour and Lazaretto creek would lie the destroyer and submarine flotillas, MTBs and sloops. There would be many parties every night, not only on board ships, but at Army barracks and RAF stations round the island too, and so another fleet would gather, the 'fishing fleet' of hopeful husband-hunting girls, the nieces, cousins, and friends of officers in the command. Diana and I did not count ourselves part of it, as we reckoned that as Father was based in Malta we were there on legitimate grounds.

Girls of the fishing-fleet could, and often did, become blasé and spoilt and Father made a firm rule that Diana and I were only permitted three late nights each week. A 'late night' was one on which we returned home after 11.00 pm. Ships regularly used to show the latest films after supper in their ward-rooms (officers' messes) on

Sunday evenings, and Father allowed these invitations to be excluded from his ruling. Such duty occasions as the Governor's ball, which were obligatory, were also excused, and these were certainly never late nights, as Father would shepherd us to say our good-byes at 10.45 pm at the latest! I was still only eighteen then, but Diana was twenty-five, yet Father was adamant about this rule, and said:

'I am absolutely *not* having you become pale and hollow-eyed from fatigue, or having your heads turned from too much attention. You will do as I say, and that's that!'

The word quickly got round the fleet, and young officers would ring us and ask:

'I suppose it's too much to hope that you still have an evening free this week? . . . No, I thought not. What about next week, then? . . . No! Oh Hell! It'll have to be the week after, then!'

I was only just out of school, but Diana must have found it very hard to accept, especially when she became engaged to Jimmy Prowse, a submariner, and Father still would not relent. He would only permit Diana to see Jimmy on three days a week, not even to go on another day to watch him play in hockey or cricket matches; they had to be arranged on those days when she was going out with him in the evenings. It was many years before I realised, when Mother told me, how jealous Father was of all our young men. (They were not called boyfriends in those days.)

There were three clubs in Malta; the Union club was mainly for dining and drinking, and which our family did not join, although I did later when I was working in Valletta in the war; the Sliema club had tennis and squash courts, and was near good sea bathing; the Marsa sports club was the largest, and boasted a golf course, tennis and squash courts, stables, a small race-course, and various sports fields for rugger, hockey and cricket matches. Rodney Price, Father's flag-lieutenant, kept a horse there, and also owned a black and yellow dog-cart. There was great cachet in being invited to the races by Rodney, and driving up to the course in his immaculate equipage. The Marsa had a weekly dinner-dance on Tuesdays, and the Sliema on Saturdays.

Ship's dances were very romantic occasions, to which we, as admiral's daughters, were generally invited. The host-ship would be 'dressed overall' for the party, with bunting and coloured lights stretched from bow to stern across the tops of the masts. The quarter-deck would be enclosed with tarpaulins, and decorated with more bunting, flags and lights, and there the ship's band would play for dancing. Guests would go out to the ship either in hired *dghaisers*, the beautiful gondola-like Maltese boats, gaily painted, with high prow and stern, and with large eyes painted each side of the bow, to keep the devil away, or collected at the Customs House jetty by ship's boats. One would cross the harbour, the water alive with dancing reflected lights from all the ships lying at anchor, and then, lifting one's long skirt, would climb the ship's gangway; sometimes, if the sea was a bit rough, one had to jump from the boat, but there would be gallant midshipmen and sailors to ensure one arrived safely on deck. Refreshments and supper would be served below in the wardroom during the evening. Diana and I could have gone to such parties every night, and some girls attended two or three on the same evening, but Father's inflexible rule forbade this.

The social climax of the year was during February, coinciding with the island's Carnival week, just before the fleet's spring cruise for exercises and manoeuvres. The Carnival fancy-dress ball in the lovely old Opera House was the greatest event of the season, and Diana and I organised a group of our friends to dress up as the domestic staff of a big house. Diana, dressed in black dress and saucy organdie cap and apron, was the parlour maid; Jimmy, her fiancé, was the chauffeur; Josephine Lovatt, our cousin who had come out to stay with us and join the fishing-fleet for a month, was the housemaid; I was the cook, being suitably buxom; Joe's 'man of the moment' was the butler; and mine, Michael Kyrle-Pope, whom I later married in 1947, was the boot-boy, in green baize apron.

At another fancy-dress dance, I went with the sub-lieutenant of the gunroom (responsible for all the midshipmen in my father's ship, the *Hood*) whose name was Hamilton-Miekle, always called HM. I was very fond of him, we had a lot of fun together, but with no strings attached, and my parents approved our friendship, which was helpful. We dressed up, reversing sexes, which caused much laughter but also disapproval among the older and stuffier mothers and chaperones; I borrowed an able seaman's uniform and cap, and HM dressed in one of my print cotton frocks, and I made him a poke bonnet with ringlets hanging down each cheek. He made a very fetching girl, and was delightfully coy and flirtatious, which I encouraged likewise.

Near our house was a small tennis club, which Father joined for us all. He would organise tennis parties at which Diana and I had to appear. He always insisted on partnering me, calling us the balance of the weakest and the strongest. I would feel quite sick with dread of these occasions, when my feet would be leaden, and my racket apparently stringless.

'Run girl, run!' my father would yell, and

'Good God, girl, can't you even *hit* the bloody ball?' and

'*Another* double fault! That's your tenth/twentieth this set!'

It was a nightmare, and not only for me: the other guests would be miserable with embarrassment, and I would pray for the moment when I would be sent home in disgrace, and floods of tears.

In the evenings after these sessions, I would be told:

'You'll never get married, you know; you are too fat and ugly, and no-one wants to marry a girl who can't even play tennis!'

I was cowed and stupid enough to believe him, and as I adored babies, and wanted to have one of my own (though how, I had no idea; I only knew you had to be married to get one), I vowed I'd marry the first man who asked me, in case it was my only chance.

In February 1939, Father transferred his flag to HMS *Barham* and HMS *Hood* sailed for home. By then Diana and I had got to know the young officers in *Hood* very well; I was half in love with most of the midshipmen on board, as well as HM, and Diana, who was not yet engaged, was also very fond of a lieutenant-commander, Christopher Hutchinson, known as Hutch, who was very smooth and attractive. The morning the ship sailed, Diana and I went down to the end of the breakwater which projected half-way across the harbour entrance, to wave the ship good-bye. We were both in tears as the huge ship slipped past us, and many caps were waved in farewell. As she faded from sight, Diana turned to me, blew her nose, and asked:

'Let me see: who are we going out with tonight?'

It was an extraordinary life, which ended when the war began, and was never resumed in post-war days. By then it had become customary for a girl to have one steady boyfriend, and one relationship at a time, which usually ended in histrionic drama, hurt and tears. In our day, we all went out with whomever invited us, and thus came to know many different young men, and to recognise the type we would eventually like to marry. There was little, if any, hopping in and out of bed, anyway in our circle, and our affairs did not progress beyond petting. Mother once said to me, years later:

'I never had any worries over Diana's young men, they were all so charming and sensible, and I knew I could trust them.' How dull, I thought.

'But you and Winifred seemed to attract so many bounders, I had many sleepless nights over you two!'

War nearly started six months earlier than September 1939, when Mussolini cast predatory eyes on Albania, and annexed it. The armed forces in the Mediterranean were put on alert. Valletta's Grand Harbour was very vulnerable to attack, for it would be easy to seal the narrow entrance, thus bottling up the fleet. So the ships were moved to Alexandria, where Father decided that we should follow, and that Diana should marry Jimmy as soon as possible, 'so as to be able to follow him respectably when the inevitable war begins'.

The day before the wedding, Diana and I had afternoon hair appointments in the city. Diana's hair was finished first, so she returned ahead of me to the hotel where we were living in the pretty leafy suburb of Glymenopolou. The hairdressers took three hours to do my hair, keeping me waiting between shampoo, setting, drying, combing out etc., and when I eventually emerged, the rush hour had begun. I walked to the tram centre in Mohammed Ali Square, as I had been told, and asked a policeman to direct me to my right tram.

The British were not popular in Egypt at that time, and either I was purposely told the wrong tram number, or I misunderstood the policeman's imperfect French. I boarded the tram indicated, which rapidly filled up behind me with rough Egyptian workers, so that I was pushed forward as far as possible from the conductor. When at last he reached me to collect my fare, we were well outside the built-up city area, to the west, and the road was no longer metalled, but a dust track with tram lines running down the middle, and low square mud huts each side. I was told I was on the wrong tram, and must get off, and return in another, to change and board the correct one at the city terminus.

I fought my way off, and stood by the side of the track, but every returning tram was full, with *fellahin* clinging to the outside, and none would stop for me.

The light began to fade, and a group of men behind me, squatting on the ground sharing a hubble-bubble pipe, began to edge closer to me. People stared, and began to pause in passing, to come closer and finger my dress. I began to be very frightened when, from between the mud huts across the road, a long, low, apple-green Rolls Royce slid towards me, the roof folded back, and a young man wearing a dashing green pork-pie hat (very fashionable at the time) leaned toward me, one arm resting invitingly along the back of the front seat.

'And what is such a pretty little English girl doing alone in this part of Alex at this time of the evening?' he asked with an oily leer. He had a long narrow moustache, a greenish-yellow complexion, and was an obvious example of what my father used to call a 'Dirty Dago'. I was really terrified by now; it was nearly dark, and still no tram would stop for me.

'Come along now, you get in my car and I will drive you home,' said the DD, and I very nearly did, but he made the mistake of going too far.

'I tell you what, we'll stop for a spot of dinner on the way,' and at that the alarm bells screamed, and I backed away, but the group behind me were almost touching my legs, and there was nowhere to run. The DD made to get out of the car to come round to me, but at that moment there was a shout from across the road, and a big burly man in European dress and a trilby hat charged up to me and grasped my arm; the DD started his car and was already gliding away when the newcomer turned to me shouting furiously:

'What the hell do you think you are doing, out alone at this hour and in this area? Where is your chaperone? What is your mother thinking of?' and a lot more, by which time I had burst into tears, and told him my story.

'I will take you home: I will force a tram to stop, and I will take you back from the city to your hotel, *and* I will tell your mother what I think of her!' And so he did.

A tram miraculously did stop for him, and room was found for us. He paid my fare, and we did eventually arrive back at Glymenopolou at about 10.00 pm to find Mother beside herself with anxiety. She meekly stood, while my rescuer (who turned out to be Maltese) berated and railed at her.

One of the narrower escapes of my life, I think. White slave traffic was a thriving trade at that time, and I should never have been told to travel alone by tram, but should have been given the money for a taxi home.

Perhaps I should add that Father was ill in his quarters on board

Barham, with a high temperature, and so the pre-wedding party had been cancelled, and in fact he missed Diana's wedding altogether.

After the wedding, the Middle East political situation quietened; HMS *Barham* and other ships returned to Malta and Mother and I followed.

Life in Malta resumed, but now I had to face Father's moods and tempers alone, with no sister to share the atmosphere of mounting tension, which would last two or three days until the eventual outbursts. He would come home to lunch on most days, and would insist on us going out into the country for a family walk in the afternoons, perhaps to trace the course of a *wied* (dried-up water-course), where wild flowers grew profusely, sweet smelling jonquils and little red anemones in early spring, small crimson gladioli later and many others. If a scene was brewing, these walks would be in stony silence, and Diana and I would drop behind, to conjecture on the cause this time: which one of us had given such displeasure? What had we done? How long must the misery last until the fury broke? Very occasionally it would be Mother who was the cause, and we would breathe sighs of relief.

Once he had made us cry, his anger would evaporate, and we would be bidden to sit on his knee for a forgiving cuddle. We did not much care for that either.

One night, after our return to Malta, I had been invited to a moonlight bathing picnic by Ian and Sophie Tower. I always had to ask permission to go out, and my parents knew and liked the Towers (Ian was a Captain RN) so it was considered I would be adequately chaperoned. We swam and had supper on the beach, and a bit later someone suggested driving up to Cita Vecchia (Mdina, as it is now called), the glorious old city on top of the only hill on the island, to look from the bastion which surrounds the city over the whole island in the moonlight.

A young lieutenant, Ralph Sandbach, whom I hardly knew, asked me to drive up with him, which I was delighted to do as he had a low, rather dashing sports car. We all drove off, and met on the bastion, enjoyed the marvellous view, and after a while began to disperse. Ralph offered to drive me home. He seemed quite a nice young man, not very exciting, but friendly and kind. He had 'private means', unlike most naval officers (which was enough to antagonise Father for some reason), and he asked me if I would like to learn to water-ski. By this time we had arrived outside our house, and were talking quietly, sitting in his car.

'Right,' said Ralph, 'I'll speak to Peter Howe about it, we share a little speed boat, ideal for water-skiing, and I'll ring you to arrange a day. Now, you'd better go in, it's been a lovely evening, good-night!' and with that he leaned over and planted a disappointingly chaste kiss on my forehead. I let myself into the house, and he drove away. It was about 11.45 pm.

And there, standing at the top of the stairs, holding a torch directed into my face, stood Father, shaking with rage, red in the face.

'Where the hell have you been? What the blazes were you doing with that young man in his car? You sat there for ten minutes, why didn't you come straight in? Did you let him kiss you? . . . Well, *did* you? Did he kiss you?'

'No, Daddy, we were only talking about going water-skiing.'

'He must have kissed you! He did, didn't he? You're lying.'

'No, Daddy, he didn't!' By this time I was shaking and crying with fear, but he went on and on, and in the end I said:

'Well, he only kissed me on my forehead, Daddy, there's nothing wrong in that, surely?'

'There you are! I knew you were lying, you're a horrible little liar that can't be trusted!' And so on, and so on.

Eventually I stumbled to bed.

The next day Father told me he had sent for the captain of Ralph's ship, and told him to order Ralph to keep away from me.

I felt, and still feel, bitterly ashamed, and more so since I have never had the opportunity to explain matters to Ralph and to apologise.

I did not understand any of this, but knew I absolutely must get away, and prayed someone might ask me to marry them.

Ever since Josephine Lovatt had come out in February to stay, and had travelled out by P&O with two sub-lieutenants, Michael Kyrle-Pope and his friend Geoffrey Carew-Hunt, whom she had introduced to the family, I had been seeing quite a lot of Michael and had become more and more fond of him. He had tried to teach me to ride at the Marsa Club (with little success), we played squash, and he was included in family picnics and parties to race-meetings, the opera and the like. After Father's oft-repeated derogatory remarks concerning my lack of attraction, I was always surprised when any young man so much as looked at me, and I was susceptible if they even smiled at me, let alone asked me out. Some years later, Michael told me he had enjoyed taking me out because I was always so appreciative and seemed to enjoy everything so much. It came as a surprise, then, when he told me he had a fiancée at home, who eventually arrived from England in March 1940; they were married a fortnight later.

After war was declared on 3rd September 1939, the Navy began to deploy the ships from the Mediterranean fleet to where they would be most useful in the fight against Germany (Italy did not come into the war until June 1940), and so the fleet was dispersed gradually homeward, and Father was appointed to command the 18th Cruiser Squadron in home waters, and to fly his flag in HMS *Manchester*. He left Malta, therefore, and returned to England, much to my relief.

Father was always respected and even loved by those who served under him, particularly the youngest seamen and most junior officers. He would fight through thick and thin on their behalf, and support them through their problems, whether of career or domestic origin; in that way he emulated his hero, Lord Nelson, whom he deeply revered. It was sad that he showed so little warmth and compassion in his family life, in which he was intolerant, severely critical and unapproachable, inspiring nothing but fear and dread.

By this time all the fishing-fleet, and many naval wives and families had also begun to move home as and when they could, and so the social round in Malta changed from being primarily Navy-oriented, and my circle began to absorb young Army and RAF officers; I had met John Parlby during the summer months, and he began to feature more and more in my life. He was in the 2nd Battalion of the Devonshire regiment, a pleasant young man, the youngest of four children, whose father had died when he was eight. The family home had been at Manadon, near Plymouth, but Cecil, John's elder brother, had sold it to the Admiralty before the war, and it became the engineering school, taking the place of Keyham.

John was young and immature for his age, which was twenty-four; he was quiet and kind, and a very good dancer, so it was fun to go with him to the weekly dances at the Marsa and Sliema clubs, to which his invitations became more and more frequent.

We became engaged in October, just before Father left Malta. After John had asked Father's permission to marry me, and I had joined them in the sitting-room, I took my tennis racket and broke it over the arm of Father's chair, and said to him:

'Never again! I will never play tennis again in my life!' This was accepted as a joke at the time, but I meant it, and did not play again for over twenty years.

When Father reached home, and was visiting Winifred and Diana, he told them that he couldn't think what I saw in John, and he regretted that I was marrying a 'Pongo' (the Navy's rather scathing term for a soldier). What I saw, was escape from Father at last, and I thought I loved John and was loved by him.

Soon after the outbreak of war, the Army in Malta was moved onto the previously planned war footing, with ack-ack positions manned, and the infantry battalions (the Devons, Dorsets and the Royal West Kents) sent to coastal defence posts round the perimeter of the island, and round airfields.

The Malta Amateur Dramatic Club, or MADC as it was generally known, had a reputation throughout the Mediterranean for its frequent and excellent productions, under the direction of the two famous sisters, Kay and Ella Warren. They were a legendary pair, Kay being the stronger personality of the two. She was strong-featured, with a stoutish upright figure, a commanding voice, and keen sense of humour. Ella was the same build as her sister, but a softer version than Kay. They had lived together with their mother for many years in Malta, and were much respected and loved on the island.

Night Must Fall was about to go into rehearsal when the war began, and I had been given the part of the young female lead. I was delighted, especially as the male lead was to be a naval commander of somewhat dubious reputation (anyway in Mother's eyes), so I looked forward to an interesting and possibly spicy few weeks. Mother was uneasy at this prospect, to say the least! Alas! The Fleet left Malta, and with it half the cast, including my opposite number, so the production was cancelled.

Instead, the Warrens planned to organise concert-parties, to go round the island, giving shows to the beleaguered garrison troops at their posts, from which the men could hardly ever get away. This was enormous fun, and the roving players drove in Army lorries and whatever transport could be laid on, through darkened roads, lanes and tracks, to perform in goat-sheds, barns or wherever sufficient space could be found. Stages were built of planks resting on kerosene drums, green-rooms were little alcoves screened with tarpaulins; we used whatever was to hand, took with us our own costumes, musical instruments and scenery, if any.

We sang, danced and acted sketches and scenes from Noel Coward plays and others. The troops loved it all and so did we. Michael Kyrle-Pope, when his submarine was in harbour, used to be a stage manager, and Molly Davidson, the fifteen-year-old daughter of Curly, a much-loved major in the Devons, was one of the group. Two of the favourite war-time songs we sang, with accompanying mime or chorus-type dancing, were: 'We'll hang out the washing on the Siegfried Line' and 'Run! Rabbit, Run!' in which the audience joined with great enthusiasm.

The soldiery lived in squalid conditions out at their posts round the island, and to begin with, seldom got leave to get into their barracks for a bath, or to Valletta. Mother was very good about allowing John to bring in some of his friends to our flat for baths (we had moved out of Casa Messina when Father went home, and had taken a flat a bit lower on Guardamangia). Mary, our excellent cook, used to bake large quantities of scones and cakes to fortify the young men before they had to return to their billets.

Meanwhile, preparations were going ahead for my wedding. As in Diana's case a year earlier, Father agreed with Mother by letter that I had better get married so as to stay with John and free Mother to return to England while the 'phoney war' still held, making it safe for her to cross Europe.

The date of the wedding was set for 12th April.

CHAPTER 2

Siege of Malta, 1940–42

BEFORE THE 1960s, and the advent of the Pill, sex was a subject seldom mentioned either in society or the media, and in some families it was totally taboo. My family was such a one, and Mother had been absolutely reticent concerning both menstruation and marriage. I think she simply could not bring herself to say the necessary words to tell us the facts of life. Of the sexual act I knew nothing before my wedding night, neither had I any idea of male physique, other than the fact that men had bits and pieces between their legs which seemed to fill their swimming-trunks in varying degrees.

John and I were married in St Paul's cathedral in Valletta, and crossed to Gozo for a brief honeymoon of three or four days. By that time Gozo was the only place we could go, outside Malta. It was a sleepy little island, with one hotel, which was noted neither for its comfort nor its cuisine.

That first night was memorable for our lack of achievement, although not for want of effort, on John's part at any rate. I could not imagine what he was trying to do, but was fully aware that I was not helping much. After the previous few days of hectic last-minute wedding preparations, I was exhausted, and when we eventually went to bed, all I wanted to do was to go to sleep. Poor John gave up in the end, and we did just that.

The next day I felt sick and shocked, and began for the first time to wonder what on earth I had done. That night the struggle was resumed, and I think that John eventually achieved his object, either then or on the third night.

Had Diana still been in Malta, she would have been able to tell me what to expect, but as it was, I went into marriage about as ignorant and cold as any bride of the Victorian era. John was also inexperienced and immature, so our honeymoon was an unrelieved fumbling failure.

We lived for a few weeks in a small rented flat in St Julian's, and

John went in to St Andrew's barracks each morning, which was the Devons' base, where he was temporarily working.

During that time my mother left Malta, crossing to Sicily by night in the little steamer *Knight of Malta*, and then travelling across Europe by train.

Italy declared war on 11th June 1940, and the situation in Malta at once changed to full alert. John returned to garrison duties, and moved out to rejoin his coastal billet, and the Devonshire regimental families were all called into St Andrew's barracks, where they were billeted in the officers' and other messes, or in officers' quarters already occupied by those entitled to them.

With Elisabeth Young, another captain's wife, I was allocated a room in the quartermaster's house, occupied by Tich and Midge Labbett. Tich was out at the battalion headquarters, the two Labbett boys shared a room, and Elisabeth and I each had one of the two other spare bedrooms.

Italian bombing, such as it was, began quite soon, but it was all their air force could do to hit the island, let alone any specific targets, and we were much amused to hear Italian radio news bulletins claiming they had hit 'the main railway station of Malta' (there was no rail system on the island), or had sunk 'HMS *St Angelo* in Valletta harbour' (HMS *St Angelo* being the naval headquarters, a mediaeval stone fortress on the western side of the harbour entrance). However, we had been ordered to take cover during the periods between the warnings and the All Clear sirens, and spent many hours in the slit trench just outside the house, having made it comfortable with deck chairs, rugs and cushions, a tin of biscuits, bottles of water, torches and insect repellent against the sandflies which lived in the rock, and which could be a menace.

There was an ack-ack gun emplacement quite close to the Labbetts' house, and the noise from the guns was ear-splitting when they were firing. We used to sing to try to drown the noise, and Peter (aged eleven) taught us all the words of 'Waltzing Matilda', and also the delightfully lewd army song 'In the quartermaster's stores', which we all belted out with gusto during the air-raids.

We three women all got on very well indeed; we divided the domestic chores between us, although I seem to remember that Midge did most of the cooking. Food had not begun to be rationed, and I recall sitting round the tea-table, consuming large quantities of bread and golden syrup, with dictionaries of various kinds piled beside our places. We used to play many word games, and all of us read a great deal. There were discussions, arguments and bets as to the exact meaning and spelling of words; we even kept a Pears encyclopedia in the air-raid shelter.

Our husbands came in to see us when they could, which amounted to an hour or two about once a week. On one occasion all three of them managed to come on the same afternoon, so we each took tea-trays up to our rooms, and were able to enjoy a brief hour in private together. Later on, when life under siege conditions became more organised, the forces were all allowed one whole day off each week.

The officers' wives had a duty roster for dishing out meals to the other ranks' families in barracks, and Elisabeth and I were also VADs, and used to be on regular duty at the MI room during surgery hours, where the families would come for medical treatment. I was just learning how to give injections when the island state of Red Alert was slightly relaxed and we families were told we could move out of barracks.

We had given up the lease of our flat when I had to move into St Andrew's, so I had to find somewhere to live.

The daughter of the previous colonel of the Devons had married a naval officer in St Angelo, and they were already living in a small family-run hotel in Valletta; I went there as well, and had a pleasant room on the top floor overlooking the central square courtyard. The St James Hotel was a lovely old building, with wrought-iron galleries round each floor of the inner courtyard. Under the hotel was a huge natural cavern in the rock, which made an ideal air-raid shelter, large enough to accommodate all the hotel staff and guests, and the Maltese family who owned it as well.

The Germans had by now realised that their Italian allies were achieving very little in the air attacks on the island, and so the Luftwaffe moved south to take on the bombing themselves. Malta was a great thorn in the enemy's side, for we operated a very successful flotilla of submarines from the island, which were a constant and effective threat to enemy shipping taking reinforcements and supplies to their campaign in North Africa. We also were able, with submarines and aircraft, to protect our own convoys doing the same, passing into the Mediterranean from Gibraltar. There was every reason, therefore, to try to bomb our island base into submission, and from the autumn of 1940 to the winter of 1942 the bombing of the island became fierce and accurate, and was sustained both by day and by night.

I started to work in Military Intelligence when I moved into Valletta to live. It was only ten minutes walk from the St James Hotel to the Auberge de Castille where I worked in the cipher office, encoding and decoding messages. At first these came through in groups of numbers, which required the relevant books to de- or en-code: the keys changed daily. Then Typex machines arrived, which automatically encoded messages typed in clear, or decoded when the groups of numbers or letters were typed. These also had keys which changed daily, and if the correct key was not typed in at the beginning of the message, then only gobbledy-gook emerged from the machines. The machines made a loud metallic clatter, with which we lived throughout our eight-hour shifts.

We had an hour off for lunch, and I joined the Union Club in Strada Reale (now known as Republic Street), which was only five minutes walk from the Castille, where I went most days for a sandwich lunch in the 'snakepit': this was a long room used as the mixed bar, in which before the war morning coffee was served, and which became the centre of island gossip, where wives and the fishing-fleet would gather after shopping or hair-do's. In the war it became the focal point

The devastation left by bombing during the siege of Malta.

for officers on their weekly day's leave, for assignations with their wives or the few women remaining on the island. I very often sat with Dorothy Davidson, wife of Curly in the regiment, whom I mentioned earlier. She was short and square, always laughing and friendly. She was very popular and there was always a group of men round us, either those whose wives and families had been evacuated, or bachelors at a loose end on their day off. I think Dorothy was a sort of universal aunt to us all, and her daughter, Molly, fifty-three years later, has become very like her. I would often be asked out to dinner, and sometimes lunch, by the many lonely officers on their day off, and I was lonely too, only seeing John one day each week. It was then that I, at last, began to develop my own personality, to sparkle and show some character and wit, without fear of parental snubbing, and I began to acquire confidence and spirit.

The raids steadily increased in duration and accuracy. When the aircraft-carrier HMS *Illustrious* limped into harbour, badly damaged by bombing, the Germans came over almost without break, day and night, dive-bombing the Grand Harbour and dock area, where it had been hoped she could be patched up sufficiently to sail home.

One morning, during the heaviest bombing, I woke to find I was covered with small blister-like spots. I had had chicken-pox as a child, and had also done a course of Home Nursing, and so it was easy to recognise that I had caught it again. Luckily there were few spots on my face, and I did not feel particularly unwell, so I said nothing in the hotel, and only told my boss in the cipher office, who told me to take a few days off work.

The Army padre who ministered to the 2nd Devons was Johnny White, an Irishman whom I had got to know well, who had an endless fund of funny stories, could play a penny whistle and dance an Irish jig, and also sing 'Phil the fluter's ball' to perfection. He heard that I had chicken-pox and was off work, and he came into Valletta with his bicycle for his day off, collected me, and we went off into the country on our bikes, taking a packet of sandwiches. It was a glorious sunny clear day, ideal for bombing, and all day the raids continued over Valletta and RAF airfields, which we avoided. We watched dogfights between the Messerschmidts and what few fighter aircraft we could still send up; their white vapour trails wove like threads of wool in the blue sky. We were nowhere near any target or village, but suddenly we heard the unmistakable whine of a diving aircraft behind us.

'Quick! Into the ditch!' yelled Johnny, and we half fell off our bikes into the road-side ditch, and scuttled into a stone culvert which luckily ran under the road at that point, just as a Messerschmidt flew down the road we had left, strafing it with machine-gun bullets, then screamed up into the sky again and away. I expect the pilot thought it good sport, and we laughed somewhat shakily as we brushed ourselves down and resumed our cycle ride.

We all slept in the big cave under the hotel now. Every night I took down with me a basket in which was my jewellery, a torch, my gas-mask and a wide-necked Thermos of water, and there came a night when I was very glad that I had.

Buildings in Malta are constructed of large hewn blocks of the soft sandstone which comprises the island itself. It was fascinating to watch the masons building a house, and cutting the rock almost like butter, along lines drawn with a pencil on the stone. When bombed, these did not break or fragment, but shook and emitted clouds of gritty dust. The Germans started to drop land-mines on parachutes, to achieve greater destruction; they succeeded, and one night such a mine hit the St James Hotel, which collapsed. The big square boulders which had comprised the walls of the building entirely blocked the entrance to, or rather in our case the exit from, our underground shelter, trapping us below ground. The cave remained intact, so we were entombed but able to move about had we wished. The air was filled with thick choking dust, and so I at once put on my gas-mask. No-one else had theirs with them, neither had they any water, so my Thermos was passed round for everyone to soak handkerchiefs or other cloths to tie across their mouths and noses. There was a baby, whose nappies came in useful for this purpose! From a steady hiss above us we realised the gas main had fractured, but a certain amount of air seeped down between the lumps of rock over the entrance.

We were trapped for only a few hours, although it seemed longer, and then we heard the welcome muffled voices of rescuers:

'Anyone down there?' and

'Are we near the entrance? Give us a shout so we can hear where you are!' and

'How many of you are there?'

'Anyone hurt?'

'OK! We'll soon get you out! Just hold on a jiffy, we won't be long.'

That was a wonderful moment to remember.

The next sound was of stones being moved and of more voices:

'Hey, mate, give us a hand lifting this one off!' and

'No, over 'ere, this is where the 'ole is, you git!' and

'You still all right down there? We're nearly through!' and then a rumble and slithering sound, a rock moved overhead; we drew back, and another was levered up and away, and after a few more were cleared, there was a hole, and faces looking down, and beyond them, praise the Lord, the stars.

'Right then! Let's have the first one!' a burly sailor shouted down.

There were about forty of us, but the mother of the Maltese hotel owner, a lady of considerable age and bulk, had had enough, and at that last moment she panicked and pushed her way into the hole; as she was being pulled from above, and pushed from below, she became stuck fast, and in her terror she seemed to collapse into her stays, if you understand me, and became even more firmly wedged. Looking back it is very funny, but at the time, with many of us waiting to escape, it was not!

There were many soldiers and sailors above, who helped us out with encouragement and jokes; it was marvellous to breathe fresh air again, and from somewhere mugs of tea appeared. Three walls of the hotel had been demolished, but the fourth still stood, and on the top floor, the gallery hanging in mid-air, I could see my room, and a bottle of scent and a vase of flowers on my dressing-table standing unscathed. Bomb blast is extraordinary in its unpredictability.

I was homeless of course, after the St James Hotel was hit, but the Dobbies very kindly invited me to stay with them in St Anton Palace, which was the official residence of the Governor of Malta, two or three miles west of Valletta. General Sir William and Lady Dobbie had been friends of my parents before the latter left the island, and so I already knew them, but not well. They were extremely hospitable, and offered accommodation to many who were homeless or recovering from injuries, and to exhausted fighter pilots and submariners, for a few days rest and peace in the country. General Dobbie was deeply religious, a Plymouth Brother, I believe, and all guests at the palace were expected to attend morning and evening prayers, which he read in one of the large palace rooms; this somewhat startled some of the fighter pilots at first, but I think everyone came to value the daily brief period of quiet prayer after a couple of days.

While I was at San Anton, Johnny White had been looking at the St

The aftermath of the bombing near the St James Hotel, Malta, 1941.

James Hotel ruins, and he decided that it might be possible for a team of sappers to climb up to my old bedroom and salvage some of my belongings.

One sunny morning, during a lull in the bombing, a group of soldiers arrived in an Army lorry, and while Johnny and I sat on boulders of rock below, they roped up and climbed to the second floor. I had to shout up to tell them where the items of greatest value were, and they took my clothes from cupboards and drawers, and threw them down. An interested crowd gathered in the street, to watch and cheer the soldiers on; imagine my scarlet face when they came to my underclothes drawer, and with wolf-whistles and whoops of delight threw down one by one, items from my trousseau of silk French panties, bras and petticoats, which filled with air as they fluttered down in the breeze!

Cosmetics were by then almost unobtainable, and when a voice bellowed down to me:

'Anything else, Madam? Have we got it all?'

'Well,' I shouted back, 'In the little top drawer of the dressing-table you'll find some lipsticks ... I'd love to have those ... and also the bottle of Guerlain scent if you can manage it!'

'Oh yes! Got 'em! I'll bring 'em in my pocket, better 'n throwing 'em down. Only 'ope the perfume don't leak, ma'am, or I'll stink like a ... Oh, beggin' yer pardon, ma'am!'

And so it was that I was lucky enough to salvage nearly all my trousseau, and at the same time we, and the large crowd of onlookers, had enjoyed a splendid spectacle, and much laughter.

Another young wife and I found a flat to move into, in the Mountbattens' house in Guardamangia, which, although occupied as a whole by them when resident in the island, could be divided into four flats to lease in their absence. Anne and I had little in common other than our recent experience in the St James Hotel, and we quite soon decided to live separately. Our accommodation comprised the spacious ground floor of the house and rather a dark semi-basement; we agreed that she should take the ground floor, and I the lower one, which had the advantage of opening on to a small walled garden in which were an orange and several grapefruit trees.

At about this time, a naval friend who lived in Valletta was about to leave and he asked me if I would like to take on his Maltese maid, Nina. I went to lunch to say good-bye to Jacko and to meet her. There was the usual raid in progress, but Jacko had to get back to his office in headquarters, so he left after lunch, urging me to take cover in the basement with Nina for a little while, until the worst of the bombing was over. While downstairs, I looked out through the barred grill which was at street level, and watched two monks hurry by, their tonsured heads gleaming in the sun, their brown robes and white cords round their waists swinging out as they ran back to their monastery at the bottom of the narrow street. Just after they had passed came the familiar whine of a diving aircraft, which flew along the street at roof-top level, and gunned down the monks before climbing away back into the sky.

Nina moved in to join me soon after that. She was a darling, gentle and smiling, and also an excellent cook.

The Marsa club had been commandeered by the Army, and ack-ack guns established on the sportsgrounds, but the Sliema club was still open to members, and its weekly dances were still held on Saturdays. John tried to take his day off as often as possible on a Saturday, and we would whirl round the dance-floor doing Viennese waltzes, trying to be the first couple on the floor so as to have it to ourselves, if only for a few moments. We were really rather good at waltzing, and dipped and whirled tirelessly, calling for encore after encore.

No petrol was available except for service requirements, but that did not stop us all cycling to Sliema for the dances, wearing trousers and our clothes for sleeping underground overnight in whatever air-raid shelter we were near when the warning sounded. I carried my long evening dress and shoes in a cardboard box on the carrier of my bike, and would change on arrival at the club, and back again to ride home. On occasions when John was on duty, I would be invited by other lone bachelors or grass-widowers, and one such was Hubert Marsham, the second-in-command at the Manoel Island submarine base. He would sometimes collect me on his motor-bike, and I would ride pillion behind him, my evening dress box strapped on behind. We became so accustomed to the continuous bombing over the island (which is only 24 miles by 13 miles), that it was decided we need only take cover when a red flag was hoisted over a particular area, denoting that that was the immediate target, otherwise the whole population would be permanently underground and life would come to a standstill.

When it became apparent that the submarine base was the likely target, and the CO, Captain 'Shrimp' Simpson, knew I was in my flat alone, he would sometimes send Hubert Marsham on his motor-bike to fetch me back to Manoel Island, where the shelters were very deep, and I would sit with the submarine crews until the raid was over. I remember one day the bombing began as Hubert and I were on our way. He increased speed, and we raced through the deserted streets, leaning into corners and roaring along, at one point being strafed by machine guns along a straight bit of the road; we got to the shelter entrance, and Hubert shouted:

'Jump! Go on! Don't wait for me.'

I ran for the tunnel, and he flung down the bike and pelted after me. That was the day the sick-bay overhead had a direct hit, and the wardroom next to it was badly damaged. No boats were hit (submarines are called boats, never ships) for they were dived, i.e.

submerged, so as to be less visible from the air. When the immediate bombing slackened, we all rushed up to the sick-bay, where sadly there had been several men too ill to be moved down to the shelter. I was not allowed to go to help there, but was sent to start cleaning the wardroom, sweeping up glass, and so on.

I knew the submarine officers well, having met many before the war through Michael Kyrle-Pope and my brother-in-law, Jimmy Prowse. They have always been a part of the Navy that has its own tight-knit unity, a brotherhood almost. When in action, each man relies completely on his mates, regardless of rank; an error of judgement by one endangers all, and this is reflected in the attitude of officer to rating, and vice-versa, and in the whole spirit of the submarine service.

My father was a submariner, who had volunteered to join in 1907, when submarines were first introduced into the Navy, and when the crews never knew if a boat would safely surface again from a dive, I had been brought up in the shadow of the service, and in a way have felt part of it all my life.

Michael was Third Hand as a sub-lieutenant in HMS *Oswald*, a submarine based at Manoel Island. When out on patrol off Sicily, she was sighted by an Italian destroyer while she was on the surface at night re-charging her batteries (this cannot be done when submerged, and therefore in wartime has to be done at night, when less likely to be spotted by the enemy). The enemy increased speed towards *Oswald*, and rammed her starboard side. The boat was damaged and then depth-charged. The Captain ordered the crew to abandon ship at once without firing a shot or torpedo, an order which Michael, being a junior officer, had to obey. He has regretted this inaction with sadness and shame all his life. The officers and crew were all subsequently taken prisoners of war. I did not hear in Malta that *Oswald* was lost until some months later, when I learnt that Michael had been shot while trying to escape. I assumed he had been killed.

My flat offered no protection from bombing, so I slept every night in a shelter under the road a few yards from my front door. These tunnels, with an entry from each side of the street, were enlarged into square chambers in the middle; they had been hacked out of the rock all over the island, for the public to use in air-raids. I had a deck chair there, and each night took down with me rugs and a cushion, and my inevitable basket with my jewellery, water, torch and gas-mask, which had so much proved their worth in the St James bombing. Being a public shelter, many Maltese also used it, those who lived in the little terraced houses lower down Guardamangia, and being a volatile nation they voiced their anxiety and fear throughout the night, in ceaseless chanting of prayers and wailing. Another disadvantage was their standard of hygiene, and the stench of urine became quite overpowering by morning. However, one felt safe in the shelter, and it was comforting not to be alone during the worst night raids.

A submarine, *Sokol*, manned by a Polish crew, had joined the Tenth Flotilla early in 1941. The crew had all escaped from Poland during the Nazi invasion of their country, and all were fully aware of the appalling conditions under which their families must be living, and of the true nature of what life under the Nazi heel meant. This made their determination to fight the Germans all the greater, and the tonnage of Axis shipping sunk by *Sokol* was considerable. The Captain was Boris Karnicki, and his second-in-command (or first lieutenant) was Georg Kojiokovski. There were three or four other officers whom I knew less well. They were a wild, and utterly charming bunch: Boris used to take me out to lunch or dinner quite often when *Sokol* was in harbour, *à deux*, and on my place at table there would always be, awaiting me, a posy of tiny pink rose-buds, which he would tell me were 'For my little English rose!'

Who could resist such charms? But I did (reluctantly), while he tried every wile to get me into bed. I had a shrewd suspicion that others succumbed, and who could blame them? Boris was devastatingly sexy and attractive, and had a beautiful speaking voice, with a delicious accent; he was also a superb dancer.

When the grapefruit ripened in the garden of my flat, I gave away many, but also would have liked to make some marmalade; however, by then sugar was strictly rationed, so that was out of the question. While taking cover in the submarine base air raid shelter one day, I mentioned my large grapefruit crop, regretting the lack of sugar, and saying how I would have liked to make some marmalade for the boats' crews. Shrimp Simpson said:

'That's no problem! We'll give you a sack of Navy issue sugar, but it will be brown demerara, not white, I'm afraid.'

The brown sugar darkened the grapefruit nicely, so the end product looked the same as my usual home-made Seville orange marmalade, and tasted just as good. I seem to remember a naval Jeep collecting about 300 lbs from my flat a week or so later, and the Navy must have supplied me with the necessary sticking plasters for all my blistered fingers from cutting up so much fruit.

Life in Malta after my marriage was lived at polarised extremes of emotion: fear; joy; grief; happiness; terror; laughter; and tears. One came to know other people far more deeply than in peacetime; we helped each other, comforted one another, shared love and laughter, and sorrows and fears. This was something that, when I reached England in the summer of 1942, my mother and sisters simply could not understand; they were shocked and horrified when a cable came for me from Hubert Marsham, saying:

'Heard you arrived safely. Thank God, darling.'

He had never even kissed me, except chastely on both cheeks on my twenty-first birthday, but my family were convinced I had been having an affair with him, and nothing I could say would disabuse them, solely on account of that one word of endearment. My sisters had been living in the country together, looking after their small children and seeing their husbands only seldom when they could get leave, and I don't think they could even begin to imagine what life in Malta had been like.

Everyone in Malta worked hard and played hard; submarines were lost on patrol, and I would hear things like:

'*Urge* is twenty-four hours overdue . . .' 'Two days overdue now . . .' and then the final statement:

'Must be presumed lost.'

We knew the crew, and also the wives who had perhaps returned to England early in the war; but life had to go on, none of us knew how long we had; never before or since has the phrase 'Life is for living' seemed so poignant. Some faces would be missing at the daily gatherings at the Union Club, but there was no point in thinking, 'Whose turn next?' or 'How long can Malta hold out?' Food was getting short, in spite of the rationing system (Hubert Marsham started up a pig farm on Manoel Island, to augment the submariners' diet). Aircraft fuel and ammunition were almost exhausted, then totally exhausted; convoys were torpedoed and shot to pieces trying to get through to us, and still the heavy bombing continued. Will the Germans land? Will there be a parachute drop of invaders? One asked oneself these questions constantly, but the greatest of all the fears was the fear of showing one's fear.

All this time I was invited out, seeing John only one day a week. I did not hop into bed with anyone, but it was often suggested. Small wonder then, that I began to look beyond the war, to the possibility of survival, and settling down in peacetime with John ... for *life*?

Our office was moved from the Castille in 1941, down into Lascaris Headquarters, which was a system of offices blasted out of the rock below the Castille in the cliff above the Customs House jetty. We had our own Typex room at the end of a tunnelled passage. One morning I left it to go to the lavatory, and while out of the office, the other operators were evacuated so that some blasting could be done to extend the complex at the end of our tunnel. I returned, knowing nothing of this, and resumed work at my machine, only to be blown from one end of the office to the other, suffering excruciating pain in my ears, when the charge was detonated only feet away. It was all considered a great joke, and I went on working, my ears recovering after a few days, but I have had recurrent ear problems ever since, and began to go prematurely deaf several years ago. I find this can be very useful at times!

I had bicycled home for lunch one day, and was about to sit down to eat when the air-raid warning sounded, and the red flag went up over Valletta. Nina became very upset, which was quite out of character:

'Please come to the street shelter, Signora,' she said, 'I know we are going to be hit this time!'

'Don't be silly, Nina,' I replied, 'It's only the usual mid-day raid, and I must have my lunch and get back to the office.'

'Oh, please listen to me, Signora. Please, please come! I am certain a bomb will hit us.'

'No, Nina, I can't. I have no time, but you go. Go on, you go and take cover. Take your door key, so you can get in after the raid, when I will have left.'

With a little more encouragement, she went. This was totally unlike Nina, and I was quite surprised.

I began to eat my cold salad, and after a few minutes, I heard a stick of bombs start to whistle down a little distance away. By this time we were all quite able to judge the line in which a stick would fall, and the distance between each explosion. I heard three go off, getting nearer, and I realised Nina had been right, and it was highly likely that the sixth bomb might directly hit the house in which was my flat. In fact it exploded just on my front door-step, blowing in the door, breaking all the windows, and cracking walls. Some furniture was blown across rooms; other pieces, including wine glasses on a tray, were untouched.

By the time Dorothy Davidson and her daughter Molly had run down the hill from their house, to see if I was all right, I had somehow crossed the length of the dining-room, and seized the bottle of brandy off the drinks tray; they found me under the dining room table gulping brandy from a tablespoon! Which just shows how well brought up I was: today I would dispense with the spoon! It took a long time to live this down. Nina's premonition was extraordinary, and when the All Clear sounded, she came running back, sobbing and crying:

'Signora, I *told* you! Oh, are you all right? Oh, Signora! Why wouldn't you listen to me?' I was certainly more inclined to after that.

By the spring of 1942, I had been having to take time off from the cipher office, going sick, more and more often. I had had a miscarriage, and had been admitted to M'tarfa hospital on two occasions. There were other women who had also begun to fall sick to a greater or lesser degree, and the authorities started to plan a scheme whereby a few could be evacuated from the island, and eventually be repatriated to UK.

Food was becoming increasingly short, although the rationing system was very well organised, but the months of bombing, interrupted nights, and shortage of sleep, were beginning to take their toll. Convoys to Malta were decimated by German submarine and air attack, and very few ships got through. The siege was not broken until August 1942, and then only partly. The island had to wait until November before supplies were arriving in any quantity.

John came home one day and told me I was to leave a few days later. Squadrons of Wellington bombers were flying out from UK to reinforce the Allied troops in North Africa, and they landed in Malta *en route*, bringing mail and medical supplies in place of bomb weight, and it had been decided to send one woman out in each aircraft. I went the first night this scheme was tried out.

I was told to pack one suitcase only, and John took me out to Luqa airfield the evening we left, where I met Elisabeth Young, another

Devon captain's wife, who was pregnant, not at all well, and who was to leave Malta the same night. There were also five other ranks' wives with their husbands.

It was dark, and the Wellingtons were waiting; an air-raid was in progress, but not in the immediate vicinity, so we were taken out to our respective aircraft, and I boarded the squadron-leader's as directed. Inside there was a strap and netting hammock-like seat fitted fore to aft down one side, and I was told to sit down. The door was shut and we taxied out to the runway; as we took off a lot of noise broke out, I presumed from nearby ack-ack guns. I hoped not from bombs.

Suddenly, after we'd left the coast of Malta behind, there came a furious rat-tat-tat of machine-gun fire, which startled me somewhat, until one of the crew explained it was only our own routine check that our guns were firing correctly. After a short time I was asked if I would like to go to sit next to the pilot in the cockpit, where I remained until just before we landed in the desert about thirty miles outside Cairo. It was a clear moonlit night. The sea was calm and empty of shipping, the sky full of stars; it was hard to believe that heavy ground fighting was going on in North Africa, and ceaseless bombing behind us in Malta.

I had been told by the Army Movement Control officials in Malta that we would be met by one of their representatives when we landed, accommodation would have been arranged, and that an advance of local currency would be given to each of us, which would be deducted from our husband's pay. The squadron-leader's was the first Wellington to touch down, and when I emerged and stepped on to the sand, there was a gasp from the waiting RAF ground crew:

'Cor, stone the crows! That's a . . . woman!'

'Yes,' I said, 'and there are six more to follow . . . just like me!'

No-one expected us or knew of our evacuation from Malta; no military movement control officer met us, and there was no accommodation prepared for us. We had landed at 3.30 am.

The small airfield staff were very quick to organise a welcome, though, and as soon as we all seven had landed, and our luggage been unloaded, we were taken to a tent and sat down to a Lucullan feast of fried eggs and bacon, and unlimited bananas to follow. We had not seen so much food for a long time, nor seen any bananas at all for months; we were all encouraged to eat as much as we liked, it was marvellous!

Meanwhile a tent was being made ready with camp-beds and blankets, where we slept the rest of the night.

After a generous breakfast next morning, we were taken in a lorry to Cairo, and dropped at GHQ where we were shown into the NAAFI canteen, and I was instructed to go and find the Movement Control office; our escort drove away.

GHQ at that time, March 1942, was not known for the industry of its staff officers. Work was from 8.30 am to 12.30 pm, when offices were abandoned and everyone went off to lunch, and to play or watch whatever sport they liked in the afternoons. We arrived at 11.30 am, so I was told I had an hour to get something organised for our little group. GHQ was four or five stories high, I seem to remember, filled with offices which had little sign-posts projecting into the passage outside each door, stating the rank and name of the occupant, and his official designation. No-one I asked knew the name of the senior Movement Control Officer, nor where I could find his office; I seemed to walk miles, peering at name-boards which read Brigadier This, or Colonel That, with RA; RE; RAMC; Intelligence Corps etc. etc. but no Movement Control.

Time was running out, and I began to run too, round and round those endless corridors, upstairs and down them, then hearing doors slam, and:

'I'm off now, old boy, see you at the club at 2.30.'

'Yes, right you are!' and so forth.

I was responsible for six women, all tired and unwell, none with a bed for that night, nor with money to buy food; all depending on me to find someone, anyone, who would take on the responsibility of their immediate welfare, and onward transport to England. I became desperate, and then, Oh Wonder of Wonders! I came to a name-board which stated 'Brigadier —— MC'. Pushing the door open without even knocking, I fell into the office, crying:

'Thank God I've found you at last! I've been hunting all over the building for the last hour! There are six more women down in the NAAFI canteen; we have nowhere to sleep tonight and no money. Why the hell wasn't anyone there to meet us when we landed from Malta last night? We were told . . .' and my voice petered out as I looked round the walls at serried rows of photographs of tanks, and then at the astonished face of the brigadier sitting behind his desk.

'Well, you *are* the Movement Control Officer aren't you? Your name-board outside says Brigadier —— MC ... Oh, *God!*' as realisation dawned that MC can stand for something other than Movement Control, and I burst into tears.

The Brigadier had not achieved his rank, nor won his Military Cross, for nothing, and he very quickly had the situation, and me, under control; the authentic Movement Control Officer was summoned, and then the second miracle in half an hour occurred, when the telephone rang, and I heard a voice say:

'Admiral Baillie-Grohman to speak to you, sir,' and I begged to be allowed to speak to him.

'Oh, Uncle Tom! Please help me! It's Suzanne ... Suzanne Layton that was; I'm an Army wife now, and I arrived from Malta last night, and no-one here knew we were coming ...' and I told him the whole story.

After that things were sorted out. The proper authorities did at last acknowledge our presence, and took over responsibility for the other ranks' wives and their accompanying husbands and Elisabeth Young and I were invited to stay with the Baillie-Grohmans until plans were made for our onward travel round the Cape.

I remember very little about the ten days we spent in Cairo, except for sleeping and eating: sleeping undisturbed, in a bed, through every night, and eating unlimited and varied delicious meals.

My father, until just before Singapore fell, had been based there as C-in-C China Station. He had correctly forecast the fall of Singapore, and the reasons for it, many months before the Japanese landed on the north-east coast of Malaya; he had personally warned Winston Churchill, and been snubbed for his pains, to the extent of being relieved of his post by Admiral Tom Philips, who was almost immediately lost at sea in HMS *Prince of Wales*.

At the time I reached Cairo on my way home, Father had got as far as Colombo, also homeward bound. Admiral Baillie-Grohman, a close friend of the family, signalled him telling him of my whereabouts, and it was planned that Father would pick me up on his way, and we would fly home together from Cairo.

By this time, however, Father's appreciation of Japanese strategy and tactics had been acknowledged in Whitehall, and he was peremptorily appointed Governor and Commander-in-Chief Ceylon, to prepare that island for the next expected Japanese assault. He therefore stayed in Colombo, where he remained for the next two years.

After ten days luxury and idleness staying with the Baillie-Grohmans, Elisabeth and I, both feeling greatly restored, rejoined the Army sausage-machine for repatriation, and were instructed to report to a troop train to travel to Port Tewfik, at the southern end of the Suez Canal. There we embarked in SS *Viceroy of India*, a P&O liner, converted for wartime use as a troopship. This was her penultimate voyage, for on the following one, she was sunk.

Elisabeth and I shared a cabin, and were very comfortable; we already knew each other well, after living with Midge Labbett in St Andrew's barracks for several weeks in 1940, and we had become good friends.

Viceroy of India carried about fifty women on that voyage, a number of British and Allied officers and troops, and eight hundred German prisoners of war, who had been captured in North Africa and were to go to Durban to work on farms up-country. A major called Jack Jobey was in command of the POWs, and I came to know him quite well. The prisoners lived down below, but were allowed up on deck for an hour twice daily, in the morning for PT and in the evening for fresh air; it was in the evenings that they would sit cross-legged on deck and sing, both in unison and in harmony, and it was very stirring to watch and listen to them. They were a magnificent crowd of young men, their average age twenty-three; and they were the cream of the Afrika Korps. They wore only shorts and their small cotton kepis (cotton uniform caps), and were bronzed and fit.

Preceding us down the Red Sea to Durban, was another troopship called the *Louis Pasteur* which had been a French liner before the war. She too was carrying German POWs, and when we reached Durban we heard that there had been a plot by the Germans to take over the ship. There were two German generals among the prisoners, who had cabins to themselves. They had asked the OC Troops if they might be allowed to have other German officers in to play chess with them after dinner in the evenings. One evening they were overheard by their guard, who understood German, discussing a plan to rush the ship. This was reported immediately, and at once all the officers were put into cells, and the other ranks were mustered on deck and searched; it was found that the feeding utensils with which they had been issued had been altered to make effective weapons; the knives had been

sharpened down to short-bladed daggers, and the forks had had two
tines broken off, and the remaining two bent at right-angles, to use as
knuckle-dusters.

Jack Jobey, the OC Troops in *Viceroy of India*, kept a firm control
over the POWs, who were well watched and guarded.

In Durban, the Germans were disembarked, and were replaced by a
thousand Italian POWs. These were very different from the Germans,
being lazy and apathetic; in the rough Atlantic weather which
followed, they were sea-sick and constantly moaning, took no pride in
their appearance, as the Germans had done, and made no effort to
keep their decks clean and hygienic, nor themselves.

I learned to play chess during this six-week voyage; there were
many officers to teach me, for there was very little to do other than
play deck games or read. A Greek lieutenant, whose submarine had
been sunk in the Mediterranean, was one of my tutors, and a Polish
Merchant Navy captain, whose ship had also been lost; there was also a
lively young subaltern called Patrick Shovelton, who started me off. It
was very entertaining listening to the three of them arguing as to what
move I should make next. It was an excellent way of learning, and we
played for hours every day. I measured my skill by how long I could
keep a game going before losing.

We reached Durban on 23rd March, and stayed there four days. I
did much shopping there, collecting together as much food as I could,
which I knew was rationed in England. I was going to go to my sisters
on arrival in England. They shared a cottage in Shropshire, and my
mother lived with them. With three small boys to feed and keep clean,
I realised soap was one priority, and I also took sugar, dried fruit, tinned
butter and bacon, also tinned meat and sardines. We reached Cape Town
three days after leaving Durban, and had two days there. I did more
shopping, and also went up to the top of Table Mountain, from where
there were spectacular views. We sailed on 2nd April, and began the
long haul into the Atlantic, out towards America, hoping to avoid the
packs of U-boats which were decimating our convoys. We were not in
convoy because our maximum speed was 14 knots, which was
considered fast enough to sail safely unaccompanied; nearing Freetown,
however, one of our two engines broke down, and so our speed was
reduced to 7 knots. We still carried on alone, hoping for the best. I did
not enjoy this part of the long journey and was glad to disembark in
Liverpool on 25th April, having left Malta on 27th February.

In the market at Cape Town I had bought a small net of eight dozen lemons, and two each holding about sixty oranges. I did not succeed in getting all the lemons safely home though, for when we reached Liverpool we had to stay overnight at the Adelphi Hotel, and next morning, when getting myself and my by now copious amount of luggage to the station to catch a train to Stafford, the net of lemons burst, and the fruit rolled everywhere; at once people materialised out of nowhere, like Arabs do in the desert, and everyone picked up the lemons and brought them to me with expressions of yearning, which clearly said:

'Here are your lemons, we know they're yours, but we haven't seen one for years!'

I suppose I took home about half the contents of the net! An aunt to whom I gave two kept them in a bucket of damp sand, which she had heard would preserve them indefinitely, while she decided how best to use such riches; alas, she dallied too long, and by the time she had made up her mind to have them with pancakes, and disinterred them, they had gone bad!

CHAPTER 3

England, 1942–47

'AND YOU'LL BE WANTING twelve bars of laundry soap, and two dozen packets of soap-flakes, this week, Mrs Prowse.'

'No thank you,' said Diana, completely mystified, 'we don't need that much!'

'Oh yes, I think so, Madam,' replied Mr Midgeley, 'I'll send your order out tomorrow!'

The next day it was announced that soap was to be rationed immediately. Mr Midgeley, the Newport grocer, was a good friend to my sisters on many occasions.

After my brother-in-law, Jimmy Prowse, was lost with his submarine, HMS *Snapper*, in 1941, my sister Diana, who was pregnant, joined forces with Winifred, who was also pregnant and already had four-year-old Jeremy. The two sisters rented a cottage in Shropshire, near my mother's sister, our aunt Olive. Winifred's husband, Ian Riches, was a Royal Marine Commando on active service, who could only get home intermittently on leave.

The two sisters lived a hard but quiet life, struggling on the severe rations available to feed their families and keep the babies' unending nappies white: both girls had baby boys only a few months apart.

My mother joined my sisters when she arrived home from Singapore, and it was there that I also first went on my return from Malta.

The boxes, baskets and bags of supplies I had brought home from South Africa were greeted with delight, and to start with, so was I, but it soon became apparent that I was not welcome, and one reason, I think, was that my sisters envied me in a way, for my experiences in Malta.

'You always have to be the centre of a drama,' they said, and of course it had all been very exciting, but not very enjoyably so.

After two or three weeks, I decided I must move on, and in any case, I had to find war work of some kind, preferably in Intelligence, leading on from my cipher experience in Malta, and I wanted to join the naval side this time. After writing to apply, I was summoned to an interview with an Admiralty civil servant in London called Mr Grey. In my letter of application I particularly did not mention my father's name, being anxious to be assessed on my own merits, without any string-pulling. I was therefore surprised when Mr Grey, after an extremely brief interview, told me to report a few days later to the Inter-Services Topographical Department in Oxford, at the new Bodleian Library, to Mr Rodney Slessor, who would be my boss. I said I was amazed that he could appoint me so quickly, without further investigation of my *bona fides*.

'Oh, we know all about you already, don't worry!' he said with a twinkle. I imagine they had had means of making their inquiries, using the sparse information I had given in my letter of application.

My husband's family, the Parlbys, had friends living in Oxford, and it was arranged that I would go and lodge with them as a paying guest. Sir Charles Harper was a delightful man, tall and burly, who had been governor of both St Helena and Ashanti; he had been retired some years when I met him and his wife. Lady Harper was a little woman, hyperactive and nervous, like a little red squirrel. I was given a charming small room looking over the garden, at the top of their house in Banbury Road, North Oxford, and lived there happily for eighteen months.

The BBC had broadcast a radio appeal for holiday snaps and photographs to be sent in, of any country outside Britain. Thousands of albums, postcards and photographs were received, and all came to the new Bodleian Library, where I joined the team whose job it was to go through them, selecting those of which we would like copies. To do this we had to check through the existing library of photographs stored in boxes standing on endless shelves. The albums would go to the printers, with labels between the pages marking the required prints:

'Left page top right' or 'right page middle row centre'. In due course they would come back with the prints, and the collections would be parcelled up and returned to the owners who never knew which of their photos had been copied. Meanwhile we had to caption the prints with as much detail as possible. I was in the section dealing with Europe; to help us, we had complete sets of Michelin road maps, Admiralty charts and Pilots, Baedeker and many other travel guides.

The Coat of Arms for Section 'C', Inter-Services Topographical Department, Oxford, designed by George Staempfli.

We had to give the grid reference of each photograph as accurately as possible.

Often there would be visitors, unnamed and in plain clothes, who would come and study the photographs prior to landings or raids of one sort or another, and sometimes special reconnaissance flights would be flown, or commandos would be landed by submarine to obtain more detailed information regarding beach gradients, cliff accessibility and 'chimneys', and deployment available for vehicles in the hinterland. These information-gathering sorties became more frequent as time wore on, and the preparatory topographical work was starting in earnest on the Normandy coast prior to Operation Overlord, and D-Day.

I was moved from the Bodleian after a few months, at my own request, to Manchester College, where the work was even more interesting. There my job was to study photographs brought in from RAF reconnaissance flights, which had been taken at '0 ft' (below 1000 ft) along the Normandy coast-line. In each film were hundreds of prints, which I had to fit together, selecting some, but not all, to make one long panoramic view; then the fun began of annotating with mapping-pen and Indian ink, the landmarks which could be seen and recognised from landing-craft. These could be lighthouses, churches, hotels; certain rocks, piers, and breakwaters; beaches and headlands, hills and woods etc. Again, Michelin maps, charts and Admiralty Pilots were invaluable for this.

On D-Day each landing-craft carried one of these photographic panoramas, together with detailed explanatory notes on gradients and type of beach, that is, whether of sand, pebbles, rock etc, and also of inland roads, deployment and cover.

The first time such intelligence was prepared was for the landings on Sicily. My Section 'C' was not responsible for the photographic intelligence, but when the landing date was brought forward by a week or so, the written reports were not ready, and it was a question of all hands to the pumps; there had to be a considerable number of these reports, each forming a pile of about $1^{1}/_{2}$ inches thick of foolscap, which had been run off a Roneo machine. We worked all night, first putting the pages together in numerical order: ten or more girls, each with an armful of pages 1; pages 2; pages 3, etc, running round a long trestle table along the gallery overlooking the hall in which Section 'C' worked, slapping down the pages in turn, slowly building up piles of pages.

Only then was it discovered that the pages had no holes, so there was no means of clipping or lacing each pile into one cohesive book.

The reports had to be ready by 6.00 am, to be driven to Northolt and flown direct to the Middle East. We all scratched our heads, and then I suggested that if we had a bit and brace (there were still no such things as electric drills), we could drill holes through each report, which could then be tied with tape. This was approved, and a RN lieutenant, John Boex, dashed off on his bicycle to his digs, where he had some tools. When he returned, the next problem arose, for as John turned the brace, the pages swirled round in a spiral, no matter how firmly they were held. We had no vice available, so I suggested that I, being the heaviest girl present, should sit on each pile of paper, while John manfully drilled the holes, dangerously near my backside, I should add! This ruse succeeded, and John went off in a naval jeep at 6.00 am with the reports, and carrying a loaded revolver, in case of a hold-up by an enemy agent, we were told!

I am glad to say that we were better organised for the subsequent preparations for the landings on Italy and Normandy. That whole episode illustrates only too well how amateurish the British are when they first have to tackle any national emergency in war-time. It seems to take a long time before a really efficient organisation is up and running.

There were many Allied officers also working in ISTD: Norwegians, Belgians, Free French, Americans and Poles. King Haakon of Norway visited us on one occasion, and some of us were presented to him.

Across the road from Manchester College was the University School of Geography, presided over by Professor Kenneth Mason, who worked closely with ISTD. His daughter Helen worked in Section 'C' with me. We became firm friends, and I came to know the family very well indeed. The top floor of the School of Geography became an informal club used by everyone in ISTD. It was known as the Beer Club, and was well patronised in the lunch-hour and the evenings. Only beer was available, for spirits were almost unobtainable in the war. If one had a friendly wine merchant, sometimes it was possible to buy a bottle of gin per month, but this was not always available, and no wine was imported, the existing stocks being soon exhausted.

In Section 'C' there was an American Army captain called George Staempfli; he was a Swiss, but became a naturalised American early in

The visit of King Haakon of Norway to ISTD, 18th May 1943. He is seen arriving at Manchester College, being greeted by Lt Colonel Sam Bassett RM.

the war, so as to be able to join up and fight. He was very tall, going bald, with brilliant blue eyes and a delightful twitching smile. I think he bedded every girl in the office, all with equal fun and gay enjoyment; everyone liked and enjoyed him, and there was never any jealousy or heavy regrets. He was a talented artist and cartoonist, and designed an amusing coat of arms for Section 'C', reproduced on p. 56.

The head of Section 'C' was Commander Bill Dickinson, a naval hydrographer. My desk adjoined his, and he used me as his secretary when he needed letters drafted and typed. He was a small dark man with bright eyes and a long pointed nose, a wide smile and ears which stuck out like jug-handles resembling a garden gnome. He was very good-tempered at our mistakes, and very popular.

One day he said he had to go to London, so I would have to interview a French 'Contact' who was being flown over to give us some topographical information.

'Contacts' were sometimes brought over from their countries of origin by submarine, fishing-boat or aircraft. There were some Norwegians who regularly came by fishing-boat, who were met in the North Sea by MTB or submarine, and brought to Scotland, where they were interviewed by our ISTD representative from the Norwegian section, before being returned to Norway by the same route.

My 'Contact' was wanted for information regarding the possibility of landing gliders or parachutists in the area in which he lived in central France, where there were many small vineyards. I was told to try to discover where there might be open fields, pasture or downland, without letting the 'Contact' know why I wanted this information. The conversation had to be in French, as the man spoke no English. I was very doubtful as to my ability successfully to do this, but Bill seemed confident that I could, and departed for London.

The man arrived, looking lost and bewildered, and we were left alone in a small office, with a large map of the area in question; the interview seemed to go all right, and I was able to report back to Bill on his return with the information he wanted. I am glad to say he was never called away again when 'Contacts' were expected; I found it all rather nerve-racking.

The summer of 1943 was hot, and one evening I organised a supper picnic on the river. I went to London that day and bought three long rectangular pork-pies from Harrods (these could be bought off-ration), and also six pounds of ripe cherries from a street market. That evening about ten of us cycled out to the Trout Inn at Godstow, and hired punts. It was a glorious quiet summer evening, the dragon-flies flitting over the river, and coots and moorhens plopping and puddling in the reeds along the banks. All the pork-pie disappeared, and the cherries followed. I forget what we drank, no doubt some beer or cider which the men brought. George was of course in the party, Helen Mason, and John Boex, who was then courting a beautiful blonde Danish WRAF officer in Section 'C', whom he subsequently married.

I used to go to London sometimes on my days off, and would meet friends from Malta: John Bridger and Bobby Timbrell, now a Canadian naval lieutenant, who had been a midshipman in HMS *Hood* in 1939. We would dine and dance at the Berkeley, which was always full of service people with wives and girlfriends. Restaurants were not permitted to charge more than five shillings for a meal, so dining out was not expensive.

John (Parlby) was still in the Mediterranean, though he had left Malta in March 1943. The 2nd Devons, Dorsets, and Hampshires had gone to Egypt to train for the Sicily landing, as the 231 (Malta) Brigade, and after that, moved on to land in Italy and fight in that campaign.

There had been many hurried weddings during the war, 'Let's get married while we can!' being the sentiment of the uncertainty and urgency of the moment. Many couples regretted it when the war ended and they were faced with the changes war had wrought in them, and the different, quieter demands of peacetime life. There were many divorces during those first post-war years, while people were sorting out their relationships in the changed circumstances of peacetime.

John arrived home with the battalion in November 1943; they were to go to Halstead in Essex, to train for operation 'Overlord', the Allied landing in France.

After some leave, partly spent with John's mother at Bishops Lydeard, near Taunton, and partly at a hotel in Tewkesbury, we went to Halstead to house-hunt. We found a minute thatched cottage, where there was no electricity or running water. There was an outside privy, and we had to collect water from a spring at the bottom of the garden, where we left a bucket permanently under the trickle from a rocky bank, which took about an hour to fill.

Helen Mason came to stay for Christmas, and brought a goose. There was a Calor gas cooker, which burned lower and lower while we cooked the bird; we had hoped to have it for lunch, but it was still only half done at 9.00 pm so we gave up and opened a tin of Spam instead. The goose was finally cooked for us in the officers' mess on Boxing Day. After Christmas it began to snow, and became bitterly cold; a kind lady in a large house in the village heard of our predicament, and invited us to go and have baths in her house twice a week. Helen and I used to cycle there, along lanes rutted with ice; it was bliss to soak in hot water and get really warm.

I became pregnant early in the New Year, and when John's battalion was moved to the New Forest military area, where families were not permitted, I returned to Oxford and lodged with the Mason family.

My mother had left Shropshire and taken a house outside

Lymington, and my sisters and their three children joined her. Diana had married again, to John Armstrong, a naval chaplain with the Commandos, who had been among her many pre-war admirers. By living near the south coast with Mother, both girls were able to see more of their husbands, both of whom were training with Commando units for D-Day.

The Second Front, as it was called, started when the Allied forces landed in Normandy on 6th June 1944. John's battalion was in the first assault, and suffered many casualties. John was wounded on 8th June, and was eventually evacuated to the Queen Elizabeth Hospital in Birmingham, where I visited him one day, travelling the hot, slow return journey from Oxford. War-time trains were slow, and subject to long delays and sudden unexplained halts between stations. I was quite large with my pregnancy by then, and I remember buying a pound of cherries to relieve my thirst during the interminable journey. I suffered for it the next day, and made an emergency visit to Mr Stallworthy, my consultant obstetrician, thinking I was starting to miscarry again.

'How many cherries have you been eating?' he astutely inquired. He appeared to bear me no ill-will for so frivolously wasting his time.

From Birmingham, John was sent to an officers' convalescent hospital in Lord Normanton's large mansion outside Ringwood. Through the hospital welfare representative, John arranged for me to go to visit him, and that I could be put up in the house occupied by the old parson of the church on the estate. I arrived by taxi to be greeted by a bent old man with a shock of long unkempt white hair, with blood-shot eyes, and slack mouth, but who nevertheless seemed rather over-pleased to see me. No-one else appeared to live in the house, and he showed me to my room upstairs, which I quickly realised was next to his. His leering and fulsome remarks I found unpleasant, and I was glad to leave my suitcase, and walk up the long drive to visit John, with whom I had supper. It was late July, but by the time I had walked back to the vicarage, it was beginning to get dark.

'Come in and have a little drink with me, my dear, before we go up to bed!' suggested the old parson, who, it was obvious, had already had several little drinks. I edged toward the stairs, firmly refusing the invitation; he followed me up, and entered my room, going over to show me how soft my bed was, and then he said:

'Now, you go to the bathroom first, my dear, and I'll . . .'

'Yes, thank you. I am very tired, so GOODNIGHT!' I said as loudly as I could, almost pushing him out of the room.

I rushed to the bathroom, and back to my room, where I turned to lock my door: there was no key. I pushed the chest of drawers across the door, and climbed nervously into bed; sure enough, a little while later, the door handle turned, and there was the sound of grunting effort, which was repeated ... I watched, paralysed with fear, but the footsteps shuffled away, and after a long time I must have slept.

The next morning I was up and packed by 6.30, and slipped out of the house: I could not face breakfast with the awful old lecher. John was somewhat surprised to see me, and the nurses gave me some breakfast. I did not stay a second night.

It was during this visit to see John that I learned he was having an affair with a Wren, who also intended visiting him at the Ringwood hospital. I wondered where she stayed!

John's wound was not serious, and when fit again, he was appointed to Lowestoft. I remained in Oxford awaiting my baby. Virginia was born on 26th September in the Radcliffe Infirmary, and after a week, I took her down to my mother's house at Lymington. John did not visit me in hospital, nor come down to Lymington until Virginia was two months old. I was surprised and hurt, because all servicemen were allowed forty-eight hours compassionate leave to go to see their wives and new-born babies.

John was appointed to the Staff College at Camberley in January 1945, and we took rooms there until his course ended in June. He was then appointed to the army of occupation in Germany, where families were not allowed, so we rented a small house in Alverstoke, where Virginia and I lived for over a year.

My father had returned from Ceylon, and was now Commander-in-Chief Portsmouth, especially bidden to pull up naval discipline in the port to pre-war standards, particularly in matters of dress, which had been allowed to lapse during the war.

Living near HMS *Dolphin*, the submarine base, I was in touch with many old friends from Malta. Shrimp Simpson was the Commanding Officer, and Hubert Marsham, once again, his second-in-command.

Father used to enjoy walking round the dockyard on Sunday mornings after church, hailing ships from the foot of their gangways. If the Quartermaster appeared to answer his hail wearing the incorrect rig of the day, Father would summon the ship's captain to his office in

Admiralty House on Monday morning, and one could only pity the poor man.

One Saturday, I was lunching with my parents, and Father said, rubbing his hands with glee:

'I am going to enjoy myself tomorrow! After church I am going over to Blockhouse [the Navy's name for HMS *Dolphin*] in my barge; the submarine crews will never expect me on a Sunday, let alone on the sea-ward side, and I shall catch the lot of them out improperly dressed!'

I said nothing, but when I returned home that evening, I rang Hubert Marsham to warn him, who was very grateful indeed. When I saw Father again a day or so later, I asked him innocently how he had got on in his weekend sleuthing exercise.

'Extraordinary thing!' he barked, 'I didn't catch anyone out . . . they were all perfectly correctly turned out! Most disappointing!'

I didn't have the courage then to tell him of my part in this, and it was eighteen years before I did so; even then he was furious with me, and saw nothing funny in the incident at all.

It was a relief to me that Army families were not permitted to accompany their husbands to Germany. I enjoyed being back in Alverstoke again, which I remembered so well from my childhood. Many families still lived there whom I had known before the war, and of course, there were the submarine officers at Blockhouse, many of whom I had known well in Malta, who used to come in groups for walks and a large tea at weekends, and sometimes for supper. Rationing was still strict, meat, fats, sugar and other commodities being in short supply, and also coal in particular. This affected the power supply, and there were frequent power cuts; housewives kept a good stock of household candles, which became harder the longer they were kept, therefore then burning more slowly. For the same reason, my mother, surely the most economical housewife there had ever been, had always bought her household and toilet soaps in the January sales, for use the following year, by which time they were hard as rock, and had lost all their scent, but lasted twice as long!

One evening in September 1945, when I had just put Virginia to bed, the telephone rang; I answered it, and a voice said:

'This is Michael Kyrle-Pope. I am speaking from Blockhouse.'

Completely dumbfounded, I replied:

'It can't be! Michael was killed while trying to escape from a POW camp in Italy!'

'I assure you it is!' he said, 'and I am very much alive! May I cycle round to see you?'

'Yes, of course; do!' I said, thinking wildly what I had in the larder. 'Come to supper,' as I remembered thankfully that I had been given six eggs that day (the ration was still one per week).

I managed to save one for Virginia's breakfast. In later years Michael was often heard to say that the reason he married me was for my scrambled eggs. He arrived looking pale, thin and strained; when I asked after his wife, Elizabeth, to start with he simply said she was not with him. It was quite a little time before he told me he did not know where she was ... 'somewhere in the Middle East' ... and eventually he said he had heard that she did not intend to return to England, that she was living with someone else, and would not be returning to him.

He had reached home from his last POW camp at Lübeck in May after 5½ years away. The let-down of arriving home after looking forward through five years to reunion with his wife, and finding she had left him, must have been intense, and he was full of tension and wounded pride. It took some time for him to be able to talk freely about this and his experiences as a prisoner of war, and he came round often to see me and talk, sometimes bringing two or three friends from Blockhouse, and we would all go out for walks, pushing Virginia in her pram, and return for tea and large quantities of toast, made by the fire.

The return of Michael into my life so precipitately was the final straw in the break-up of my marriage, but before our problems could be finally resolved, there was a difficult period to get through.

The decision made to leave John, I had to wait for him to come home on leave in August 1946 to tell him, as I thought it would be cowardly to do so in a letter.

Divorce in those days was extremely uncommon, and divorcees, both husbands and wives, were mistrusted and despised. Anyone who had been divorced would not be invited to my parents' house, nor to those of their friends. I knew that by leaving John, I would probably be thrown out of the family and disinherited. John and I discussed the custody of Virginia, then aged two, and we agreed that she should stay with me, and that he should have access when on leave. Michael had come to know Virginia and grown fond of her, and was anxious to welcome her as his step-daughter.

It all took a great deal of agonising thought, and I had had to ask myself: had I the necessary courage to go through with it? Was I prepared to hurt my mother so much, as I knew it undoubtedly would?

And what about Virginia? John and I had agreed that she should be brought up by me, and I knew she would have a loving, caring and wise step-father, as well as the continued love and influence of her own father, whom she would see no less frequently than she had done since she was born.

If John and I stayed together, then what were the chances of our own happiness? We had both matured and changed in the five years since our marriage, during which we had hardly seen each other, and never had a home together.

The decision made, I rang Father's secretary to make an appointment to go and seen him in his office in Admiralty House.

I bicycled up to Gosport ferry, crossed the harbour, and then cycled along Portsmouth Hard and into the dockyard.

Father was sitting at his desk; I stood facing him, and told him my intentions, omitting to mention Michael's name. I felt sick with nervousness, and found it difficult to stop my hands from shaking. As expected, Father erupted in fury:

'How dare you? I've never heard such nonsense! You will go back to John at once! We do not have divorces in our family!' and a lot more in the same vein.

'No Father,' I said, quietly, when I could get a word in. 'I have thought about this for a long time. My mind is made up, and you will not change it.'

'You will not enter my house again if you persist in this course,' he said, white with anger. 'I shall stop your allowance and cut you out of my will. I shall never mention your name again, and I shall tell your sisters they are to have nothing more to do with you!'

'Yes, Father,' I said, 'all that I had anticipated, but I repeat, nothing you say will make any difference to my decision.'

'Who is this man you are leaving John for?' he demanded.

'I am not telling you. You will find out in due course, I expect,' I replied.

'I shall, you are right; and if he is in the Navy, I will break him! I will smash his career! Now, GET OUT!' he roared.

I left, and cycled shakily home. Michael was in Scotland: he had just been appointed to HMS *Vanguard*, which was a battleship being built in John Brown's yard on the Clyde. She was to take King George VI, Queen Elizabeth and the two princesses on a six-month cruise to South Africa early in 1947, and her officers had been especially selected for this. My father would soon find out Michael's identity, of course, but I hoped I had bought a little time for him to make counter plans to Father's mission of discredit.

Michael rang up that evening, and I told him what had transpired, and of the threat to his career, which we had half expected; the next day, he asked for a private interview with the captain of *Vanguard*, Bill Agnew, and told him of the situation. Bill had been hand-picked for the command of the ship during the royal cruise, and he told Michael he was a personal friend of the King's private secretary, and would have a word with him.

Divorce was anathema to the royal family, and no divorced person was received at court, or knowingly presented to any member of the family, so we were not very optimistic as to the outcome of this, even though my divorce proceedings had not begun. However, a few days later, the captain sent for Michael and told him that the King had been told the whole story, and so long as no further mention was made of it, he wished to hear no more about it, and Michael should stay in *Vanguard*.

History does not relate what my Father said or felt when he discovered that Michael had got one step ahead of him and thwarted his policy of career-breaking.

Soon after this, I was telephoned by the wife of a naval captain on my father's staff; she asked me to call one morning at 10.00 am, and when I arrived, I was kept standing while she told me what she thought of me, ending:

'We no longer wish to have anything to do with you.' I hardly knew her, and have often wondered why she thought I would mind.

Father had another ace up his sleeve, however. He decided I was not fit to have custody of my daughter, and I received a letter from him saying that if I persisted in claiming it, he would personally fight me in court, and would of course, win, bearing in mind his public position as Commander-in-Chief, Portsmouth. He had arranged that my sister Diana should have the care of Virginia until such time as John remarried and could make a home for her. I don't know if John had any say in this but I doubt it.

I had no money to pay for a court action, having no capital whatever, no income, and of course, no allowance. I also assumed that Father, in his rank as full admiral and position of power, could and would over-rule my case. Michael wanted me to fight, but there was absolutely no financial possibility of it (which Father would have realised).

So one wet cold day in March, I took Virginia down to Denmead, where Diana was living, by hired car from Michael's home in Herefordshire, where we had moved from Alverstoke in October.

I remember Diana saying:

'We will divert Virginia to play with Nicky [her four-year-old son], in another room, then you had better leave without saying good-bye, which would upset the child.'

I left, and was driven in the same hired car to Ringwood, to stay with Sheila Mott and her mother; Sheila had been married to John's cousin, David Mott, a naval lieutenant who had gone down in his submarine. Sheila and her mother showed me the charity and mercy which my family lacked.

By this time Michael had sailed for South Africa on the royal cruise. I was on my own, and had to earn my living. Michael's parents had been marvellously kind in giving Virginia and me accommodation on the top spacious floor of their house in Much Marcle, but with Michael away, and Virginia also, it became imperative for me to find a job.

I had no qualification except my experience in bringing up my own child, and the London diploma in Domestic Economy which I had obtained at Harcombe, so I went to Mrs Boucher's agency in Basil Street, which provided nannies, Mothers' Helps, and other domestic servants to the wealthy. I was interviewed very sympathetically, and offered a temporary position with a stockbroker's family in Essex, looking after Ap and Joy Adams' twins of twelve months, while their nanny was on holiday.

It was a very happy three weeks; within twenty-four hours I had packed away my uniform white overalls, and a day later I had taken over the cooking, the babies having decided they preferred being looked after by their mother. I was treated as one of the family, and we all became firm friends. Francis Ellis, another stock-broker and friend of Ap's, spent much time with the family, and in due course became god-father to our son, James.

After that job with the Adams', the agency sent me to Surrey, to look after a three-year-old child who was living with his grandparents. I never learned where the parents were, but the boy was delicate and nervous, and I had to sleep on a camp-bed in his room. It was a dark house, silent and depressing, and I was glad to leave when the child's nanny returned from holiday.

In the intervals between jobs, I went back to Oxford, where Professor and Mrs Mason put me up: theirs became my second home.

Then Joy Adams wrote to ask me to return to Ingatestone, and to go with the family to Norfolk, where they had taken a seaside holiday house for a month, and where I was asked to go to cook for them. It was a very happy few weeks, for one of which Francis Ellis came to stay; he was god-father to Joy and Ap's eldest child Marigold, aged eight, to whom I read *The Secret Garden* each afternoon on the beach.

I received a letter from Diana soon after Virginia had gone to live with her; it consisted of two or three lines:

'We have changed Virginia's name to Ginny, which we think nicer. She now calls me Mummy.'

I am sure she would have said that the hurt this caused was no more than I deserved.

My divorce was finalised in August (Michael's had come through earlier) and we were married in Oxford from the Masons' house. Many of Michael's relations came, including his parents, but none of mine, of course.

I think this is the moment to relate how, many years later, after both my parents had died, I learned that all that time when my father was condemning me, and railing against me, telling me of Mother's unhappiness, and that I could never again go to Holy Communion, etc., he himself was enjoying two mistresses at once, a pair of Australian sisters whom he had met when he was Governor and C-in-C in Ceylon, and they were in the WRNS. As C-in-C Portsmouth, he would tell Mother he was going to London for meetings, and would stay overnight at his club. In fact he met his girlfriends who had a convenient flat. Mother learned of this quite by chance, when a telegram from the girls to Father confirming arrangements for the following evening was taken to her in error by a steward at Admiralty House; as it was addressed simply to 'Layton', my mother opened it. I still can't bear to think what she must have suffered, first from my betrayal, and then, so soon afterwards, from her husband's.

No words can ever express my feelings of disgust for my father and his cant and hypocrisy.

John remarried within two years of our divorce, and he and his wife were able to make a home for Ginny, who now called a third woman 'Mummy'.

I told John when he remarried that I would claim no access until Ginny was in her mid-teens, so that she should have one stable unchanging family background, without disruptive pulls from or through one or other parent. I would keep in touch with her by letter, but would not interfere in any way, and if he could send me photographs of her from time to time, I would be very grateful. I also said I would like her to call me 'Mother', thinking privately that surely there was no-one else she could call by that name.

CHAPTER 4

Scotland, Gibraltar and Spain, 1947–51

Soon after we were married, Michael was appointed to command HMS *Swiftsure*, a cruiser which had to be sailed up to Rosyth, and there 'put into mothballs', i.e. laid up in reserve.

We found rooms with Mrs Marshall in North Queensferry, whose house was high on the cliff at the north end of the Forth bridge, where we stayed for the winter of 1947-48. On foggy nights we would lie in bed listening to the fog warnings being detonated along the railway line atop the bridge. The house looked out on to the North Sea, and we would climb down the cliff across the road from the house, to look for driftwood on the beach. Fuel, and much food, was still strictly rationed, and any wood we could salvage and man-handle up the cliff was of value. Hot water in the house was heated by a solid fuel boiler, and we were limited to two hot baths a week, which we shared.

It was a bitter winter, and our breath froze in droplets on the folds of the blankets at night, but nothing could detract from our happiness, and the enjoyment of living in the Marshall household.

Michael bicycled to work each morning, and I was alone all day with little to do once I had cleaned our rooms, and with no possibility of finding a job. I started to take orders for knitting, and then, becoming bored with making ladies' jerseys and men's pullovers, I decided to try taking some matinee jackets and bootee sets to a London store. The finishing of these little garments was as important as the knitting, and it took me two days to make a set. When I had half a dozen ready, and I next went down to London, I took them to Fortnum and Mason, and asked to see the buyer in the baby-wear department; she was not available, but the assistant buyer accepted my parcel, and said I would hear from them in due course.

I heard nothing for a month, and so I wrote and asked for my garments to be returned to me if they had been rejected. By return of post, the parcel arrived and, disappointed, I did not bother to open it for several days.

The author and Michael Kyrle-Pope on their wedding day in 1947.

'Hadn't you better open it and see what they say?' eventually said Michael; I did so, and was electrified to find a letter thanking me for my samples, and ordering six dozen of each design, offering me 12s.6d. per set, and saying they would give me the two clothing coupons they had by law to demand for each. The annual allowance of clothing coupons was sixty, and as this was 100 per cent mark-up on the coupon value of the wool used, it was a great bonus; I had calculated that each set cost me 3s.6d., so I also earned a good financial profit. It was hard work trying to complete the order; I knitted all day, and long into each evening, and when I had made a dozen of each pattern, and we were leaving Scotland to go south, I took them to Fortnums, and this time I did see the buyer. I explained that I was knitting as fast as I could, but it would be some time before I could complete the order.

'Good Heavens!' she said, 'Do you make them all yourself? I assumed that you employed out-workers.'

She was extremely appreciative and helpful, and when I asked if she would like some small cable-stitch jerseys to fit two-year-old boys, she replied:

'I'll take anything you make, and leave the styles to you; just bring in what you have ready whenever you happen to be in London. Don't feel pressurised, and I'll look forward to seeing you again when it is convenient for you.'

After that I worked for Fortnums intermittently until 1951 when we went to America.

During 1948, Michael did the Royal Naval Staff Course at Greenwich, and then was appointed to a staff job at the Admiralty. This coincided most conveniently with his youngest brother Ernle, who was also in the Navy, being sent to Australia. Ernle and Pam owned a small house in Waterlooville, outside Portsmouth, so we rented this from them, and Michael found digs in London and came home for weekends. I have always thought this the ideal *modus vivendi*: each partner free to pursue his/her own interests from Monday to Friday, gradually building in excited anticipation to the weekend reunion, and shared days together. I used to plan a special supper of welcome, trying to obtain the ingredients for Michael's favourite dishes on Friday evenings.

One Friday morning I went to see what the fishmonger in the village had to offer; on his slab was one plump sole, lying amid the usual herrings, kippers and cod. 'Ah', I thought, 'just the thing, what a treat for him!' and I joined the long queue. I slowly drew nearer my prey, eyeing it and the customers in front of me anxiously. With only one woman left to be served, the sole still lay there, and when the woman said:

'I'll 'ave a pair of kippers, Mr Brown, they'll just do me and 'ubby nicely for tea, and 'alf a pound o' cod for a nice fish pie for termorrer,' I thought the sole and I were home and dry, but then the wretched creature added:

'Oh, and I'll 'ave that sole too. My pussy just *luvs* a bit o' sole, it'll be a nice treat for 'er!' and I felt I could happily have strangled her, and done worse things to her cat.

There was a small draper's shop in Waterlooville, and one day I noticed a card in the window advertising for a part-time manageress. I applied, and was interviewed by the owner, an elderly man nearing retirement, who wanted someone to take over the three days a week that he served in the shop himself. I was offered the job, and I asked if I could take over the window-dressing, which had remained unchanged for months; he agreed, and I enjoyed enormously changing it each week to a more restrained display, removing weeks of clutter, and promoting a different theme or colour-scheme with each Monday's renewal. The number of customers increased, as did the takings, so I was allowed more freedom, and took on some of the ordering and choice of stock. It was all great fun, and I enjoyed it enormously.

I had been in touch with my mother by letter since Father had broken off relations with me, but I had not seen her. One day in 1949, I had a letter from her, saying she would like to see me again, and suggesting we meet on Southsea Common one morning. (She had by then found out about Father's *ménage à trois* in London, but I was not to know that.)

I remember approaching the agreed meeting place and seeing her sitting on a seat, with my sister Diana beside her. I was shocked at Mother's appearance, she looked so pale and sad. It was an awkward encounter, but served to break the ice for further intermittent contact.

Ginny had her tonsils out in the spring of 1949, and Diana and John wanted to go on holiday just then, so I was asked to have Ginny for ten days; this disruption in her life was exactly what I had hoped to avoid when I voluntarily renounced any of my entitled access until she was older, and it was not a happy visit. The poor little girl, pale and run down from her recent operation, a stranger to our house, who had not seen me, or Michael either, for two years, was utterly confused and miserable, a little girl lost.

Michael and I went to Brittany for a week's holiday in August. No-one had been permitted to travel abroad through the war years, nor since, but the law had just been relaxed, although one was only allowed to take about £10 currency out of the country. We crossed the Channel from Southampton to St Malo, where we hired bicycles and proceeded to Erquy-les-Bains, where we stayed in the Hotel de la Plage, across the road from the beach. We cycled for miles, enjoying wonderful French meals like nothing we had had for years; we visited Lisieux by train, and also the grave of Michael's younger brother Alec in a tiny village churchyard, near where he had been shot down on D-Day behind German lines. On our return, we were not even able to afford the meagre duty-free allowance of wine or spirits, but I must have caught the malevolent eye of a fierce busty Customs Officer; she searched me intimately, and even shook the covers of my library book, expecting what? I wondered, to slip from between the pages!

That autumn I had appendicitis and was admitted to hospital in

Portsmouth. Forty-eight hours later I was transferred to the Queen Alexandra hospital in Cosham. This was a gruesome experience, the ward of fifty women occupying the whole length of an almost unheated Nissen hut. I was so cold that I asked for a hot water bottle, but the dragon of a nurse said:

'Nonsense! You're far too young to need a hot water bottle! You certainly shan't have one!'

The next day the hospital was officially visited by my mother, in her capacity as the wife of the C-in-C Portsmouth, and the matron who escorted her round the wards, when they came to my bed, was surprised that I was greeted so warmly.

'Is there anything you want or need that I can send in to you, darling?' asked my mother.

'Oh, yes please, Mother, I am not allowed a hot water bottle and my feet are icy; could you possibly send me one, or a pair of bedsocks?'

'Not allowed a hot water bottle?' cried the matron, in some consternation, 'why ever not?!'

'I was told I was too young to need one, and it was too much trouble for a nurse to get me one,' I replied.

Mother looked appalled and the matron furious, and surprise, surprise, a hot water bottle materialised within minutes! This did not endear me to the bullying nurses, who took it out on me in other ways until, thankfully, I was discharged and allowed to go home.

Meanwhile, my elder sister Winifred had had a row with my father. He had blazed with fury when she told him she intended going to look after me when I first came home from hospital, for the few days until Michael returned for the weekend. He forbade her to do any such thing, but she stood her ground, and came, and was a wonderful help, giving me time to get on my feet again.

When she returned home to the house in Alverstoke which she and Diana were sharing, she went to see Father, and remonstrated with him again, on my behalf, saying she insisted he reinstate me in his will. I do not know how the scene transpired, except that she did overrule him, and when his residual estate was finally divided between us three daughters on the death of our mother, my sisters were each left three sevenths, and I received one. I have always been grateful to Winifred for this intervention on my behalf.

Michael's next appointment to the Admiralty was in the Operations Division, attached to the section called Ship Target Trials. This work included controlled explosive tests of all types of naval weapons, shells, bombs, depth charges and mines, against different classes of ships.

Michael joined the department when most of the programme had been completed, leaving only those to be carried out on submarines. Most of the explosive tests firing depth charges against submarines at varying depths, and explosions set at different distances away, had also been completed. The remaining trials involved lowering the submarines in deep water to the point at which the hull began to crush and collapse from pressure. The last trial of all had to be conducted in extremely deep water, and as there was no area of sufficient depth round the British Isles, it was decided to do it in Gibraltar Bay in the early summer of 1950. It looked as though the trial would take several weeks, if not months, so Michael suggested that I should accompany him. He would be living in *Flamborough Head*, the depot ship to the specially converted lifting-craft which would lower the submarine in a wire cradle of six-inch wire hawsers; the Admiralty scientists and construction engineers working on the trial would also be accommodated on board, and we thought that I could probably find digs of some sort once I arrived in Gib.

I was lucky enough to get a passage out in the Admiralty Fleet Auxiliary *Bacchus*, which was carrying stores to Malta, calling at Gibraltar.

We sailed toward the end of April from Chatham. I shared a cabin with Sally Cocup, the pretty eighteen-year-old daughter of a naval Chaplain and his wife, who were doing the round trip to Malta and back as a holiday cruise. There were twelve passengers, including a scientist going to Malta to do experiments on gravity and magnetic fields on the sea-bed from a submarine.

We sailed into a freshening wind with a north-westerly gale forecast just ahead of us. The weather quickly deteriorated, and within twenty-four hours of sailing, china, glass, and even tables and chairs were crashing and sliding from one side of the saloon to the other. The gale increased, and the little ship seemed to do everything but stand on her head; the dining-room emptied, and at meals Sally and I and the young scientist were the only passengers to appear. We maintained a relay of large pots of tea and quantities of sandwiches to fortify the crew, who were all busy about the ship, trying to keep up with the damage being caused by the heavy seas. After forty-eight hours, as we left the Bay of Biscay behind us, the wind began to abate, and we all caught up with a little sleep, and nursed our bruises.

We reached Gibraltar six days after leaving Chatham. Michael met me and took me to the house in Rosia Bay, which was the official quarter of the Secretary to the Flag Officer Gibraltar. He, Geoffrey Palmer, had very kindly offered us accommodation, his wife having already returned to England, ahead of Geoffrey, who was nearing the end of his appointment. It was a lovely old house of yellow washed stone, with green shutters at the windows and a roof of Spanish red tiles; the walled garden was full of flowers, plumbago, hibiscus, bougainvillaea, oleanders, arum lilies, and one or two olives and palm trees. The house was that to which Nelson's body was brought after the battle of Trafalgar; the body was embalmed in a cask of brandy, and rested in the room Geoffrey was using as his study, until it could be sent back to England.

Life in Gib was very social and full of gaiety and colour. Relations between Spain and Britain were strained at that time, over the recurring problem of Gibraltar and Spain's claim to it. In 1704, after Gibraltar had been captured by the English, Queen Isabella is reputed to have sat on the semi-circular hill north of the Spanish border at La Linea, which overlooks Gib, and to have vowed that she would never move, nor wash again, until the Spanish flag flew once more over Gibraltar. The legend goes that after a few weeks, the English, with traditional chivalry, hoisted the flag of Spain for a few hours, to enable the lady to go down and have a wash and change her underwear! The hill is still known as the Queen of Spain's Chair.

When we were there, the British in Gib had to obtain passes from the Spanish Consulate whenever they wished to cross the border, and on passing through the frontier, in both directions, all cars and their passengers were searched thoroughly. This caused long queues of cars to build up, particularly at weekends, on both sides. We were lucky enough on several occasions to be invited to go over with the Flag Officer Gibraltar, Rear-Admiral Brooking, in his official car, when he was going into Spain for a game of golf. He was swept through the border posts with great pomp and bugle-blowing by the Spanish guards, which was great fun, and saved a lot of time.

One Sunday we were invited to join a party of about sixteen to go to an annual festival, (called a *feria* in Spain), up in the cork oak woods at Al Miraima, a little village in the hills to the north-west of La Linea. The further we progressed, the more crowded the road became, with Spaniards converging from all directions, in cars, on horses, mules, and donkeys, and on foot. Many of the vehicles were decorated with sprays and branches of bracken and oak leaves.

On entering the forest the road deteriorated to a dusty track, threading between the stunted and twisted oaks, many of which had been stripped of their cork bark to any height from 6–20 feet.

The fair extended over about two square miles, and consisted of family parties round their fires, over which were cooking the traditional Andalucian dishes of paella in large shallow pans. Each party was singing and laughing and greeting friends round other fires nearby; many groups had tied a rope high up in a tree, up which young men climbed to do acrobatics in the branches, and from which girls and children swung.

During the afternoon the tempo quickened: there were groups singing and dancing flamenco, clapping to the rhythm, the girls' castanets clicking as they swirled their long frilled dresses, and the young men stamping and twisting sinuously between the trees. Everyone had plenty of *vino*, and drank from goat skins held high above their mouths. In and out of the trees, horses, mules and donkeys were being ridden by young men wearing high-waisted tight trousers, bloused shirts, and hard black or grey hats with stiff wide brims: behind them, riding pillion, sat their girls, sitting sideways, a scarlet flower in their hair, red or blue frilled skirts cascading almost to the ground.

It was a hot sunny day, and among the trees were stalls selling wide straw hats, and bottles of rather ominous looking cloudy water. The atmosphere was irresistibly infectious, of gaiety, laughter and fun; everyone was flirting and drinking wine, and all were happy and carefree. As we wandered through the forest dark-eyed handsome young men winked and waved at me, and pretty dusky girls cocked eyebrows at Michael, and of course we waved back.

The dust was thick in the air, and our throats became dry, so we stopped at a little *venta*, a wine stall, and drank draught beer, sweet and aromatic stuff, not unpleasant and deliciously cool; I longed for a glass of water, but was firmly warned off the suspect bottles for sale. We continued our wandering, and found the little chapel of Al Miraima, where it is said that one wish made is always granted. The doors were wide, and a continual stream of people were going in to say a prayer and make their wish. Outside the babble and chatter of the fair came right up to the walls, but inside all was quiet and reverent, people moving slowly forward to light a candle and kneel.

We began our journey home at about 6.00 pm. Some of the Spaniards were also packing up, though many would stay on far into the night; the roads were full of people, and every imaginable form of transport, which had bracken threaded into harness, cartwheels, and headlights; the crowds all were still singing, shouting to each other, laughing and waving bottles of *vino*.

On our way home we stopped at our favourite *venta* to have a glass of wine, and found a group of three children there, a boy of about ten, who played a violin, and a girl of about the same age who played the guitar; they were both dressed in black and were good looking little urchins; the third child, a younger girl, handed round a plate hopefully, after they had come to the end of their repertoire, and then with many shouts of encouragement from all, the three of them clambered on to one adult bicycle with their instruments, and rode off.

By this time it was nearly dark, and people were pouring along the road from Al Miraima. A van full of young men stopped at the *venta*, and came to sit near us on the terrace; they had more sophisticated instruments than the previous youthful trio, and after passing round a leather wine-skin between them, they settled down to play. The music was Spanish, folk songs and dances, and played very well, with the insidious rhythms held by a superb drummer; some of the young men sang, and beat time on anything to hand. After a while they stopped to pass round the wine again, and a member of the party began to sing flamenco; the listeners began to clap the rhythm, and this went on until the singer had to stop for further refreshment. I had not heard spontaneous flamenco before, and found it hypnotising, in a quite intoxicating way.

The following Sunday, Michael and I walked through the dockyard tunnel under the rock to Sandy Bay, on the east side, which had a long shingle beach, with no houses or buildings near it. We walked along the road above the beach and round to Catalan Bay to the north, where in those days there was a little village tucked in under the rock face, peopled by emigrants from Genoa. They kept entirely separate from the Gibraltarians, returning to Genoa for their husbands and wives. They hardly ever went into the town of Gibraltar at all, although the men would pass through the dockyard tunnel to work each day, otherwise they remained an entirely separate community, even doing their own foreign trading. Nowadays I think the ubiquitous tourist trade has developed and spoiled that east coast, and I don't know if the little Genoese village has survived.

Meanwhile Michael's submarine trial had been proceeding according to plan, but on Whit Sunday a strong easterly wind rose, and he was recalled to *Flamborough Head* after lunch, as the trial ships and barges were bumping dangerously, and the submarine herself had received some damage, so all had to be moved back into the harbour. This not only delayed the trial, but brought to a head many political questions which had been simmering for the previous two or three weeks.

The site of the trial was an area of water in Gibraltar Bay, to which both the British and the Spanish have laid claim for over two hundred years, since the Treaty of Utrecht. The dispute had reared its ugly head at intervals, until Joseph Chamberlain, in 1897, made a sensible speech in the House of Commons, in which he advised that as there obviously was no answer to the vexed question, it would be better to avoid any further discussion of the matter. Since then neither nation had mentioned it, both quietly claiming the area as their own.

When this siting of the trial was first mooted, the Flag Officer Gibraltar had strongly vetoed it, foreseeing trouble. His advice was over-ridden by the Foreign Office, and the go ahead was given for the trial to continue as planned, so the lifting craft, spud pontoon and barges took up station and were moored in the middle of the bay, and the trial began.

This action was rather more than the Spanish were prepared to overlook, and after a few days, first motor-boats, then motor torpedo boats, and then sloops of the Spanish Navy came out to circle the trial ships, and presumably they sent agitated signals to Madrid, from which angry demands were sent to London that the trial should be aborted immediately, if not sooner.

In Gib, Michael's orders were to carry on as quickly as possible, and it should be added here that there were only two other possible sites in the world where the sea was sufficiently deep to carry out the trial, one of which was in Russian waters, and the other inaccessible for other reasons.

The removal of the unit from the disputed area owing to bad

weather conditions must have looked to the Spanish very much like British capitulation, so there was some speculation as to what the reaction would be when the weather improved, and the trial was resumed. A Spanish destroyer had arrived on the scene, and stood by to observe the dismantling of the trial site with interest. Although the Foreign Office attitude regarding this matter, and in their general dealing with Franco's Spain, had been anything but co-operative during the past years, in Gibraltar, relations between the Governor, the Flag Officer and the Spanish authorities had been excellent, so it was hoped that their diplomatic and friendly exchanges could be extended to overcome the current difficulty, and permit the trial to resume in due course. This is what occurred.

One day we drove along the Spanish coast to Torremolinos, which was then a very small village, for lunch, and on to Malaga. The road was not the wide highway it is today, and we passed through little villages, and round sandy and rocky bays, looking down through clear water to the sea-bed. The country was green and cultivated, fields of barley being cut by men with reaping-hooks, who cut, gathered up, and bound the sheaves as they worked. Men and women in the fields wore wide straw hats, and we overtook many groups of women carrying water jars on their shoulders, and baskets on their heads.

The dwellings we passed, in many cases they could hardly be called houses, were of mud bricks, whitewashed, with roofing of dried palm leaves, and round all these hovels there were invariably to be seen large bushes of scarlet geraniums, and prickly pears over-grown with vines of deep blue morning glory in full flower. On the inland side of the road, beyond the narrow coastal strip of agriculture, rose high severe mountains. We drove along roads lined with silver-grey leafed eucalyptus trees, and through cork woods, and later, a forest of squat Mediterranean pines, their vivid green a sharp contrast to the brilliant blue sea. All that has gone now, over-taken by so-called progress, which has brought miles of ribbon development of high-rise hotels and apartment blocks, almost continuous from Gibraltar to Barcelona.

Through my host, Geoffrey Palmer, we had met Elizabeth Cresswell, a very attractive Russian woman, married to, but separated from an English diplomat. She lived in Spain with her son aged seven, and her elderly mother, a white Russian baroness who spoke Russian, French and German, but no English. Elizabeth and I became friends, and when Geoffrey's posting ended and he left to return to England, she invited me to go and stay with her in her house in Campamento, a village beyond La Linea, on the coast road round the bay to Algeciras. Michael was by then nearing the critical moment of the trial, and could come ashore less frequently, so it was very convenient for me to move into Spain and join Elizabeth's unusual household.

Her typical small old Spanish house opened directly off the village street; my bedroom was on the immediate right, with a wrought iron barred window on to the same street. Beyond my bedroom door, the stone entrance passage widened into a small open patio, from which doors led into other bedrooms and a stone stairway rose to the first floor sitting room, and continued on higher to the flat roof; this was where Elizabeth did her entertaining.

In the passage between the front door and patio, and all round the walls of the patio itself, were many swallows' nests, one on top of a wrought iron bracket lantern, and when we went to bed we would see all the parents roosting on old hooks in the walls, while the nestlings, fully grown except for the length of their tails, were sitting round the edges of their nests, heads to the middle, rumps sticking out, like little groups of gossiping old women, a most enchanting sight.

One evening Elizabeth had a party; about a dozen of us gathered up on her roof, and drank the local red wine, Corriente, which she bought in large carboys and decanted into jugs. We sat at small candle-lit tables, and ate her cook's delicious paella, which I had watched being made in a huge wide shallow pan over the open kitchen fire. Rice, saffron, garlic, onions, chicken, prawns, pimientos, peas all went into it, the scent and flavour was ambrosial. Later, while listening to Elizabeth's Russian and Spanish gramophone records, we watched crowds gathering in the street below for the eve of Corpus Christi celebrations: strings of lights were switched on across the street, and eventually we went down and mingled with the crowd. We found a fairground at the outskirts of the village, so we all went on the big wheel, bought balloons, and generally behaved like children, until those who had to return to Gib before the frontier closed had to leave.

Michael was able to get ashore one day, so I went into Gib by bus and met him for lunch, after which we walked to the lighthouse on the southern-most tip of the Rock, Europa Point. As a Younger Brother of Trinity House, Michael had arranged for us to be shown round the lighthouse, which was the only one outside the United

Kingdom that was maintained by Trinity House. Mr Gregory, the head keeper of the three, explained the working clearly and concisely.

It was an old-fashioned type of light even then, running on pressurised oil in the same way as a Primus stove; the timing of the beams was run by clockwork, a canister like a huge inverted cocoa tin dropping right over the light, thus obscuring it at the required intervals, and lifting again. The light was 12,500 candle-power, and could be seen in normal Mediterranean visibility over a distance of 18–20 miles. We were shown the mantle which was beginning to hole round the edge and which was to be renewed that evening: it was shaped like a small balloon, about $3^1/2$ inches in diameter, and tied to its metal holder with a piece of thin cord, like a jam-pot cover; it disintegrated into powder in my hand when I touched it. The new mantle was a small limp knitted bag of shiny white silk, soft and stretchy, about ten inches in diameter; the moment this, on its holder, was dropped over the light, which was turned to full pressure, it was blown up like a balloon, then settled and shrank to a perfect globe: if the globe was not true, or if it settled into a cone, the light would be out of focus with the lens. This light was replaced by a modern electrically operated one soon after our visit.

We were taken out on to the narrow balcony encircling the lens tower, and looked down 160 ft into the sea. I noticed a wide muddy stream spewing out of the rock into the sea below the lighthouse.

'That is the main Gibraltar sewer,' said Mr. Gregory, 'and do you see the mass of well-fed fish in it?' We were amused to see a local fisherman with a rod and line lowered in to the middle of it.

We went to Tangier once or twice, crossing the Straits very early in the morning, exploring the town on its steep hill, wandering in narrow streets, mingling with the throngs of North Africans in every kind of tribal dress and colour, and returning to Gib in the evening. I thought it a rather frightening place, suggestive of my narrow escape in the Arab quarter of Alexandria in 1939, and I did not wish to tarry there after dark.

Meanwhile the submarine trial ships and equipment had been re-established in Gibraltar Bay, and work was to recommence. The Spaniards seemed resigned, and the weather was ideal. The atmosphere on board *Flamborough Head* resembled that of a maternity home, with everyone talking in bated breath about 'Her'.

'Is all going well?'

'Will the weather hold?'

'Zero hour tomorrow.'

'Will she do it at 600 ft? Or less? Or more?'

'Will she slip her wires and sink irretrievably to the bottom when she "goes"?'

This was a modern submarine, and the Admiralty were anxious to know exactly how much stress and pressure her hull could take before it collapsed, and where the plates would give first, etc. Michael had my telephone number in Campamento so I could be told when the literal crunch occurred. I felt almost as if I were to be told if it was a girl or a boy, and if mother and child were doing well.

While awaiting the momentous news, Elizabeth and I were to go to a big Spanish wedding in Algeciras, between an Air Force officer and the sixth daughter of the Larios family, in which there were seven girls and one son, who was the Duque de Lerma. The marriage took place at 6.00 pm in a small church near the bull-ring; accommodation inside was so limited that only women guests were ushered to seats, while the men waited outside.

The east wall of the church, above and on each side of the altar, was carved in niches, which had been filled with blue hydrangeas, completely covering the whole wall, so that the altar seemed to stand against a vast curtain of blue flowers. There was no other floral decoration, nor any bridesmaids. The bride wore conventional white, and was escorted right up to the altar by her uncle who was giving her away, and also by her mother, a tall and beautiful lady who wore an exquisite black mantilla of Chantilly lace over a high tortoise-shell comb in her hair; the mantilla hung round her shoulders down to her waist, and was shown off to perfection over her dress, which was of a soft banana-beige crepe.

The service, in Latin and with no music, only took twenty minutes, and then we all emerged to go to the Larios' house, where champagne and many dishes of rather solid canapés were served out on a large patio, from which magnolias, jasmine, plumbago and bougainvillaea climbed the walls. Many of the guests had come down from Madrid for the wedding, and the women wore gorgeous couture dresses and hats. Elizabeth knew many people, and introduced me to them, including Pepito, the bride's brother, who was quite the most handsome and flirtatious man I had ever met. As the evening wore on, we began to pair off, and dancing began. Elizabeth and I must have been the only guests there who were not Spanish and I found my partners were all superb dancers. There was one amusing incident when a Spanish general asked me to dance; he was a small fat man, wearing full uniform, and he spoke a little French (badly) but no English. The dance floor was L-shaped, the end of one arm being used for sitting out, and there my partner's little fat wife was sitting. The general and I sallied forth to dance a tango, and little by little, I was clasped closer and closer, till I was unavoidably dancing cheek to cheek, but only when we danced round the corner of the room out of Mrs General's sight; as soon as we neared the angle of the room from which we could be seen, our cheeks miraculously disengaged, to cleave together once more only after the danger area was transversed. In spite of this drama (or because of it?), I enjoyed the dance very much.

After a while a guitarist appeared with two men flamenco singers, and a girl of fourteen wearing a beautiful flamenco dress, rather unusually in white; the skirt had stiff lace-edged frills from waist to hem and a lace-edged bodice; she wore it with a deeply fringed scarlet silk shawl and scarlet shoes, and on top of her head, Madrid fashion, she wore a scarlet carnation. Girl flamenco dancers always wore a flower in their hair, and where they wore it, behind the left ear, or the right, or on top of their head, etc, indicated from which part of Spain they came. This child, who was a cousin of the bride, danced quite perfectly, with exquisite precision, delicacy and grace; her hands, her face and her body expressed all she was feeling in her dance. It was an amazing spectacle, quite breath-taking, and all the more so because as soon as she stopped her adult dancing, she became a shy, self-conscious child again. Pepito and all the other Spaniards to whom I talked said it was the best flamenco dancing they had ever seen, and that no better would be found anywhere in Spain.

At about 1.30 am it was suggested by Pepito and Raphael, Duque of Alcala, with whom Elizabeth had been watching the flamenco, that the four of us should go on to the Reina Christina hotel to dine. We danced on the sunken glass floor in the garden, which was lit from beneath, and sat on the terrace looking through the trees to the bay. When the band stopped playing at 3.30 am two men took over from it, and sang flamenco; they became totally emotionally absorbed in their singing, trembling all over, eyes shut, fists clenched as though in agony; Pepito and Raphael became quite rapt, but after an hour or two, I wandered out into the garden and down to the shore, to watch the dawn breaking across the bay, where the trial ships were silhouetted against the sky.

Elizabeth and I eventually got back to her house at 7.00 am, having been drinking champagne for twelve hours on end, but seeming none the worse for it; we fell into bed, and at 8.30 am Michael rang.

'How did you enjoy the wedding? What time did you get home?' he asked.

'It was wonderful!' I replied, 'we got in at seven o'clock.'

'It didn't last very long then, did it?' said Michael in surprise, 'it began at six, didn't it?'

'Seven o'clock this morning!' I replied, 'one and a half hours ago!'

'In that case, you'd better go back to bed!' said Michael, 'and come on board later, for lunch: the submarine well and truly burst yesterday, and is now being hauled to the surface for examination, so we are all celebrating.'

I returned to Campamento after lunch, and slept all afternoon, and so was ready to go out to dinner with some British expatriates in their lovely house in the country. After the meal we all went on to the *feria* in San Rocce, and the evening ended with Elizabeth and me being taken home by two naval officers from Gib, who came in for a drink, when we went up on to her roof, took off our shoes and danced by moonlight to the gramophone. When the two men left to catch the frontier before it closed at 3.00 am Elizabeth and I sat on talking for another half hour before going to bed.

Two days later, Michael started a few days leave, and we crossed the Bay by ferry to Algeciras, there catching a little single coach diesel train, which took seven hours to climb up through the hills to Granada. It was a wonderful journey except for the temperature; the train radiated searing heat from roof, sides, and floor. It was quite appalling, but the scenery we passed through, so slowly that we had ample time to study it all, was magnificent.

In Granada we stayed in the Parador, a government run hotel, which is part of the Alhambra itself. It was a magical few days, exploring Granada, and then wandering in the beautiful courts and gardens of the palace, and crossing to the Generalife, which we thought almost more lovely in its less formal and detailed design than the Alhambra palace.

The journey back was less uncomfortable and shorter, for our train left in the early cool part of the morning, and the track was downhill all the way.

Four days later I said a sad farewell to Elizabeth, and we left Gibraltar. I was allowed to take passage with Michael in *Flamborough Head* as she was a Merchant Navy vessel, and not of the Royal Navy. It was rough again, crossing the Bay of Biscay, but not so severe as on the outward voyage, and we berthed at Plymouth on 12th July, where it was cold and wet, and where everyone looked depressed and worried about the war in Korea.

We moved back to Waterlooville on our return from Gib, and within a fortnight Michael had been appointed to HMS *Warrior* as her first lieutenant. *Warrior* was a light fleet carrier which was being used as a ferry carrier, taking troops and stores out to Korea. She was based in Portsmouth, and Michael joined her early in August and sailed for the Far East at the end of the month.

Meanwhile, Father had retired from the Navy and left Portsmouth, and he and Mother were living at Curdridge, near Southampton. We had not been home long when, to my amazement, Mother rang up to invite me to go and spend a night with them, Father having said he thought 'it was about time he saw me again'. Michael was not invited.

I drove over to arrive in time for tea, and was greeted by Mother, who told me Father was gardening, and I had better go and find him; he was hoeing, I remember, and said:

'Oh, hello!' without looking up. I was rather nervous, and he remained silently working, so after some innocuous remark, I left him and returned to Mother on the terrace. The atmosphere eased somewhat over tea, and then I was invited to pick the raspberries for dinner, which took care of the hour before drinks were offered. I left the next morning thankfully; nothing personal had been mentioned and it was an awkward meeting, but it had at least served to thaw the three-year-old glacier.

Mother came over to Waterlooville occasionally after that, and I visited Curdridge. *Warrior* returned to Portsmouth at the end of November, and was home over Christmas, but Michael was 'day on' (the naval term for being on duty twenty-four hours), and so I was invited to spend it at Curdridge, which seemed to confirm my re-acceptance into the family.

We had to move out of Ernle's house in December, as he and his family returned from Australia.

We bought a small cottage in Purbrook, just south of Waterlooville, which had 2½ bedrooms, which was all that we required. I had had two miscarriages, which had been disappointments, for we very much wanted to start a family, but for the moment we only needed a small house.

Warrior did another trooping voyage to Korea in the new year, and Michael was away another four months.

CHAPTER 5

USA, 1951–53

'MICHAEL, YOU MUST KEEP an eye on Suzanne, for as you know, she is very susceptible to good-looking men!' said my mother, and then, turning to me, she added:

'And you must never accept a lift from a man alone in a car, darling, for all American men are wolves, and something very unpleasant could happen to you!' Keeping a straight face, I assured her that I would be very circumspect (she had never in her life been to America!).

This was the first time that my parents had received Michael, when we went together to say good-bye before leaving for Washington DC in June 1951, where Michael was to join the British Joint Services Mission (BJSM) as Staff Officer (Plans) to the NATO section. This was an 'accompanied' appointment, meaning that I could go with him, my travelling expenses being paid.

We sailed in the Cunard ship *Caronia* to New York. After years of strict rationing, which still continued in England (this was six years after the war had ended), we very much enjoyed the rich food onboard, and tucked in rashly, learning our lesson swiftly!

Caronia called at Le Havre, where she berthed at 7.00 pm; after dinner we went on deck to watch the Chief Purser and chefs buying fresh food from vans parked at the foot of the gangway. The chef examined the crates of fruit, greens, eggs, etc. carefully burrowing to the bottom before passing the consignment for purchase; they were then carried onboard by the waiting lines of underlings. He and the purser then bartered with the salesmen, who were typically verbose Frenchmen; there was a lot of argument about the eggs before a price was agreed, and four or five were taken onboard to be tested before the deal went through. This also happened over asparagus, when a small bundle was taken to be boiled and tasted before that consignment was accepted.

The day we arrived in Washington, Michael heard that he had 'got his brass hat', naval slang for being promoted to Commander. This was very exciting, as this is the first rank to which promotion is selective:

up to this step, it is automatic; the increase in pay would also be a great help with the cost of living in America, which to us was high.

We arrived in the heat of a Washington summer; the temperature and humidity were both in the 90°s. On arrival, until we could find a house, we were lent one across the river Potomac, in Alexandria. It was a pleasant house on a hill, and until we could buy a car and generally get ourselves organised, I had to walk half a mile down the road to the nearest supermarket, and then back again up the hill, carrying everything we needed: milk, bread, potatoes, fruit, meat, cleaning materials etc.

One day I was labouring home with a huge brown paper grocery sack in each arm, when I was overtaken by a large Plymouth estate car; it stopped and a handsome man leant out and called back to me:

'Say, you look kinda hot, could you do with a ride?' to which I replied:

'To hell with Mother, I certainly could!'

He told me he was a US Navy commander called Bill McCormick, known as Mac, and we immediately found we had a lot in common.

One afternoon, a few days later, I was doing the ironing, and because of the tremendous heat and humidity, I was wearing a bikini, when the front door-bell rang; wondering who on earth it could be, I answered it, to find Mac on the door-step wearing an immaculate suit, with a most glamorous woman wearing a hat and gloves, whom he introduced as his wife, Lolly. They had come formally to call, to welcome us, but all formality flew out of the window when I told them of Mother's warning, and how I could not resist Mac's offer of a lift. We became great friends, and although Mac is now dead, Lolly and I remain close friends to this day; a few years ago Michael gave me the fare to go to California to visit her, as my seventieth birthday present, and she tries to fit us into her itinerary when she comes to Europe each summer to visit her married daughter, who lives in Paris.

Michael's work was largely to liaise with the American NATO headquarters at Norfolk, Virginia, whither he commuted regularly, and where the American NATO staff were quartered. I therefore met few Americans, but the other NATO nations' representatives were, like us, based at Washington, so we came to know them very well indeed, and lived a very social life, attending not only private parties, but also the formal receptions celebrating each nation's various anniversaries and national days. I found that my French improved the

longer we stayed, for the Portuguese, Belgians, some Italians and
Spanish, as well as the French themselves, of course, all preferred to
speak it rather than English.

When we had acquired a second-hand Chevrolet, I drove to
Alexandria to shop one day, and parked in a public parking lot. It was
supervised by an elderly coloured man with frizzy grey hair, and a
kindly benign expression; we talked for a little while and then he asked
me where I came from.

'I'm British,' I replied, and told him I was in the States with my
naval husband.

'Gee! Yes,' he said, 'I just knew you were foreign as soon as I heard
your broken English accent!'

Lolly McCormick had a part-time job at Garfinkles, the
Washington equivalent of Fortnum and Mason's at that time, and she
offered to try to get me work there too. I could not work full time,
having no work permit, but would be permitted to take part-time
employment. I was offered work as a sales-girl on three days a week,
and began in the debutante's department, which sold moderately
priced fashions. I was the only non-American working the floor, and
found the first few days quite daunting; generally I was welcomed and
helped by the other sales girls, but there were those who eyed
me suspiciously, if not with thinly veiled hostility; one such was a
brassy blonde, hard and harsh-voiced, but eventually one day she said
to me:

'Now we've got used to you, we think you're OK, in spite of being
British!'

The customers were varied, and not always easy to please. The stock
was not in view out on the floor, but held on racks and rails in long
rows in the huge stock-room behind the show-room. We had to step
forward to our customers and appraise them, their requirements, and
their likely taste; we then dived into the stock-room to select five or
six models, and bring them out to show the customer. If you were
lucky, or astute in your assessment of her, you should not have to
return to the stock-room more than once, before suiting her; she
would then retire to a fitting-room, to try on the chosen two or three
garments for size and fit. A difficult customer, though, could be very
demanding and tiresome, and one's patience sorely tried. Of course we
had to know our stock thoroughly, keeping up with new deliveries,
and what sizes were still available or had sold out.

One day I had a French customer, who almost at once remarked with obvious pleasure:

'You're English, aren't you?' I was so delighted to be called English for once, instead of the usual term 'Britisher', that I liked her at once; she went on:

'Oh! It is such a pleasure to hear English being properly spoken; I have been over here for eighteen months, and how tired I am of American voices!' She told me she was often taken for English (her accent sounded very French to me!), and I said I was frequently asked if I was French.

'You see,' she said, 'we all learn English in England, or from an English teacher, so of course we have an English intonation to an American ear.'

We went on to enjoy a friendly conversation in a fitting-room, while she tried on dresses. Although we ended up fast friends, she bought nothing, so the *entente cordiale* was not materially profitable to either of us.

After that I had better luck, for my next customers were a mother and daughter who were looking for clothes for the latter's trousseau; she was a pretty little thing, size 7, and looked adorable in anything she put on; they bought three dresses, and I enjoyed every minute I spent with them.

I had quite a lot to learn when I began working in Garfinkles: my first day, I advanced toward a customer, and said:

'Good morning, Madam, may I serve you?'

The customer, and the floor manager (my boss), who was hovering nearby to see how I would conduct myself, both looked equally appalled, and another sales girl was summoned to take over from me; I was led apart a discreet distance, and the floor manager, who was a tall and very intimidating woman, said to me, rather fiercely:

'You must *never* say that to a customer, Pope,' (she called us all by our surnames in a very autocratic way).

'Why not?' I asked in some bewilderment.

'Because stallions serve mares, or bulls serve cows, in this country; here we offer to *help* customers!' and I gratefully saw a twinkle in her eye, and her lips twitching, but I did not make that mistake again.

One evening, only half an hour before we were due to close at 5.45 pm, two tall good-looking men came into the department, wearing large white cowboy hats. We sales girls were allowed to sit down between customers after 5.15 pm and I jumped up, hissing at the other girls:

'These are *mine*! My very first rich Texan Oil Kings!'

'Good evening, gentlemen! How may I help you?' I asked with a warm smile.

'Waal,' one of them drawled, 'we're up here on a convention, and we go home tomorrow; we're both looking for somep'n to take to our wives back home.'

'Oh yes,' I said encouragingly, sizing them up and thinking of what we had in the stock-room that they might like: something fairly flashy, I reckoned.

'Were you thinking of a little cocktail number, perhaps? We have a very chic little red velvet dress which I will bring out for you to see, or have you different ideas?'

'Gee, that sounds just the thing,' they both agreed.

'What about size, then?' I asked.

'Waa-a-l,' said the one who had so far done most of the talking, 'somep'n just about your size, I'd guess,' drawing my outline with his hands through the air, 'what do you think, Al?'

'Yeah, that's right, and the two gals are much the same, I'd say.'

I left to go and get the dress and picked up its duplicate in black velvet, at the same time.

'Jeez! Just take a look at that!' said Al as I emerged from the stock-room.

'That looks just fine!' said the other one, and then, looking at me a touch provocatively, 'but it would be kinda nice to see them on; would you model them for us?'

'Of course I will, with the greatest of pleasure,' I said, thoroughly enjoying the game. To cut a long story short, Al and his friend each bought one of the dresses, I didn't have to show them any others, and they went off highly pleased with themselves. The other sales girls had enjoyed the pantomime too, and I had to take a lot of ribbing. That evening at a NATO dinner party I made a good story of the incident, but I was deflated the next day when I went to work, and the floor manager called me over, and said:

'Say, Pope, I thought you'd like to know that the only convention on in Washington this week has been one of dentists from Arkansas! Sorry, no Texan oil men!'

Just before Christmas I was transferred to the lingerie department for a week, where I had the excitement one day of spotting a customer swiftly transferring a pair of silk panties into her handbag. We had a drill for this, and I made an excuse to her to call over another sales girl, and then went and rang the store detective, who wandered the store all day looking like a customer, with a bleeper in her handbag; she arrived on the scene very quickly and I pointed out the thief, who was tailed until she left the store, when she was stopped and asked to open her bag; I was disappointed that I was unable to see the dénouement of the affair.

For the last of the Christmas rush, I was transferred again, to the men's tie department on the ground floor. In those days, English taste in ties was still very conservative, but the Americans had already gone overboard in both colours and designs. One morning a large, extremely opulent looking lady came and sat down at the counter.

'Now, honey,' she said, 'I want to buy nineteen ties for all my nephews and sons-in-law for Christmas; let me see what you have.'

I showed her drawer after drawer of what I thought were almost wearable ties.

'No, honey, haven't you some a bit more cheerful than that?' she asked, so I brought out more of those in what I considered the worst possible taste.

'Yes, that's better,' she said, her eyes lighting up. And sure enough she chose nineteen of the most hideous and expensive silk ties. I was delighted, for her purchases bumped up my commission in the most gratifying way. Two days later, I was called to the telephone; the sales girl who summoned me said:

'It's a lady who says she wants to speak to the "cute little English gal" who sold her ties on Tuesday.'

Thinking she was going to ask to return some of them, I picked up the telephone and asked cautiously:

'Yes, Madam, how can I help you?'

'You sold me all those ties which you thought were real horrors, didn't you, honey?' she asked.

'Yes, Madam, do you want to return them? I can credit your charge account quite easily,' I offered.

'No, no, of course not! I've remembered seven more presents I want; will you choose the seven designs you think are the most goddam awfullest, and have them charged and sent to me? And I know they'll be just fine.'

Working in Garfinkles was the most marvellous experience; I met so many interesting, amusing and nice people, but not all customers were pleasant to deal with. I had to serve Merle Oberon, the Hollywood film-star, one day when she too was buying men's ties prior to Christmas; she was rude and offensive, and I found it hard to control my own tongue. She had with her a female companion, to whom she was even more unpleasant; when she returned on a later occasion, I avoided her, and called over another sales girl.

While working in Garfinkles, I paid in every cent I earned to my charge account credit, so I could spend it in the store, using my employee's 20 per cent discount. I have never since had such lovely or expensive clothes, and during the January sale, I hid the particular olive green wool crepe shirt-waister dress, edged in black silk braid, which I had my eye on, among the other reduced price stock, and begged the other sales girls not to show it to any of their customers. They didn't, and at the end of the sale I was able to bear it home in triumph. I wore it for years.

We travelled about as much as we could in America, although Michael was not able to take much leave; we managed to get down to South Carolina, and visited Charleston, and the amazing cypress gardens in spring, where we punted along the waterways, between curtains of azaleas, magnolias, forsythia and other vivid plants, ducking under the ghostly grey Spanish moss, the lichen which hung from the trees like trailing tresses of drowned maidens.

We went to Lake Mattamuskeet, near the coast of North Carolina, in the autumn of 1951, with two other couples. The purpose of this trip was for the men to shoot wild geese, for which they had to obtain hunting licences at vast cost. They had three days shooting, in misty, still weather, while the geese snuggled comfortably in the reeds, knowing what was good for them. The men's total bag was seven bob-whites (small quail)! However we all enjoyed the expedition, and we three wives explored the countryside each day; we found a weird old woman whom we visited in her cottage to see her collection of thousands of buttons, which included some from Napoleon's uniform. She also showed us a shelf of specimens in bottles of formaldehyde, which included the foetus of a two-headed baby. Suki Bailey, who was pregnant, rather understandably 'came over all queer' at this horrid exhibit, and beat a hasty retreat into the fresh air.

*Lake Mattamuskett shooting party, 1951. Standing: the author, Michael,
Phyllis and Dick Bryers. Sitting: Suki and Tony Bailey.*

Mac McCormick's posting to the Pentagon finished at Christmas, and
he was appointed to Coronado, near San Diego, so the family had to
prepare to move to the West Coast. Mac went ahead to find a house,
and then Lolly started packing. Michael thought with pity of her
driving across the continent with the four children, and suggested I
should volunteer to accompany her to help with the driving and with
the younger boys. Lolly jumped at the idea, and I became wildly
excited, and one chilly day toward the end of January we set off. We
planned to go by the southern states, as the middle west was snowed
up. The family consisted of Bill Junior, aged fourteen, Cary of
thirteen, and Jamey and Johnny of four and three; with three thousand
miles to traverse, the planning had to be meticulously thought out.
Lolly had a married sister living in Dallas, so we were aiming to stay
there a few days to break the journey. They all decided that because
they had a 'poor ignorant English girl' with them, the journey should
be leisurely, with diversions here and there to visit places of interest
such as the Grand Canyon and the Petrified Forest.

The back of the McCormick 6-cylinder Plymouth shooting brake
was prepared: the rear seats were folded down, suitcases were then laid,

exactly fitting the floor area, and two large cot mattresses were laid on top. Each child had a pillow and small case of its toys, books, etc., and thus the back of the car made a comfortable stable for all four children.

We eventually set off in sleet and rain, after lunch and many delays. We found a motel in North Carolina, and after searching for somewhere to eat, we all settled for the night, the boys in one room, and Cary with Lolly and me in another. Lolly and I sat on our beds drinking whisky and water before putting out the light, congratulating ourselves that we had got away at last.

The next morning we all over-slept, and then had to improve the comfort for the travellers in the back by putting more suitcases on the roof-rack. The weather had improved, and it became increasingly sunny and warm the further south we drove. Even so, we did not make very good time as our 'comfort stop' drill was not yet brought to the fine art it later became. Someone would want to stop, and we'd look for, find, and stop at a reasonable looking gas station, the afflicted one would alight and get on with it, and then just as we'd be preparing to move on, one of the babies, at last understanding the purpose of the stop, would pipe up:

'I want to go to the bathroom too, Marmee!' which of course became a matter of increasing urgency, the more the unsympathetic elders tried to persuade him otherwise. We eventually decreed that the following day, whenever we stopped, no matter at whose request, the whole party would take advantage of the facilities, willy-nilly.

The next day I drove until lunch and relieved Lolly again at 3.00 pm. She sat in the back with the little ones for the last lap, with marked effect, for they were soothed and comforted, and stopped worrying about 'not finding Daddy' or 'going home', so we were able to drive on till 5.45 pm, when we reached Camden, South Carolina, and found the AAA recommended Court Inn Hotel. I was sent in to prospect, on account of my 'English accent', which Americans seemed to find so fascinating. The results were fabulous, the management falling over themselves to make us welcome, offering us three double rooms and two bathrooms for $10 in all. We had an excellent dinner, then baths and beds for all, Lolly and I once more enjoying our whisky night-cap. Our bottle of whisky became the most important item of our luggage, and when Bill climbed up to load and unload the roof-rack each day, he soon learned it was the first thing to be unloaded in the evenings, and the last to be stowed in the mornings.

We reached Georgia the next day, and with the straight roads, fewer towns and little traffic we made good progress. The general appearance of the state was less prosperous though, villages and towns being shabby and mean, and road surfaces patched and irregular. We drove through large areas of cotton fields, and beautiful pine forests with brilliant orange-red soil.

We entered Alabama in the evening, and stopped at Phenix at a comfortable motel. The day's run totalled 340 miles, so Lolly and I felt we had earned our pre-dinner drink. Supper, in a coffee-house across the road, was quite a hilarious affair, for the little boys were highly entertained by the revolving stools up at the counter, where we sat. It had been a really good day; our routine and discipline improved as we went on. Bill and I were responsible for loading the car in the morning, and Cary for tidying and preparing the interior for the day's drive. Our stopping drill has already been described, and in the evening, Bill and I unloaded, while Lolly and Cary coped with the little boys. In the car, the children sat in the back in the morning, and Lolly changed with one of the big ones after lunch, while I drove, so she was behind to nurse and soothe the little ones for their afternoon naps. Then she and I changed over for the last lap.

We sang in the car the next day, and I taught them to sing rounds, and the words of 'Waltzing Matilda'. We passed a seedy and run-down farm, and saw on its gate-post a sign saying 'Struggle Ranch', very aptly named, we thought.

The following day we entered Mississippi, and it rained most of the day. Johnny was restless and weepy; he couldn't understand why we never arrived home when we stopped in the evenings, and fretted for his father. Jamey, aged four, was far more robust, and inclined to be mischievous.

Jamey was a beautiful child: he had sleek, thick corn-gold hair, blue eyes, and rosy cheeks in a golden complexion; he also had a wicked smile and matching sense of humour. He and I hit it off from the moment we met, and in the car he would position himself right behind me so as to whisper into my ear, telling me long stories he made up. Soon after we started the journey, he discovered I loved having the back of my neck tickled, and that was fine so long as I was not driving, and I could relax into a state of semi-somnolent bliss, but when he persisted whilst I was at the wheel, it became rather dangerous. I therefore asked him to stop; he did, for about five minutes and then started again, his small (slightly sticky) fingers caressing my skin in a most delightful way.

'Jamey, will you please stop it!' I said, firmly; I might as well have saved my breath.

'Jamey, I am *telling* you to stop tickling my neck, *now*, or I'll drive us all into the ditch!'

The only answer was a low chuckle, so his mother joined in:

'Jamey, you're to do what Sue tells you, or there'll be trouble!'

The tickling continued, and Jamey, with an expression of affronted innocence, said:

'I'm not doing anything, Marmee, I'm just holding up Bear so he can see out the front!' Bear was his soft toy, behind which Jamey's fingers continued their lethal massage.

'Jamey,' I said, 'tell Bear to stop whatever he's doing to my neck, or I'll stop the car, and we'll have to camp by the road for the night!'

Still the tickling went on, and I stopped the car.

'JAMEY!' roared his mother, 'you do it once more and you'll get a belting.'

I drove on. He did. I stopped again.

'Right!' said Lolly, 'Sue, please stop at the next gas station.' I drew up as instructed a mile or two further on.

'Pull down the shades,' Lolly told us, and we obediently pulled down the sun-screens over all the windows. 'Come here and bend over my knees, Jamey,' and, not looking quite so cocky now, Jamey did so, and using the strap from her handbag, Lolly gave him three sharp ones across his small bottom. The resulting yells were deafening.

'Quick, everyone, shut all the windows, and drive off, Sue, as fast as you can!'

We sped away, keeping a look-out to make sure we weren't being followed by the American version of the NSPCC. The bellows and yells continued for a few minutes then the shades were raised, the windows mercifully lowered, and Jamey, having said he was sorry, was given a cuddle, and peace was restored. He did not tickle my neck again.

American children at that time, to our British way of thinking, were spoilt and tiresome, and apparently undisciplined, but the McCormick parents believed in firm Navy-type discipline, with a smack administered when necessary; as a result their children were delightful, full of fun, and with very good manners. I met Jamey and his wife and family in California when I visited Lolly in 1991, and he is as attractive as ever. Lolly has now made her home with them, at their invitation, and it is a very happy household.

Mississippi was an even poorer state than Alabama and Georgia, but with more varied scenery. We crossed numerous rivers and creeks, tributaries of the Mississippi river, and the land changed from flat expanses of cotton, corn and sugar cane to rolling hills covered with pine-woods; we saw increasing numbers of trees festooned with the eerie grey beards of Spanish moss.

It was quite a shock entering Louisiana the next day and seeing the rotten and precariously leaning log cabins in which the coloured people were living, the roofs patched with cardboard and sacking. I remarked to Lolly that I could not understand why the men didn't repair them, or even build new houses, for there was plenty of timber to be had for the cutting of it. She replied:

'It's not laziness only which accounts for their lethargy, but also ill-health due to malnutrition and pellagra, which is very prevalent in the southern states.'

We drove along a built up causeway through miles of swamps, from which grew trees, their boles swollen obscenely at the water-line, their branches smothered in the drooping grey Spanish moss. Although interesting, I found it oppressive and depressing. Lolly told me that in the Civil War, the local people took refuge in the swamps, and lived in them in hiding.

The roads in Louisiana were poor, narrow and pot-holed; the towns and villages were scruffy, dirty, and untidy, the paint peeling off buildings. The coloured people all had large cars, and washing-machines out on their screen porches (balconies), but their homes would compare unfavourably with an English garden potting shed.

We crossed into Texas just as we needed to fill up with petrol, which was very convenient, as gas is much cheaper in the great oil-producing state. As soon as we entered Texas the smell of crude oil was strong; I did not find it unpleasant, but almost herbal and clean. It was unbelievably flat, monotonously so, and the road, perfectly straight, went on and on, bordered by brown grass and scrubby bushes. We made excellent time, in spite of an unnecessary detour which I took through Long View, a busy town, instead of taking the by-pass which I should have followed. The trouble was due to a new Plymouth in front of us, being driven by a gorgeous young man in a spotless white ten-gallon hat and a maroon silk shirt, whom the older children and I swore was a cowboy, the first one I had seen. I overtook him so as to have a closer look, and found that yes, he was even more handsome than I'd thought. He caught my eye as I passed, and a few moments later, he overtook me; and so we went on, overtaking each other, until I felt I knew him quite well; but then I found myself behind him approaching some traffic-lights in Long View, having been paying not the slightest attention to our route; the lights changed to red just after allowing him through, and I was forced to stop. He disappeared into the town, and in panic, I whispered to Cary beside me:

'Quick, Cary, look at the map, where are we?' and from the back came a sleepy voice from Lolly:

'That'll teach you to follow a drug-store cowboy!'

A little later we did see a genuine cowboy: he had a dirty wavy-brimmed cowboy hat, blue shirt and jeans, and worn and scratched high-heeled boots: which sounds like today's fashion, but in 1952, in Texas, spelled out COWHAND. I was thrilled.

We arrived at Dallas in the early evening, and found our way to the house where Lolly's sister, Barbie, lived, and where the family were to stay. Pem, Barbie's husband, took me to the hotel where I had a room, and fetched me back for supper a little later.

The next day I was taken on a tour of Dallas, which was a large city even then, being the oil centre of Texas and the main banking centre in the south-west. It was obviously a very prosperous place, with huge areas of large and lovely houses. A woman friend of Pem and Barbie's came to supper, a secretary to some big commercial concern; she was middle-aged, unmarried and most entertaining: she caused some amusement when she said:

'I've been looking for a two-legged oil-well for some time now!' I wonder if she ever found one.

Another friend had managed to get four tickets to go to a rodeo at Fort Worth the following evening, and so Lolly, Bill, Cary and I went. It took place in a huge oval stadium rather like the Earls Court exhibition centre, with an area encircling the arena, in which stalls selling hot-dogs, drinks and souvenirs were doing a brisk trade. We were amazed at the number of women wearing grotesque cowboy style clothes in bright colours, accompanied by flashing jewellery. The genuine cowhands had on wide battered and sweaty hats, the brims curling up at the sides, plain coloured or check shirts, and narrow tight jeans, which showed off their thin and very bandy legs.

Our seats were half-way down one of the long sides of the stadium, so we had an excellent view. The competitors entered through boarded passages from behind the seating, directly into the arena. The programme consisted of various contests in horsemanship, interspersed with equestrian circus turns. There were riding broncs bareback; calf roping; steer wrestling; horse cutting contest; Brahman bull riding (bareback). These all represented the activities that cowboys have to do in the normal course of their work. The rodeo was a championship occasion of the south-west, and cowboys had come great distances to take part, having won the first rounds in their own localities.

The contents were all judged by timing. The cowboys had to stay on the backs of the bucking broncs for eight seconds, and as the animals entered the arena, a girth just in front of their hind legs was yanked very tight by a man hanging over the high fence of the entry; this maddened the beast, and only a few riders managed to stay on for the required eight seconds. It was the same procedure when the Brahman bull-riding took place, which was the last and most exciting event of the evening.

The calf roping was a more interesting display of mutual understanding between the cowboy and his horse. A calf would be released into the arena, and be pursued by the mounted cowboy and lassoed, the rope being tied to the horse's harness; the rider then dismounted, with another length of rope between his teeth; from then on, the horse had to keep the lasso rope taut, so the calf could not work free, while the cowboy tied three of its legs together. This event was timed.

Wrestling with a steer can be dangerous: the animal is released into the arena, and is followed by two mounted cowboys. The contestant spurs his horse on to one side of the steer, and the second mounted man goes to the other side, to prevent the steer from running out and goring the contestant's horse when he dismounts; he leaps from the saddle and grasps the steer's horns, and must wrestle and throw it to the ground, where he must hold it for a prescribed number of seconds.

By far the most fascinating event was the horse cutting contest, when a herd of young steers were released into the arena, and the contestant's horse had to cut out one beast and prevent it from returning to the herd during a set period of time. Although the horse remains mounted throughout, the skill in this is entirely on the part of the horse, for once the cowboy has made known to his mount which beast he wants singled out, his reins lie slack on the horse's neck, and the rider takes no further part; it is entirely his horse which controls the situation, never taking its eyes off the calf, anticipating its every move and countering it. The vast audience was silent and wholly engrossed during this contest, which was enthralling to watch.

When we left Dallas on 30th January, the territory changed completely; we drove through huge flat prairie, and came to an area of sudden little square flat-topped rocky hills, the rock strata horizontal and colourful. We drove for over four hundred miles, seeing few humans or habitations, and crossed into New Mexico in the late afternoon. The Carlsbad caverns were nearby, so we visited them the next morning, walking through subterranean cathedrals and gardens of stalactites and stalagmites in every shade of apricot, pink and dark red, all artistically lit to great effect. Toward evening we passed through the Guadalupe mountains, which were deep purple-blue in the sunset, shot through with shafts of pink sun-beams shining between the peaks. We passed several salt lakes, white rimmed where the water level had dropped, leaving the glittering crystalline edge.

As we neared the Grand Canyon, the terrain became more and more colourful. The Painted Desert at sunset was magnificent, with the rocks, sand, soil and hills all glowing in pinks, purples, reds, browns, gold and blue in the rays of the setting sun.

We were stopped as we entered Arizona at an inspection post, and were told to give up any fruit we might be carrying, which would be destroyed. This was for fear of introducing any pests into the state, which produced large quantities of fruit, and most of the grapefruit consumed in USA.

Nearing Flagstaff, we passed through a corner of the Petrified Forest, and saw large fossilised trees lying by the road-side, an amazing development of nature. We stopped to buy pieces of petrified wood at a road-side stall, and the children made great friends with the owner.

'Good-bye, good luck!' he called, as we climbed back into the car.

'Good-bye, good love!' shouted Jamey in return.

That night we stopped in Cameron, and met several Red Indians; the women had long straight black hair, almond eyes, and dark skins; they wore striped Indian rugs over their shoulders, and bound their hair with tape in long plaits. The men wore theirs in the same way, and had wide-brimmed, square-crowned black hats, one with a bandeau round his brow. All wore cowboy type shirts and jeans, with many strings of beads round their necks. They worked the local silver and turquoise mines, and made very attractive jewellery to sell.

There was an ominous grey-yellow cloud overhanging Grand Canyon when we rose the next morning, and by the time we had breakfasted it had grown larger and nearer. However we optimistically started off on the Canyon road, passing several Indian *hogans*, which are the adobe houses in which they live; they are shaped like igloos, with a short length of pipe projecting out of the top, presumably to act as a chimney or ventilating shaft.

As we climbed, it began to rain, and then to snow, and by the time we were half-way up the mountain-side, we were in a sharp blizzard, and visibility was down to only a few feet. Our spirits sank, and we all became more and more silent, for we had been so looking forward to seeing the Grand Canyon: it was to be the climax of our journey. There was no point in going on in the risky weather conditions, and Lolly turned back. It was maddening to have got so near, and then to be thwarted, but the storm looked to be lasting, and the road was becoming unpleasant, winding up the mountain, with an awe-inspiring drop on one side, and it would be no fun to be skidding about on snow and ice on the higher and colder levels.

We had descended about thirty miles on the return route, when I looked back, to see to my amazement that the storm had entirely blown over, and the mountains were bathed in sunshine from a clear blue sky. I asked Lolly to stop and look for herself, and without a word, she turned the car once more, and we resumed the climb. The tarmac road cleared quickly of snow in the sunshine and as we got higher, it levelled out on to a high forested plateau of pines, which against the bright blue sky, and with the carpet of snow, looked like a scene from a Hans Andersen fairy story, and the more so when a little white-tailed doe stepped out on to the road only a few yards ahead of the car; it stopped and watched us slowly approaching, before it crossed over, and bounded away between the trees.

We left the car when we reached the Canyon, and walked to the rim; the panorama was breath-taking: imagine looking down on a world of deep rocky ravines and gorges, mountains and valleys, eighteen miles broad at its widest point and 145 miles long; visualise it through a rosy haze, and add sunshine in a blue sky, with small wind-

driven clouds making dancing purple shadows across this world, and
then perhaps you will have some idea what it was like. The rocks vary
in colour through gold and red, to purple, but mostly pink and red.
No vegetation grows in this part of the Canyon, and one might be in
the bowels of the earth, or in hell, were it not for the sun and sky
above. It is a terrifying place of indescribable beauty, the ever-
changing colours and shadows seeming to make it almost alive.

We descended to the desert again to continue our journey west.
There was a high wind blowing, and we watched the tumbleweed
spinning across the landscape; it is a low bushy, almost spherical plant,
with very shallow roots, and when it dries up in the rainless season, it
turns silvery-grey, and the winds blow it loose from the soil, and send
it spinning across the desert like giant puffs of cotton-wool.

The next day we crossed into California, which was another change
of scenery, from desert to mile on mile of fruit farms and orchards,
orange and grapefruit groves; the trees were laden with fruit, and the
heady scent of the flowers filled the air. Date palms grew in serried
rows, clipped and spruce, 'newly shaved', Lolly called them; there were
acres of vineyards too.

We crossed the Sierra Nevada mountains, to drop gradually down
to San Diego on the coast, the country becoming greener, and the air
warmer all the time. Excitement in the car built up, as Lolly and the
two elder children began to recognise familiar landmarks, and as we
neared the ferry to cross to Coronado Island, Johnny, not to be
outdone and left out of the nostalgic memories, suddenly shouted
triumphantly:

'And there's a Shell station!'

It was wonderful to reach the house Mac had prepared for us, and
he was there to meet us, and to show us round it.

It had been an epic journey. The children had travelled remarkably
well, although all were beginning to get a bit bored by the end.
Johnny picked up after the break in Dallas, but Jamey had thrived from
the start, bursting with life and energy. There had been the usual
scenes with him, which one expects with a four-year-old; Lolly's
leather strap from her handbag had been in regular use, and Jamey's
lungs well exercised accordingly, but apart from one tyre blow-out,
which occurred in a small town where there was plenty of help, we
had no mishaps.

On 6th February, Mac came home for lunch, and told me the news of the death of King George VI. I had not known he had been ill again, so it came as a sad shock, and I regretted that I was so far from home and other British people.

That afternoon Mac and Lolly took me down into Mexico, to see Tijuana, a border town very like La Linea, in Spain, I thought. It was a sleazy place, the abject poverty quite shocking to see. It had a bad reputation at that time for vice of all kinds, and was the source of much of the drug-smuggling into the US which remains the case today. It was a shopper's paradise, even then, as it still is, and I was glad to have seen it.

I flew back to Washington a few days later, my head full of the experiences of the previous three weeks.

Soon after we were married, we decided that we'd like to start a family, but were unsuccessful. We hoped we would have better luck in America. There the miracle happened, and James made a rather dramatic appearance in March 1953. As I was coming round from the anaesthetic I dimly heard a baby crying.

'Is that my baby?' I asked from the operating table.

'Yes,' said a voice from behind my head, 'you have a beautiful little boy, what is his name?'

'James,' I answered, which had already been decided.

'Hi, Jimmy!' called out the voice, 'welcome to the world!'

'NO, NOT JIMMY!' I shouted, waking up sharply, 'he's to be called JAMES.'

'OK! OK!' said a laughing young interne who had come to peer down at me. He came to my room a day or two later, and on entering, he said:

'How's my friend Jim?' so there was more backchat and fun. The staff in the George Washington University Hospital were marvellous, and so friendly and caring.

The joy and happiness of James' safe arrival were euphoric after the disappointments of so many miscarriages, and we returned home to England three months later to a delighted welcome from all the grandparents.

CHAPTER 6

Germany, 1955–57

THE NEXT PRIORITY was to have another baby while I remembered how to do it.

Michael next had two short appointments in the Portsmouth area, which enabled us to live in our house in Waterlooville, and he then attended a course at the Joint Services' Staff College at Latimer, from where he came home for weekends. During this time I became pregnant again, and Emma arrived safely, albeit prematurely, after another difficult pregnancy and an emergency Caesarean birth. I remember holding her in my arms, sleeping peacefully, and swearing that nothing and nobody would ever take her away from me.

She was a frail little scrap, and it became obvious that we were going to need professional help in rearing her. An aunt of Michael's told us of her god-daughter, Ruth Pruen, who had just finished her

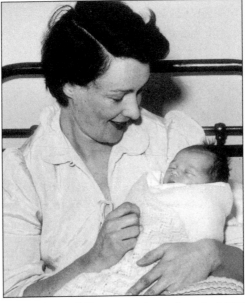

The author and Emma, aged two days, in 1954.

training as a nursery nurse and was looking for a job. She joined the family the day Emma and I returned home from hospital, and she stayed with us for two very happy years.

Early in 1955 Michael was appointed as the Staff Officer (Intelligence) on the staff of the Flag Officer, Germany, who at that time was Keith Campbell-Walter; for the first of the two years we spent in Germany, Michael was also the Senior Naval Officer, Hamburg, so it was to Hamburg that Ruth and I set out with the two babies in March, to join Michael who had gone out a month or so ahead of us.

Ruth was then nineteen years old. This was the first time she had been abroad, and also the first time she had been parted from her identical twin sister Margaret for longer than a few days.

The Army Movements authorities were responsible for all travel to and from Germany by the Forces and their families. We had been sent an enormous amount of military instructions regarding the journey and had accumulated a large pile of typed foolscap paper, which necessitated the addition of yet another bag to our already daunting number of suitcases, trunks, hold-alls, zipper-bags, baskets and other items of baggage. Also included was the cumbersome enamel steriliser for Emma's bottles, which contained for the journey all the filled bottles it was capable of holding.

We had to report at King's Cross Station at 2.00 pm, and from there travel to Harwich, where we were herded into a transit shed to wait for between two and three hours while we were 'documented'. This military language was new to us, but we soon became all too familiar with it, and also with the shouted orders which were constantly being relayed over the loud-speaker system. The families who were travelling were herded together to go through each formality in turn, and no-one was allowed to move on to the next procedure until the whole group of a hundred or so had completed the previous one. Long queues formed, the sheds were chilly, and in only one were there chairs to sit down on; small children cried with exhaustion, tired mothers scolded and slapped them, and the time dragged on. When the last document had been stamped, we were told that at last we could go on board the boat. By this time it was 11.00 pm. There was a walk of two or three hundred yards across railway lines and between warehouses, no porters were available, and we were told to carry our own hand luggage. For Ruth and me this was impossible, as she was carrying Emma in her carrycot and I was carrying James, who was crying and worn out by this time: yet it was only by demanding that we should be allowed help, and quite a bit of unpleasantness, that a nice soldier eventually was allocated to help us embark. There were many Other Ranks' families with four and five children who must have been far worse off than us but who did not dare raise their voices. We were the only naval family travelling that night. I think the Army Movements Control officer on duty must have been thankful when at last he got rid of us on board the ferry!

We were lucky enough to be allocated a four-berth cabin, small and cramped, but perfectly adequate, until we started washing the children, and looked round for towels. There were none.

'They must have forgotten to put them out,' I said, 'I'll ring for the stewardess.' Nothing happened, so I rang again; still nothing happened, so I tried a third time, keeping my finger on the bell-push for a considerable time. At last a large angry-faced woman in a grubby overall came to the door and barked:

'What do you want? What are you making so much noise about?'

Keeping my temper (for the moment), I replied:

'May we have some towels please, there do not seem to be any put out.'

'No, of course there ain't; you don't get no towels 'ere: this ain't the bloody *Queen Mary*!'

'Oh yes, I do! I demand that towels be provided at once, and don't speak to me like that, either!' I said.

'There ain't no towels! Did'n' you 'ear me? Think yourself lucky you've got a cabin! I'll report you to the Captain!' she shouted.

'Yes, you do that, and tell him from me that there's a naval officer's wife with two babies who have been travelling since nine o'clock this morning, and who intends to wash them before putting them to bed, and unless towels are brought down to the cabin at once, the sheets from the berths will be used instead!'

The woman's jaw dropped, and she went quite pale (it was really most satisfactory!) and surprise, surprise, towels were produced within five minutes!

The crossing was a rough one, but we were lucky enough to have our cabin to ourselves, so we could endure any sea-sickness in privacy. The babies both slept and the next morning we found we had reached the Hook of Holland, and were bidden to go ashore at once for breakfast in the transit shed, and yet more documentation! This time it only took an hour and a half, and I found a soldier who would help us again, to walk the length of the quay and find our train with all our luggage; we left the Hook at 9.00 am, and proceeded by troop train across Holland, and round three sides of Germany, it seemed, till we finally reached Hamburg eleven hours later.

This was James' second birthday, and Ruth and I had packed a whole bag of small presents which were produced one by one through the day, to provide constant and oft-recurring diversion from the frustration and boredom of being cooped up for so many hours in the railway carriage.

We were fortunate in having the compartment to ourselves; one look through the window at us was enough to send other boarding passengers scurrying elsewhere in search of less infantile fellow passengers! Emma in her carrycot was consigned to the high and conveniently wide Continental type luggage rack, from where she was lifted down at regular intervals to be 'bottled'. We had mixed ready twelve bottles with her formula before leaving home, which we hoped would be enough to see her through to Hamburg, but the problem of how to warm them was a rather difficult one, as the wash-basins in the train boasted no such luxury as hot water. Ruth proved her resourcefulness by dashing up the platform at one of our stops, clutching an enamel jug, and by sign language and miming, she successfully indicated to the engine-driver what was required; he kindly drew off some boiling water from the engine. Ruth managed to regain our compartment before the train drew out, and shortly afterwards Emma's hungry wails were quietened. Subsequently Ruth took a Thermos as well as the jug, and then we felt less dependent on halts to embark or disembark troops, of which, of course, we had no schedule.

Soon came the inevitable request from James so, putting on his coat to brave the bitter cold outside the compartment, I led him off down the corridor; the state of the lavatory when we reached it was beyond description, and we hastily retreated back to our now cosy home-base.

'Ruth, we can't take James along there! It is filthy! Too disgusting even for him to stand on the seat!' I said.

'I can easily get out his pot, I know just where I've put it,' said Ruth, whom nothing seemed to daunt, and find it she did, just in time!

'I'll go and empty it,' she said, 'be back in a minute, and I'll take Emma's used nappy to dispose of too.'

Poor Ruth! It was her first experience of England's traditionally licentious soldiery! But you cannot blame them for finding the sight of a pretty, petite curly-headed blonde walking along the corridor bearing such a burden, too much to refrain from suitable comment and appreciation! She returned at last, scarlet in the face, and saying either I could empty the next instalment, or we would tip it out of the window!

James, of course, being a naturally active and inquisitive child, climbed all over the carriage: up on to the luggage rack to see how his sister was getting on, but mostly on to the floor and under the seats, from where he emerged covered from head to foot in dust and grime as old as the train itself, which, judging from its rate of progress, was one of the first locomotives invented.

As the long day wore on into dusk, Ruth and I longed for a snooze, but James had had a good night and felt no such need, and there was no chance of us dropping off with him bouncing around and over us.

With huge relief we heard the warning being called: 'Hamburg in twenty minutes! Get ready to de-train!' Immediately all was chaos, as we hunted for toys, books, a lost knitting-needle, passports, mittens, gloves, caps and woollies, as well as all the other essential impedimenta of travel with two babies. Miraculously we were ready as the train drew to a halt, and there on the platform, as calm and imperturbable as ever, stood Michael waiting for us, with a peak-capped man who seized our baggage, and we all piled into a waiting Volkswagen minibus. We drove through the city out to Marienburg, to the house Michael had prepared for us, where a smiling German woman greeted us.

During the journey when James had explored under the seats in the filthy train, he must have picked up the gastro-enteritis which developed with alarming violence two days after our arrival. Ruth diagnosed it at once, and the doctors in the British Military Hospital confirmed it. James was admitted, and was very ill indeed, and within twenty-four hours Emma had joined him, and we had a very anxious few days.

Michael was away, and so, as many service wives have found since time began, I had to cope alone in this emergency, not speaking the language, in a strange country; the babies were so poorly I wondered if

I was going to need a black hat and funeral clothes. Surprisingly Emma was the first to recover, but James was in hospital for over two weeks.

The house in Hamburg was temporary, and after six weeks we moved to a very luxurious residence on the Elbechaussee, which had belonged to Goering's sister, where he had often stayed. However, before that, we had to get rid of the cook. She and I had taken agin one another from the first; I thought she might well have been one of those brawny she-devils who made lampshades from human skins in Belsen: she also produced disgusting food.

At first she tried to rule me, and run the house according to her own wishes, calling herself the cook-housekeeper. Ruth and I were rather over-awed to begin with, and I found it difficult to remonstrate with her, as she spoke no English, and I no German. There came the day that I decided she must go, and so that morning Ruth built up my courage with two stiff double gins, before I marched into the kitchen and gave the woman notice. She was dumbfounded and lashed out at me, shouting and screaming. I wasn't going to stand for this, and told her she could pack and leave at once. I beat what I hoped was a dignified retreat, and Ruth had another gin ready for me; shortly afterwards we heard the front door bang, and peace reigned.

I then had to interview applicants for the vacant post. I had not employed servants before, but under German War Reparations, we were entitled to three and a half; the half was the *Putzfrau*, or daily char-woman, who 'only' worked a seven-hour day. The others lived in.

The first applicant arrived one morning, and was old enough to be my mother; we sized each other up, and I remembered my mother's advice: 'Always look at their shoes, darling; don't ever employ anyone with down-at-heel or un-polished shoes.' Fräulein Lundstedt's were worn but gleaming. It was really the Fräulein who interviewed me:

'How many children you haf?'

'How many years they haf?'

'Vill you be parties haffing?' and so forth. Her final question was:

'Do you animeels haf? I cannot cook where there animeels are.'

We evidently satisfied her requirements, and she finally stood up and announced:

'Is gut! Tomorrow morningk here I vill be at eight o'clock! Auf Wiedersehn!' and with a firm handshake, she left. She would not live

in, but came each day in time to cook breakfast, and left after dinner
in the evenings, and she was a superb cook.

We also had Helga, a dark, winsome and plump little pigeon, with
flashing eyes and a naughty grin; she adored the children, and was very
good with them, begging to be allowed to bath and 'bottle' Emma on
Ruth's days off; this was good practice for her, for quite soon, she told
us, a little shame-facedly, that she was pregnant, and when we left to
move to Cologne, she also left to get married, just in time for the birth
of her baby.

The third servant was Anni, red-haired, less flighty than Helga, and
also an excellent worker. She came to Cologne with us, and became
our cook.

Frau Schultz, the *Putzfrau*, arrived at 7.00 am and left at 2.00 pm.
Under the immediate post-war rules for the British Army of
occupation, we were not allowed to give the staff meals or food of any
kind, but I found ways of getting round this. Frau Schultz and I taught
each other ten words of English/German every day, and tested each
other regularly on our previously learned vocabulary. We were a very
happy household, and all had much fun together.

I found it quite easy to pick up enough German to carry on a
conversation, although my grammar was appalling; it seemed to me
that there were so many words in a sentence quite extraneous to its
meaning, that really only one word in five needed to be understood!

A few weeks after our arrival, we had to attend an official cocktail-
party, at which Michael introduced me to the German who
commanded the Hamburg Water-Police, who spoke no English; after
the introduction, Michael walked away, and left us. I felt utterly
betrayed, and quite desperate, but there was nothing to do other than
dive in at the deep end: heaven knows what we talked about, but for
twenty minutes we gabbled away, no doubt the drinks helping, both of
us greatly amused at the other's linguistic efforts, and I, anyway,
thoroughly enjoyed myself.

While doing the household shopping, I resorted to miming if
necessary, to get what I wanted. One day I was in the butcher's, slowly
moving in the long queue of *Hausfraus* toward the counter to be
served. Eventually, when my turn came, I asked:

'*Haben Sie . . .*' and I made horns with two fingers jutting from my
head, then mimed milking a cow, and then turned, bent over showing
my bottom to the butcher, and waggled my arm and hand from it to

resemble a tail, by which time both he and the queue were in fits of laughter:

'*Aaah! Ein Ochsenschwanz, ja?*' he asked, understanding my wish to have an ox-tail for lunch.

It was a good way to make friends, who then taught me more words, and if my grammar and syntax were nil, then it caused much laughter, and what better way is there of getting to know people and making friends than giving them something to laugh at? It always interested and saddened us that the British Army in Germany, and there were many thousands there with their families, never fraternised with the Germans, and still professed to dislike and mistrust them, long after the war was over. Michael had been prisoner of the Germans for three years (and of the Italians for two before that), but bore no ill-will, and we made many German friends, some of whom we keep up with to this day.

Our house on Elbechaussee faced south, and looked across the Elbe to the Deutschwerk shipyard, where work went on day and night; the river was wide enough for the noise of the yard not to incommode us. Our garden sloped steeply down to the river bank, and was full of peach and cherry trees, which were bowed down with fruit that year. Along the south front of the house was a long wide terrace where James played, Emma lay out in her pram, and we sat out in the sun through the long hot summer of 1955.

That winter the Elbe froze out almost to the middle of the river, and we could skate and slide along the bank-side. Later with the thaw, huge lumps like icebergs came floating downstream bumping and clinking as they jostled along.

Three Royal Naval destroyers paid a visit to Hamburg during that summer, and Ruth and I went out on to our bedroom balcony to wave nappies in greeting as they steamed past us up-river. I hoped that we would be given an answering whoop of their sirens, but there was no reaction. That evening there was a party on board HMS *Grenville*, the leader, and I told Captain Wilson how disappointed we had been. The next morning a motor-cyclist delivered a parcel to the house, which contained a large Union Jack, and a note saying:

'Hang this from your balcony, and we will see you when we leave.'

He did, and all the destroyers gave those wonderful spine-chilling whoops on a rising note, the sailors waved, and so did we, and so honour was satisfied. We still use that Union Jack for all celebrations concerning the Queen and the Royal Family and major occasions in our village.

Michael's Intelligence work consisted in co-ordinating all the naval intelligence matters throughout Germany. There were three bases for this, in Hamburg, Kiel and Berlin, and the main work was connected with ports in Northern Germany, running patrols in the Baltic to observe Russian shipping, and listen to their naval coast-guarding radar, and radio detection installations. For this purpose there were three fast motor boats, manned by German ex-Navy personnel. They had to work under cover, as the Germans were not permitted to have any armed forces, and their crews wore civilian clothes and were said to be carrying out Fishery Protection; if challenged by Russian motor patrols or frigates, they were fast enough to escape.

These boats were also used to infiltrate into the East, and bring out our secret agents, and there were some amusing moments at home concerning these activities.

I was told nothing of all this at the time, Michael maintaining an entirely correct (and rather pompous) air of secrecy about his activities, which I found maddening!

One evening soon after my arrival in Hamburg, he had invited some of the naval staff in for a drink to meet me. Just before they were due to arrive, the telephone rang, and after he'd rung off, he came in and said:

'There will be some people arriving in about half an hour; when the door-bell rings, you are not to answer it, I will. I shall bring in two men to join the party, whom I will introduce as Ferdie and Shergie; you are not to ask their full names, and you are on no account to go into the kitchen until I tell you you may. Is that understood?'

I felt like saluting and answering:

'Aye, Aye, Sir!'

I should add that this was just after I had sacked the cook, and we had invited a few of the guests to stay on for supper, for which I had a casserole gently cooking in the oven.

Sure enough, the door-bell rang; I stayed with our guests, and after a few minutes Ferdie and Shergie were brought in, and more drinks were dispensed.

It was a jolly party, and an hour or two later, all the guests had left except those who were staying on for supper. Michael had gone out to see Ferdie and Shergie off, and I thought the kitchen must be clear, and anyway, I needed to check the casserole. I went into the hall, looking to see if any black cloaks and false beards were hanging on the coat-hooks, and moved on into the kitchen.

There, sitting at the table, with papers spread all round them, were two blond men, who, looking up at me like frightened rabbits, hastily shovelled their papers together and covered them with their arms.

'Good evening, gentlemen,' I said, as surprised as they appeared to be, 'Not burglars, I presume?' and I went over to the oven, and left the room as quickly as possible.

Many years later I was told that they were two agents about to be infiltrated into the East, who had received some last-minute instructions which had to be decoded before their departure, so they had been brought to us, as being a 'safe house'. The next time I went into the kitchen, they had gone, and Michael told me that on pain of death (almost), I must not mention this to anyone.

On another occasion, he came home from his office one evening, and I saw him loading a case of champagne into the boot of his car.

'Oh, goody!' I exclaimed, 'are we going to a party?'

'No,' said Michael, severely, 'this is nothing to do with you, and you're to ask no questions. I shall be going out after dinner, and will not be back till quite late; you're not to stay up for me.' Obediently, I made no comment, and again, some time later I was told that when agents returned from their often dangerous missions behind the Iron Curtain, they were greeted with champagne, at the expense of the Foreign Office, before their first de-briefing. I find this a surprisingly humane gesture by our Foreign Office.

I used to go to a small row of shops not far from our house sometimes, especially on Fridays, when there was an excellent fish stall in the street. One summer's day, there was a row of barrels in front of the stall and, peering in, I saw they were full of live eels; there was a queue of *Hausfraus* at the stall, who, it being a warm day, were wearing suitably cool clothes. One very large woman, clad in a cotton dirndl dress, with a deep cleavage showing her amply curved proportions, leaned over a barrel, to select her prey; an adventurous eel, seeing its chance, leapt out of the barrel, and straight down her cleavage! It was a most wondrous moment, before the yells began, and the other waiting shoppers enjoyed the spectacle to the full, as did I!

In September, Michael was able to combine some leave with a duty visit to Berlin. We started with a few days walking in the Harz mountains, and then went on to stay with a Royal Marine colonel in the British Mission to the Soviet in Berlin who, because of his work, had more or less free access to the Eastern sector of the city (this was before the Berlin Wall had been built). We were taken to a cocktail party for the Russian equivalent of our Mission, and I still have one of my letters describing it:

'Only about twenty Russian officers came with their wives, out of the fifty expected, and none of the wives could speak English, but I found one who spoke French, and talked to her. The Russian women were all gigantic, and wearing ghastly clothes and no make-up, but what furs they had were superb; the colonel's wife I met had a most magnificent sable cape, entirely wasted on her, I rather cattily thought!'

We were taken into the Russian sector, to sight-see and shop, and with East-marks at 4½ to 1 West-mark, the exchange was very advantageous. I remember buying a complete set, cloth-bound, of all Beethoven's piano sonatas, for the equivalent of five shillings. The ruins and rubble from the bombing were still dreadful, and behind the imposing façade of Unter den Linden, which the Russians had rebuilt, we could see that there was no other construction; behind was the rubble, and people emerging from holes in the ground, where they were living. I asked to get out of our military vehicle to take some photographs, and I crossed the road to get better shots. While taking photographs, I became conscious of being watched, and looked up to see two Russians in uniform, staring at me, and beginning to walk purposefully toward me. I suddenly remembered I had left my passport in my handbag in the car, and I turned and ran back to it, falling in, just as the driver was speeding away. I was severely reprimanded for my foolishness. The Cold War was on, and occasionally solitary Westerners were abducted while walking in the East Sector, and held hostage for considerable periods in prison, in great discomfort.

After Berlin, we drove down the Rhine and Mosel valleys, and went for glorious walks up the hillsides of the Ahr valley, which were carpeted with wild gentians; we also wandered into little valleys where we couldn't help walking on pale mauve autumn crocuses (*Colchicum*), so thickly did they grow.

We gradually got to know well the three German commanders of the fast patrol boats that operated under Michael in the Baltic. They had all been in the German Navy, and when Germany was once more permitted to recruit armed forces, they rejoined the Navy, and all went on to become admirals.

The commanding officer of the flotilla was Helmut Klose, who had
served in E-boats in war-time, and so was well qualified to run the fast
patrol boats. His family came from East Pomerania, then occupied by
the Russians, and so he was very strongly anti-Russian. He was a very
formal Prussian, and would stand stiffly erect, even when *en famille* in
our house, with his hands clenched, knuckles white, at his sides.

It was the German custom when invited to dine in private houses
for a man to take the hostess flowers, but there was strict etiquette to
observe: they had to be an uneven number, three, five, seven, nine, etc,
and certain colours were taboo: yellow implied envy (of the husband),
pink was all right, but dark red flowers indicated a proposal of marriage
if the recipient was single, and of an improper nature if already married.
Helmut used to bring me either pink, or sometimes yellow ones, and
when I knew him well, I teased him one evening, by saying:

'Oh Helmut! How lovely! Thank you so much!' and then, after
kissing him, I added, 'but you know, I always hope that one day you
will give me dark red roses!' Poor Helmut blushed dark red himself,
and stuttered:

'Oh Sue! Oh Sue! You mustn't . . . I couldn't! . . .' before he joined
in the general laughter.

Within an hour's drive of Hamburg there were three camps for
Displaced Persons. These poor people had been conscripted from their
own countries by the Germans during the war, and force-marched to
work as slave labour where they were required: in munitions factories;
shipyards; road maintenance; clearing bomb damage, etc. They
originated mainly from eastern states which the Germans had
overrun: Hungary; Romania; Ukraine; Poland; Latvia; Lithuania; and
Estonia.

When the war ended, the Allies collected these people together into
camps all over Germany, tried to restore their health and find
employment for them, and then organised emigration for as many as
possible to Britain, Canada, Australia and New Zealand. Most DPs
were badly under-nourished and many were found to be suffering from
tubercular diseases; these latter were unable to emigrate, and many were
unemployable. By 1955 most of the many thousands of DPs had either
emigrated or been absorbed into the German community, and found
employment, but there was still a hard core in some of the camps, and
as the wife of the Senior Naval Officer, Hamburg, I found that I was
expected to become the local chairman of the Adoption Committees

for Aid to Displaced Persons in three camps. This was an organisation registered under the War Charities Act.

The largest of these camps, in which I was most involved, was Falkenberg. It was about an hour's drive from the city, in a semi-rural area, on a hillside covered with heather and pine-trees. The camp accommodation consisted of Nissen-type huts, in which each family had one or two small rooms, sleeping in tiered wooden bunks. There was an interdenominational church in one converted hut, where the DPs had made, carved and painted the altars, etc, and it was most inspiring to see the various examples of their native crafts, every square inch vivid in colouring, gilded and painted, unlike any English church. The DPs were mostly Roman Catholics or Greek or Russian Orthodox, and Mass was said daily.

The majority of DPs in Falkenberg were Ukrainians, with Poles, and a few from the Baltic States. Their home and community rooms were decorated with much of their brilliantly coloured embroidery. The total number in the camp was 472.

The German government ran the DP camps, and in each was a German appointed Camp Commandant. I had to work with a German Social Welfare Officer, who was a charming, plump little woman called Fräulein Pohl, who genuinely had the care of the DPs at heart, and visited the camps at least twice a week. I tried to visit one camp each week, but came to know Falkenberg and its inmates best.

These people were stateless, with no country, no passports, and no homes. They could not return to their own countries, for the Russians, then in control of the whole of the East, would have executed them for working for the Germans, albeit involuntarily. They had been offered German nationality, but only about 5 per cent had taken it up, in the hopes that the international situation would change, enabling them to return to their own countries. The children were being taught in German schools, and therefore were learning the language; they would eventually become integrated, but the adults spoke no German, had no future, and had perforce to continue to live on charity, which denuded them of self-respect and independence.

The purpose of the organisation I represented was to help those remaining in the camps to learn a trade which they could follow even if they were tubercular, so as to be able to earn some money, for although the German government provided accommodation and most of the bodily necessities of life, their post-war resources were not infinite.

Therefore we had to try to get individuals and families 'adopted' by Women's Institutes, or other such organisations in Britain, to ask them to send out clothing, sewing-machines, and fabric and thread, knitting-wool, sports equipment, musical instruments and sheet music, blankets and baby clothes, etc.

I then thought that I would like to arrange children's Christmas parties in the camps, for there had been no possibility for them ever to have seen Father Christmas, balloons, crackers, or even Christmas trees; so the next few months were filled with extensive preparations, and the huge cellars under our house, where there were wooden floors, central heating and lighting, made an excellent depot.

From Fräulein Pohl I obtained the names and ages of all the children between eighteen months and fourteen years, who numbered between 120 and 180 in each camp. I also decided to include the old people over sixty, who numbered between 40 and 60.

I wrote round to many WIs in England, telling them about the camps, and the stories of some of the families, and I received a marvellous response. I asked for sweets; toys; balloons; cocoa (for the children) and Nescafé (for the adults); soap and cigarettes also for the elders. Ruth and I evolved various fund-raising ploys as well.

The Missions to Seamen chaplain in Hamburg agreed to act as Father Christmas, but then we realised we had no outfit for him. Then I thought of writing to the Managing Director of Selfridge's, telling him of our work, and the Christmas plans, and asking if he could possibly help. By return of post (all parcels were able to be sent to us, duty-free, through Forces Mail), came a large box containing a magnificent Father Christmas outfit, the robe trimmed with real fur, and with a curly white wig, beard and moustache, all of real hair. With this there was a letter of support for the project, offering the outfit as a gift, to be used at all parties, and at any further charity affairs I might organise in the future.

The parties were magical: Fräulein Pohl arranged long tables laid with strips of white lining paper, on which she laid little sprays of green fir interspersed with white candles; each child had a mug of cocoa, two cakes, a chocolate biscuit, and a bag of sweets.

At the table for the elders, there was by each place a bar of chocolate, one of soap, and a packet of ten cigarettes: they had the same food, but mugs of Nescafé, instead of cocoa.

There was a huge Christmas tree on the stage, lit with white lights, and decorated with little bows of white ribbon.

When the old people entered the hall, many wept.

After tea, Father Christmas arrived with sacks of toys; each child was called by name to come and accept its labelled present, and I gave each one a balloon before they departed. Watching the faces of awe and incredulous delight as the children filed in on arrival was very moving, it made the weeks of preparatory work by Ruth and me well worth while.

A Christmas party at the Displaced Persons Camp, Falkenburg, 1955.

Ruth had settled into our family very well, the children loved her, and we enjoyed having her with us. She had turned Emma round in six months from the thin frail little baby she had been when she was born, to a plump and happy little person who was constantly hungry.

I have already said that Ruth was an identical twin; I had not had an experience of the phenomenon before. When she came to us she had a lot of dental treatment. A month after it was completed, she came down to breakfast one day, holding her very white face, saying she had appalling tooth-ache.

'Ruth, you've only just finished a major dental overhaul, there can't suddenly be something so wrong that it is as painful as that!' I exclaimed.

'No,' she agreed, 'I won't go back to the dentist for the moment, but will just wait a day or two.' I gave her some aspirin, and the pain abated. Two days later she had a letter from her twin, Margaret, telling her that she had had a wretched few days with an infected wisdom tooth, that had to be taken out.

Another time, Ruth was complaining of a painful elbow, and later heard that Margaret had fallen off a ladder and broken hers.

After Ruth left us, on our return to England, she became matron at the Dragon School in Oxford, and Margaret got married. Ruth then went to Rhodesia, to another job, and when Margaret started a baby in England, it was Ruth who had the morning sickness, in Africa, and she also had labour pains when the baby was about to be born!

Michael had to visit Copenhagen in December, and I was able to accompany him. The city was decorated for Christmas, and was like fairyland.

I was able to visit the Danish naval officers' training school, the equivalent of our naval college at Dartmouth, and I was shown the room where my father had been held in internment in 1915, when he withdrew his parole, and from where he escaped.

We had much entertaining to do in Hamburg, particularly of official visitors, whom we often had to have to stay in our house. This was no problem with our excellent and happy household staff. One dinner party was for Rear Admiral and Mrs Campbell-Walter, who were visiting us from Cologne. We also invited the British Consul-General, Dr Dunlop, who asked if he might bring a house-guest and old friend, Lord Inverclyde. We made the number up to ten, but on the day of the party, Dr Dunlop rang up to ask if he might bring a second house-guest, Sir Kenneth Swan, a QC who had arrived unexpectedly.

Our menu was arranged, and ten steaks had been bought, but we managed to obtain an extra one. I was not so lucky when I tried to get an eleventh roll from the bakery, where our special order of ten in the shape of swans had already been made. The bakery made them beautifully, with slim elegantly curved necks, and they were most life-like.

I laid the table, arranged a bowl of flowers, and put a swan in the centre of each water-lily I had folded from starched damask napkins.

As Lord Inverclyde and Sir Kenneth Swan were both strangers to us, I had them sit one on each side of me.

The guests arrived; Lord Inverclyde was quite young, relaxed and charming (he was tragically killed only a short time after this, when he fell from a moving train in Scotland). Sir Kenneth was older, a small thin man, rather pedantic in his speech, but very friendly. When we moved in to dinner, and he saw the swan rolls, he thought they were an intended compliment to him, and I did not disabuse him.

'Oh dear lady! Oh how truly delightful! Especially for me! How I wish my dear wife were here! I shall not break mine, but will take it home to show her. How I wish I could take a second one, so that we each could have one! Such a charming compliment!'

'Here, have mine!' said Lord Inverclyde, reaching with it across the table, and Sir Kenneth continued to bubble his appreciation well into the evening. At Christmas that year we received a card from him, in which he said the rolls were still sitting in pride of place on their drawing-room mantel-piece in London!

In the summer of 1956, Michael was required to move his office to Cologne, where the Flag Officer Germany had his base. We left Hamburg very reluctantly, and although the house we were allocated in a pleasant residential suburb of Cologne was very spacious, with a large garden, it was not to be compared with the mansion on the Elbechaussee.

Finding friends for James was now a problem, as was proved only too clearly when he set out on his own to look for some. He was three and a bit, and had been given a tricycle by his Pope grandparents when they visited us in Hamburg.

On one of Ruth's days off, I was washing Emma's nappies, and became aware that the house was ominously silent. I went to look for James, but although Emma was sleeping peacefully in her pram in the garden, there was no sign of her brother; I then saw the front gate was open and swinging in the wind. I ran out on to the pavement looking this way and that, and calling desperately for James; there was no sign, and no sound in our quiet road. I ran back and got the car out, then circled the block: no sign of James. Venturing further afield, I started down the busy main road into Cologne city centre, desperately scanning the pavements.

Eventually I spotted a small figure in blue jersey and corduroy shorts, pedalling laboriously down the centre of the road between two sets of tram-lines, looking first to one side and then the other. When I had succeeded in extricating him, and getting him on to the pavement, James watched me shaking with the fear which in relief had turned to anger, then, looking up at me, he said:

'But Mummy, I was only looking for a friend to play with me.'

I drove straight to the kindergarten not far from our house.

'Well, I don't know,' said the charming German girl who ran it, 'he is a bit young to come to me, but . . . yes, he certainly seems ready for it!' And so James started there the very next morning, and loved every minute of it.

We did not enjoy living in Cologne nearly as much as in Hamburg; the local Germans were not as friendly, either to the English as a nation, or to us. However, it was convenient for travelling further south on leave, and we drove down to Italy in the summer of 1956, stopping at Munich on the way. We visited Gavi, one of the fortress camps near Genoa, where Michael had been held as a prisoner-of-war, and looked down from the ramparts to the village square below, which reminded him of how a friendly Italian guard used to lend him his binoculars, the better to watch the pretty girls parading in the square on Saturdays and Sundays!

The Everetts all came out to stay with us in Cologne, on one of their holidays. Winn, the doctor, drove in her large car; her mother, Lady Everett, sat like a dowager in the back; Jill, Winn's niece (who was also Aunt Rita's grand-daughter), shared the driving, and there was also a cousin with them, called Marigold. After a day or two with us, I went on with them down to the Black Forest. The Everetts as a family have a tremendous capacity for enjoyment, and that holiday was hilarious, from the day when Marigold retired behind a bush for the usual reason, to come leaping out shrieking:

'Help! There's a snake! It stood up on its tail between my legs!' to the evening when we were playing one of the Everetts' favourite parlour games after dinner in our hotel, and I stood up to read out all the names of famous men of whom I could think, beginning with the letter 'H'. The whole room fell silent as I recited: 'Haydn; Handel; Hesse; Himmler; Hitler; etc.' I then had to turn to explain to the German hotel guests that we were only some mad British, playing a parlour game.

We left Germany in the spring of 1957, when Michael was

appointed as an instructor to the RAF Staff College at Bracknell, where we were given a house on the college campus.

That autumn the Admiralty made an appalling blunder. When they found they had too many Seamen or Executive Officers (without specialist qualifications) for naval peacetime requirements, they decided to divide those officers in the rank of commander into what were called Wet and Dry lists. Those who were to continue in sea-going command appointments were the Wets; the Dry would be employed in Staff and Shore work. The Admiralty also offered a generous 'Golden Bowler' to those who might like to choose an early retirement.

Michael had had some duodenal stomach trouble in the preceding four or five years, and he was told that he was to be put on the Dry list. He was so horrified that he applied for a 'Golden Bowler', and we even began to discuss the possibility of emigrating to Australia.

However, totally unexpectedly, he was promoted to Captain, his application for a 'Golden Bowler' was turned down, and he was appointed to Singapore, as Chief Staff Officer (Intelligence) to the naval C-in-C there.

We therefore left Bracknell after only one year there.

CHAPTER 7

Far East, 1958–60

'WELL, GOOD-BYE DARLING, I hope I arrive in Singapore before you do!' said my husband, as he saw us off in the troopship *Dunera* in which the children and I were about to sail from Southampton in July 1958.

His RAF flight out had already been cancelled, as all service aircraft were being held close to their bases, in case of urgent need in the Middle East, where Iraq was in a state of turmoil after the Socialist Ba'ath party had staged a revolution and had murdered the Crown Prince and King Faisal. The situation was very tense, and *Dunera* was to carry an unexpected shipment of arms and troops to Cyprus, and we had been warned might then be sent back to UK to fetch more. So we were uncertain whether we would be disembarking in Singapore or back in Southampton.

Michael was required to take over his new appointment as soon as possible, as his predecessor had already left Singapore, and there was much political instability in the Far East, also Communist terrorism had still not been brought under control in Malaya. All of this unrest was directly the result of the 1939–45 war, and the Russians and Chinese who were exploiting it as far as they could, to obtain a strong communist influence in the independent states arising out of the old British and Dutch colonies.

Having disembarked the military personnel and cargo at Limassol, *Dunera* was given the all-clear to proceed on to Singapore, and by then I had heard that Michael had been flown out by BOAC, so the children and I settled down to enjoy the rest of the voyage.

Michael's Intelligence work involved him in the political and business spheres in Singapore, and so we lived in the south of the island, near the city, and were allotted a house in the Army area of senior officers' quarters, in Pasir Panjang, on a hill above the British Military Hospital. Our house was of the old colonial style, with wide open veranda passages down each long side, on to which all the rooms opened with short double swing doors, with gaps above and below them, like those of saloon bars in Western films. There were big ceiling fans to help circulate the air, for there was no air-conditioning then, except in much more luxurious houses. The house looked out on to a deep narrow uncultivated valley, filled with jungle plants, trees and creepers; on the lip of this, just outside our front door, was a frangipani tree, and its flowers would fill the house with their strong heady scent.

We were lucky to inherit from Michael's predecessor two excellent Chinese servants; Ah Tan was the cook, and his wife, Katherine, did everything else, including looking after the children when we had to be out.

Our life was very social indeed, for we mixed not only with other British Forces personnel, but also with the Intelligence staffs of all our South-East Asian allied embassies and High Commissions, as well as our own, and with many business men in trade and industry of all nations, and their families.

I was very thankful that we did not live in the naval base on the north point of the island, for it was a large enclosed community, isolated and parochial, and it would have been rather like living in a naval quarter at Portsmouth. As it was, I was independent, and able to get to know the families of a very wide and varied circle, of all nationalities, who mostly lived in the big residential areas round the northerly outskirts of Singapore city.

The Singapore climate is hot and humid, with rain falling for a short time on most days, and during the monsoon periods, sometimes heavily and continuously for several days, causing roads to flood, with consequent dislocation of traffic, in spite of the five-foot deep open monsoon drains which bordered all the main roads, to carry away the surplus rain to the sea. When this happened, snakes and other creatures would be flushed out of their holes in the sides of the ditches, and swirled along in the floods. One evening, after several days of heavy rain, we saw an eighteen-foot python hanging up in a tree by the road-side near our house, surrounded by a group of excited Chinese boys; they had pinned it down behind its head and killed it; the skin would be sold for making shoes and hand-bags, and the meat would feed the boys' families with a much prized delicacy. They were delighted with their trophy, and we looked at it with awe, to think that it had been living within a hundred yards of our house.

The Far East Naval Command then extended from Korea to

Australia, and from Hawaii in mid-Pacific to beyond Ceylon to the west. This was all Michael's 'parish' as Chief Staff Officer (Intelligence) to the naval Commander-in-Chief. The Korean war had ended two years previously, in a stalemate armistice, but the Royal Navy still had two destroyers on detachment to the US Navy, which continued to patrol off South Korea. There was trouble in Vietnam, where both the Communist Chinese and the Russians were backing the Communist North Vietnamese in their civil war against South Vietnam.

The British Commonwealth had had to contend in Malaya with the Communist Terrorist Organisation, which had lain fallow in the jungle after the war had ended against the Japanese in August 1945, until it broke out in major insurrection against the newly created Malayan Federation and British rule from 1948 to 1957. This had been almost brought under control by the time we arrived in Singapore in 1958, although there were still pockets of CTs, notably in Johore state, and we still had troops patrolling and fighting, but by 1959 the Chinese Communists had all retreated to the north and into Thailand.

We had formed a defensive alliance called the South East Asia Treaty Organisation (SEATO), which had its headquarters in Bangkok. This was mainly a political talking-shop to keep tabs on movement and aspirations of communist elements, but it also gave authority to USA to train troops and maintain a presence in and around Thailand and South Vietnam.

There was further potential trouble brewing in Indonesia, where after the war the Javanese and Sumatrans had refused to allow the Dutch to return to control what had been the Dutch East Indies before the Japanese invasion in 1942. There was much guerrilla fighting in the islands, which the Dutch could not control, and eventually they left the government to the Indonesians under Soekarno.

In 1958 the situation was beginning to settle down, but it was uneasy, and Soekarno did not have total support throughout Indonesia, there still being resistance in Celebes, Timor and Western New Guinea.

The British had their own worries also, in Hong Kong, where Communist Chinese made occasional threatening moves against the colony's border between the New Territories and mainland China, which kept our Army in Hong Kong constantly on the alert. Further north the Nationalist Chinese had retreated to Taiwan, and the US

Navy kept a constant patrol in the Straits of Formosa to ensure that Communist China did not invade Taiwan.

There was therefore a good deal to keep Michael busy in this vast theatre, much of it in a state of political unrest, and during our two years in that first appointment in Singapore, he spent much time travelling around the command.

While the Communists were stirring up trouble in the wider context, Britain was working to create political independent states in Malaya and Singapore, away from the former colonies and dependencies.

Singapore was emerging as the political, financial and commercial centre of the Far East at that time, and was a seething city of development and intrigue. It was fascinating to be living so close to all that was going on, and to meet and get to know well so many of the principals in the battle for power and position: Chinese, Indians, Malays, Indonesians, as well as others of European origin such as Germans, Dutch and of course the British. One of these was Charles Letts, a prominent local businessman, merchant banker and entrepreneur, with many interests throughout the whole of the Far East and Australia. He spoke many local languages, and had lived in the Far East since 1936, including having been a prisoner-of-war of the Japanese during the Second World War. He became, and remains, a great family friend.

We also met, and knew well, David Marshall, a man of unknown origins, but said to be from Baghdad; he had been an outstanding lawyer, and had taken a leading political part in the development of Singapore, having at times been a considerable thorn in the flesh of the British government. In 1959 he led the opposition party to Lee Kwan Yew. He was a very colourful personality in every sense, being a big man, olive-skinned, with large dark eyes, a sensuous mouth, and a shock of curly dark hair, which was starting to go grey. David was very hospitable, and had a beach house set in lovely gardens on a cliff top, on the south-east coast of the island, where he held large family parties most Sundays, to which we were sometimes invited. One met people of every creed, colour and background there, and all the children played about freely while the adults lazed in long chairs on the lawns, drifting down to the sea along a steep winding path to cool off at intervals. Large curries of different kinds were prepared over charcoal braziers to one side of the lawns, and simpler fare was served for the children in the house. David was very susceptible to the charms of the fairer sex, and there was always a resident beauty who acted as his hostess; he was devoted to children and we used to wonder if he ever would marry. Eventually he did, and having revelled in a bachelor's life, he very soon became a doting father and family man.

Soon after our arrival in Singapore, we were invited to a large formal dinner-party, and I was warned in advance that I was to sit next to a Chinese banker called Tan Chin Tuan, who was known for being a not very easy conversationalist. He was head of the Overseas Chinese Banking Corporation, owned the Tiger Beer company, and was involved in many other commercial concerns.

'We have placed you next to him, Sue, because you talk so much, and if anyone can get him to relax, you will!' I was told. I was very pleased to have the opportunity of getting to know a Chinese, and of finding the answers to many questions that were intriguing me. By the most fortuitous chance, I started off on the best subject I could have chosen:

'I would love to try to grow orchids while we are out here; do you know anything about them, and can you advise me how to set about it?' I asked, little knowing that I was speaking to one of the expert orchid fanciers in the Far East. Chin Tuan's face lit up, and from that moment we became life-long friends. A few days later we received a gold embossed card inviting us to a Chinese dinner in Singapore city, which was to be a memorable occasion.

Tan Chin Tuan's house was surrounded by large gardens, all given over to the cultivation of every conceivable variety and specie of orchid. At dinner there were two round tables, each seating ten people. Chin Tuan presided over one, and his wife, Helene, over the other. Michael and I were the only Western guests and were seated next to our host and hostess; the centre of each table was a circular revolving mirror, on which was a low bowl of orchids to one side, and on which was set each dish in turn; places with chopsticks were set round the ebony outer perimeter; there were ten courses of the most delicious Chinese dishes, and being a novice with chopsticks, I was helped by both my host on one side, and by my neighbour on the other, to delectable morsels which they delicately lifted with their chopsticks, and dropped in my bowl. Once or twice the bowls were removed, to be replaced with another filled with sharks' fin soup and later with birds' nest soup; crisp Peking duck, sucking-pig, steamed pomfret and ginger, chicken with almonds and other delicacies followed in turn, but one only ate two or three mouthfuls of each and thus never became sated, and eventually lychees and other exotic fruit signalled the end of the feast, accompanied by fragrant Chinese tea drunk from little bowls, and then we rose from the table.

'Come along, Sue,' said Chin Tuan, 'I will show you my orchids,' and the two of us left the rest of the party and went into the garden. We entered an eight foot high steel mesh enclosure, through a padlocked gate, and wandered between beds of staked plants and graduated shelves of pots, admiring graceful arcing sprays of vandas and dendrobiums of every colour, and then Chin Tuan said:

'Now we will go into the next enclosure; stay close, Sue, for in this one, and the innermost, which holds the most valuable plants, there are guard-dogs which are trained to attack strangers!'

I indeed stayed very close while a large Alsatian was ordered off, so that we could linger and admire bigger and more beautiful blooms. The third enclosure was the smallest, and held Chin Tuan's prize orchids, many of which he had hybridised himself, which he said were worth a great deal of money; he told me that thieves came down from Thailand regularly to try to steal from orchid-growers in Malaya and Singapore. The flowers here were breath-taking, huge waxen blooms, with marbled petals veined in darker shades of their different colours, rose, lilac, apricot, cream, green and yellow. Some were scented, and all were unblemished and radiant in the subtle lighting that had been switched on as we entered the garden.

I did not have the opportunity that evening to get to know Helene, Chin Tuan's wife, but later on she became a close friend.

The children had settled well to the new life in Singapore. James was enrolled in the nearby Army Infants' school in Pasir Panjang, and our friendly neighbour, Anne Murphy, was able to get Emma into the small private kindergarten in Tanglin, where she taught. School hours were in the mornings only, and the children returned home for lunch, after which we all had a rest, and then I took them on most days to the Tanglin club to swim. Many other families also followed this routine, so it was a good way of getting to know them.

The Murphy family were our lively Irish neighbours; Desmond, an RAMC colonel, was the senior army psychiatrist in the Far East command, charming and quiet; Anne was as vivacious as Desmond was shy. Of their five children, the two youngest were twins of five years old, who paired off well with James and Emma, the two boys and two girls going off to play by the hour, which was fine, so long as the pairs didn't meet, when each brother and sister would go for the other, and bedlam ensued. It made a great difference to us having such good neighbours, who introduced us to many other families, and I found Anne a tremendous kindred spirit.

Because of Michael's appointment, we had to attend quite a few formal dinners, to some of which we were bidden to represent our naval C-in-C during his periodic absence from the island. One such was to dine with the American Consul-general and his wife, to meet the US Secretary of the Army, and a US vice defence minister, who were on an official tour of the Far East, accompanied by their wives.

At the dinner was our Governor and his wife, Sir William and Lady Goode; the British GOC (General Officer in Command); the AOC (Air Officer in Command); Lim Yu Hock (Singapore's Chief Minister) and Mrs Lim, and one or two senior American generals.

It all began very formally (and nothing can be more stickily formal than an American official occasion), but during dessert there occurred an incident which began by causing general, if politely suppressed, giggles, which ended all stiffness. Suddenly, and without warning, the wife of the senior visiting American potentate, Mrs Bruckner, jumped up, her gold be-sequinned draperies flying, and so, of course, the hostess also rose, confusion amongst the other ladies then became general, and, desperately spitting out our grape pips, and abandoning our coffee and port, we all rose to our feet, scattering napkins, bags and gloves, when a booming voice came from under the table, where Mrs Bruckner had dived, and whence came a sound like trunks and suitcases being heaved about:

'Siddown girls! It's only me and my photography! There now, I've disturbed you-all! Isn't that just too bad of me? But I must have a picture of this *lerverly* party!' Then she turned to Bill Goode, her neighbour, who by this time was quite submerged under little leather boxes and cases, and said:

'Do *you* know, Governor, I'm just crazy on photography; I've taken over two thousand shots on this trip, the folks back home are going to just *lerve* 'em!' and with that, she tripped across the veranda where we were dining, climbed nimbly on to a chair, and flash bulbs were fixed, then:

'Just look this way, please, everybody, and say "Money", No, Mrs Kyrle-Pope, not "Cheese", that is quite outmoded, "Money" gives a much more serene expression to the face! That's right! Thank you all,' by which time we were all in such a state of hilarity that the rest of the evening was a relaxed and gay affair.

Some weekends we were able to borrow or hire a naval or army launch to go to an off-shore island. Three or more families would combine, and we would set off after church, taking large supplies of drinks for all ages, a picnic lunch, and plenty of sun-burn cream. One island we particularly liked was Raffles Light, at the entrance to Singapore 'roads'. It was a small uninhabited island with a safe sandy beach for the younger members of the party to play on and swim from, but a little way off it was the edge of a reef, where with goggles and snorkel breathing gear one could watch the shoals of small brilliantly coloured fish through the clear water, and see many varieties of coral, starfish and sea anemones. At low tide the latter were almost within reach, and we could stand on a head of coral, and bend down to pick up pieces to take home to bleach and make exquisite paper-weights and table decorations. Lunch would be eaten on board the launch, where an awning gave protection from the sun, and all ages enjoyed the 'afters', which were invariably the small local finger bananas, thick slices of juicy pineapple, eaten in one's fingers, and large wedges of pink water-melon; the children would sit on the side of the boat, legs dangling, seeing how far they could spit the black melon pips into the sea.

Everyone wore stout shoes for swimming, a very necessary protection against spiky sea-urchins, and the almost invisible stone-fish, which lurked on the sea-bed, and could give an extremely painful and poisonous sting if trodden on; the fair-skinned wore old T-shirts and hats for swimming as well, to avoid sun-burn.

We would start home by 4.00 pm, hoping to avoid the heavy rainstorm which usually occurred in the late afternoon, and accompanying choppy sea, when one got both soaked and very cold; no-one minded this much and the race against the black clouds of the building storm was all part of the fun.

There was a night-flowering lily in Singapore, called a Keng-Hua. It flowered on a cactus-like plant, but only seldom. It needed a marked drop in temperature to stimulate flowering; two or three days after this had occurred, a small brown pimple would appear on the edge of a leaf, and at once the owner would plan a dinner party for three weeks ahead, hoping it would coincide with the opening of the blossom. Daily the pimple would swell, lengthening into a trumpet-shaped bud four or five inches long; the bud would be ridged with dark red-brown ribs and as it grew plumper it would curve out into a bulb at the end of the trumpet. One evening after about three weeks, the bud would start to tremble, and if you had timed your party right, your guests would be able to watch the bud slowly breaking, as it trembled and shook; its myriads of narrow petals would open like a large white water-lily, gloriously scented. It lasted only a few hours, and by the next morning would be a drooping rag of brown slime.

We would eat Chinese food as often as possible. In downtown Singapore there were areas in which there were night street markets, and some narrow streets were lined with stalls each bearing a charcoal brazier, on which a variety of dishes were cooked in a wok while you watched. There were crude wooden tables and stools, almost in the path of passing traffic, and one ate the most superb food there very cheaply indeed. We liked to join up with a few friends and go down to Albert Street, or go to the car-park opposite the Cold Store in Orchard Road, which at night was filled with these cooking stalls. Alas, all that has been swept away now, in the enormous development of the city, which has become similar to many other eastern concrete cities of sky-scrapers.

One of my friends, Marigold MacKintosh, whose husband was the Deputy Commissioner General, asked me one day if I would like to join a class of six ladies doing a course of Chinese cooking, as a vacancy had occurred. The class was organised by a Chinese lady called Mrs Ho, and she interpreted for us at the classes, which were held in a house in Chinatown belonging to a well-known chef, who could be hired to cook for private parties. We sat on high blackwood stools round a kitchen table, watching the chef prepare high-class dishes such as sharks' fin soup, Peking duck etc. He had few kitchen implements; I remember only a two inch thick segment of tree-trunk, about twenty inches in diameter, a large razor-sharp hatchet, and a long-handled ladle. With the hatchet he dismembered poultry, pork and fish, and also chopped and sliced vegetables, holding the latter on the board with one hand palm down, and slicing horizontally to and fro as quick as lightning between his hand and the board; he would then hold up a slice of cucumber or onion to show us, which we could see through, it was so fine (we never saw a drop of blood!). He cooked in a wok on a brazier on the table, and Mrs Ho gave a commentary in English while he worked.

The other four students were two Chinese ladies, one being the wife of the Deputy Chief Justice, a Dane, and an American. The kitchen was at the back of the house in a mean street; to reach it you had to pass through a large bare room, in which there were classes going on, either in Judo or in Chinese sword dancing, both students and instructors being Chinese who took not the slightest notice of us passing through; that room led into a small dark one, where an old crone would always be sitting, rocking a tightly swaddled baby which was wedged into a rough wooden cradle, between two hard holsters, so that it could not move.

I never tried to reproduce the dishes we were shown in those classes, although when I returned to Singapore ten years later, and attended another course of Chinese cookery, I did attempt some I learned then, with partial success. That second course was taught by Mrs Lee, the mother of Lee Kuan Yew, the then Prime Minister of Singapore; she taught Nonya, or Straits style of Chinese cookery.

It is almost impossible to find authentic Chinese food in England I think; the ubiquitous 'Chinese take-aways' in every town and many villages supply food which bears no resemblance to that which we ate in the Far East, appetising though the English versions may be.

We had only been in Singapore a few weeks when Michael came home from the office one day and told me that the C-in-C, Admiral Sir Gerald Gladstone, had offered me a passage to go up to Hong Kong in his 'yacht', HMS *Alert*, which was being sent up ahead of his forthcoming official visit. *Alert* was a sloop, with her own duties as part of the Far East fleet, but was partly converted to act as the C-in-C's host ship, when he travelled round his scattered command. He could not afford the time always to travel in her, but would follow by air, the ship being sent on ahead. When this happened, if the ship was not required for naval exercises *en route*, the admiral would sometimes offer the use of his private cabins to the wives of some of the officers on his staff.

I asked Michael what he had replied to this marvellous invitation.

'Oh, I said you would be very grateful for the offer, but that you couldn't possibly go so soon after we had arrived out here!' he said.

'What!' I exclaimed, 'why ever not? Of course I can! The children are settled in their schools, Katherine looks after them very well when we have to go out, and they are already very fond of her, and Anne [Murphy] will help, I am sure, and you will be here at night! Of course I can go! If I refuse, the C-in-C may never ask me again! And I'm not going to miss any opportunity that comes my way of going *anywhere* if I can possibly help it!'

Anne was as encouraging as Michael had been dampening, and said:

'Of course you must go! The children will be perfectly all right between Katherine, Michael and me, and so will he!'

So it was decided, and preparations were made. Lists of menus were made out for Ah Tan, schools notified, warmer clothes dug out of chests (some already mildewed in the humidity since we had arrived); I had about a week in which to get ready, and it was fun speculating what life would be like actually living on board an HM ship, which in those days was almost unheard of for women.

The C-in-C's accommodation on board was surprisingly spacious; there were four other wives going up as passengers, and we each had a comfortable cabin, with a bathroom to each pair of ladies. The weather to start with was hot and fine, and we sat up on deck in long chairs under an awning, reading, sewing, writing letters etc.; each evening a film was shown, to which the officers came along from the wardroom. Quite soon the wind and sea got up, as we headed into the tail end of a typhoon. Our noisy chat and laughter quietened, and Mrs Whittle disappeared to her cabin; Peggy Davies also absented herself at intervals, and I felt slightly queasy, although I am usually a good sailor. The awning then had to be removed, and a life-buoy sentry was posted in the stern, where he sat shrouded in oil-skins, ready to heave a line to any 'man overboard'. The bad weather continued all the way to Hong Kong, but we eventually found our sea-legs, even poor Mrs Whittle, who emerged pale and wan from her cabin. The Captain, Peter Anson, used to join us for dinner in the admiral's dining cabin, and one evening, Mrs Whittle, who was a rather prim and proper lady, surprised us by saying that sunflower seeds are an excellent aphrodisiac, 'even better than Durian,' (which is a delicious but evil-smelling tropical fruit, local to Malaya and Sumatra, much sought after by those in need of aphrodisical inspiration!). Mrs Whittle's remark was so unexpected and out of character, that we all spluttered slightly, and looked at her with new eyes.

As we neared the China coast, we awoke one morning to see hundreds of junks on all sides, slipping out through the mist to their fishing-grounds. More and more sailed silently past, big ones and small, with patched sails of faded purples, blues and mauves, sage and emerald greens, brown, ochre, tan and yellow. They glided by, with the picturesque agelessness of China, fading back into the morning mist as they drew clear of our wake.

The islands drew nearer, and the mainland of Hong Kong (the New Territories) rose behind, little hummocky mountains forming an encircling backdrop for the panorama of the harbour and its approaches, with the islands all humpety too, greyish-green, gilding to gold as the sun rose and slowly overcame the morning mist and haze.

By the time we passed through Li Moon passage into Hong Kong harbour, the sun was blazing, and it was hot and clear; the green and white Star ferries crossing the harbour, and the little blue *walla-wallas* (sampans) spiked the scene with points of brilliant colour, and the modern sky-scrapers of Victoria Island and Kowloon gleamed with a scrubbed whiteness against the hillsides behind.

We tied up in the naval dockyard at about noon, and we ladies were met by our various hosts. I was to stay with Brian and Diana Hewson in their quarter on Stonecutters Island, in the middle of Hong Kong harbour. Brian took me into the naval base, HMS *Tamar*, to cross in his barge to the island, where Diana awaited us. That evening there was a vivid orange sunset, reflected in the harbour, followed by a quick nightfall, and the beauty of the lights all round us, from the towns on either side, the Peak rising above Victoria Island, and the small craft still busily crossing and recrossing the harbour, was unforgettable.

The next day was a holiday, so we crossed to HMS *Tamar*, where Brian kept his car, and then set off on a tour of the island. This was 1958, and there was less than half the development that there is today; the problem of illegal immigrants from China and Vietnam had hardly begun.

We drove up the Peak, from which there was a view of the harbour all round the island, and then we came down and drove round the coast road, visiting Repulse Bay and Aberdeen: the latter is a fishing village in a creek, formed entirely of sampans and small junks, moored alongside each other in rows, with 'roads' and passages in and out between them. Thousands of Chinese lived there in their boats, large families in appalling cramped conditions, but everyone busy and calling to one another cheerfully. The smell was overpowering, sanitation nil, and water supply of extremely doubtful quality, being mainly from the creek. Seven and eight year-old children, with their baby brothers and sisters strapped on their backs, clamoured round us with hands outstretched; it was almost impossible not to give them all one had, they looked so beguiling in their jackets and long trousers, with little round faces, button mouths and slanting eyes, yet their shy smiles hardly changed as we moved on, ungenerous and unreproached.

In the afternoon we crossed the harbour to Kowloonside, and drove through the New Territories and out to the border with Red China. The country is hilly, and every square inch seemed cultivated and weed-free, with large market gardening areas and rows of brilliant green succulent vegetables, which looked mouth-watering until the only too obvious means of fertilising the soil became apparent.

The rice was being harvested by hand, and threshed in the field, sheaf by sheaf, as it was cut. The thresher had a large wooden tub and, standing in it, a rattan screen encircling four-fifths of its circumference, leaving open a foot-wide gap. The coolie raised a sheaf high in the air and brought it down hard between the open sides of the screen, so that the stalks were banged against the rim of the tub, and the grain fell into it, and was prevented from being blown away by the five-foot high screen.

We saw many duck farms, where two or three little ponds were almost obscured by the thousands of birds in every stage of development, and where the farmer lived in a mud hut, reed-roofed, on the bank of one of the ponds.

Diana Hewson was imminently expecting twins, and so was glad when I suggested that I went off on my own to explore Kowloon and Victoria, on shopping expeditions. There was much to tempt one, for unlike today, everything then was very cheap in Hong Kong.

I was able to fly back to Singapore by courtesy of the RAF Transport Command, filling a vacant seat on one of their regular flights.

There was a SEATO conference in Singapore in May 1959, and we were much involved in entertaining some of the many deputations of

Asians from Thailand, Vietnam, the Philippines, Burma, Malaya, Indonesia and Cambodia. We gave a cocktail party for some of the visiting naval officers, and thirty of them arrived by bus, all together, on the dot of the time that they were invited, and before most of our Western friends whom we had invited to meet them. The house seemed suddenly to be filled with smiling little yellow men, all wearing white uniform, and all with rows of gold teeth and entirely unpronounceable names. Although they all looked much alike, many did not know each other, and so I had to try to introduce them; I managed to master a few names, and by introducing these rather noisily, I won the reputation for being 'wonderful with names', and the owners of those I remembered were very flattered, and smiled more goldily than ever. Little did they realise that I only remembered them by the even greater number of gold teeth they possessed than the others! I lost my voice in the middle of this party, which was tiresome (although possibly only for me), and one little Cambodian came and peered up at me, and crooned in a sing-song voice:

'If I may be so bold as to suggest it, Madame, a leetle Veek massaged into your throat and, er, lower down, would relieve your discomfort, I theenk.' I received the impression that he would have quite enjoyed doing it himself!

The British Military Hospital was at the foot of the hill on which we lived. It catered for the Army and Navy in the Far East Command, and there were always some sailor patients from Hong Kong and other outposts, or left behind by their ships, who had no family or friends to visit them, so I started to visit naval patients as a regular commitment. Through our neighbour, Desmond Murphy, who was the senior army psychiatrist in the command, I became particularly interested in his patients. Other naval officers' wives visited the hospital as well, but no-one liked to visit the psychiatric wards. At first I was nervous too, but Desmond urged me on, in the belief that a regular visitor whom the men could get to know might be helpful therapy for them, and he would sometimes ask me to pay particular attention to one or other among them.

Psychiatric therapy was very prolonged, and the patients became understandably bored and listless. I was interested to notice after a while, that most of them were bachelors, between the ages of thirty-five and forty-five. Some violent ones I was not allowed to visit until they showed signs of recovery, and even then I found it a bit disturbing to be locked in a room with them alone, although I knew there was a male nurse the other side of the door who would come in if I called. Over the weeks I came to know the patients very well; it was sometimes heart-rending listening to their troubles, and trying to comfort or cheer them.

I remember one bear-like man who had been closely confined for weeks, and was said to be capable of considerable violence. Desmond asked me if I would be willing to visit him in spite of this, for he thought I might be a calming and civilising influence. I was locked in with him alone, and was very nervous. He glowered at me, and during the first visit he said nothing, while I sat and talked quietly, getting no reaction from him at all. I visited him three times a week, and I became quite fond of him; he had no family at all, no-one who cared for him, or what happened to him, and no-one to go home to. He was a merchant seaman, and so would be at sea for weeks or months at a time, seldom having the opportunity to go ashore, nor the wish to do so. The last time I saw him before he was repatriated to UK for further treatment, he startled me by walking up and putting his arms round me. I was not sure of his intentions, and stood still, and he also stood quietly, then, dropping his arms, he said:

'I have a present for you, to thank you,' and he fished into his trouser pocket, and brought out a little ¼ lb box of milk chocolates, which he gave to me, adding:

'I don't want to say good-bye. I don't want to go back to England. I don't know what will happen to me.' I left him then, he was starting to cry, and I was very near it. I wonder what became of him.

Emma was four years old by now, and beginning to show signs of some financial acumen. One Saturday, both Michael and I independently gave her her weekly pocket-money; she said nothing, and it was only later that we discovered she had been given it twice. She was wearing a new sun-dress that day, and when we taxed her with this small deception, she thought for a long time, and then, looking down at her new dress, she said:

'Well, my new dress has two pockets, so I thought you were giving me money for each pocket.' I think she deserved to get away with it, but I don't remember if she did!

Michael was always reluctant to take leave, but in May 1959, we

James and Emma in Malay dress, Singapore, 1959.

took the children up to Malacca for a week. It is a small old town on the west coast of Malaysia and, like Macao, was once a Portuguese colony. Many of the old buildings, and the fort, show a strong Portuguese influence, and are built of a dark reddish stone.

We stayed at a guest house run by an English widow, which stood in a pleasant garden opening directly on to the white sandy beach. This stretched for miles, and fishing boats would land their catch regularly twice a day, right below our hotel, which was great fun to watch.

From Malacca we visited a Dunlop rubber plantation, which was managed by an Englishman we knew of, who arranged for us to watch the tappers at work, as they incised narrow $^1/_4$ inch spiral strips of bark round half the girth of each tree twice every day, thus releasing a stream of liquid white latex to drip into a little cup wired to the tree below. This would be collected and mixed with ammonia to keep it liquid, and then it would be transported by road in tankers to factories.

Some of the village people in the country owned a few rubber trees, and they would let the latex set hard into white sheets on the ground, then the pieces, looking like large handkerchiefs of crepe rubber, would be hung on wires and over bushes by the road-sides, to be collected and pooled in a local co-operative trading system.

It was beautiful country round Malacca, with small Malay *kampongs* (villages), of wooden houses raised from the ground, with long high roofs, dipping in elegant curves between the gable ends. I later saw similar houses in the Batak tribal area of North Sumatra, just across the Straits from Malacca.

One day we watched a coconut monkey at work. When we first saw it, it was sitting on the shoulder of its owner, who was riding a bicycle into a coconut grove. The man alighted, and the monkey, which was tied to a very long leash, was sent up a palm tree, the cord being paid out as it climbed. When the animal reached the big cluster of nuts hanging below the leaves, it would twist each in turn, and if ripe, the nut would fall to the ground. If unripe, the monkey tried another. It was advisable to stand well clear while this was going on, for a coconut in its husk, full of milk, is quite heavy, and one falling has been known to kill an unwary person standing underneath.

Our drive to and from Malacca took us through varied scenery; we saw tin mines, also miles of padi, brilliant green where the rice plants were standing in water. We passed pepper and pineapple plantations, the scent from the latter heavy and sweet. There was then little road traffic, and we had to cross rivers on rickety bridges, or by primitive raft-like ferries, which we summoned with a shout when we wanted to cross. There were heavy wooden carts drawn by buffaloes, which were also used to plough the padi and do other agricultural work, and these were more numerous than cars.

We had met, and got to know well, an Englishman called Richard Tufnell. He was a retired Captain RN, and was the head of the Singapore Drug Prevention Narcotics Bureau. A great deal of opium came into Singapore from Laos (the centre of the Golden Triangle in Indo-China, where it was grown). The Customs and Police seized a certain amount, but a lot more went on westwards to Europe and America. Quite a large amount was used in Singapore and Malaya, and the Narcotics Bureau were on constant alert, and had sources of informers who tipped them off. They raided houses and known opium dens to catch the smugglers and smokers.

One night Richard Tufnell invited us to accompany him and his team on a routine evening's work, to see what went on. I was told to wear khaki trousers, and to look as much like a man as possible. We set off in a large long-wheel-based police vehicle, and drove into the China-town area of the city first, to the purlieus beyond Arab Street. There were three or four policemen, dressed in white short-sleeved shirts and khaki trousers, Richard, Michael and me. We left the vehicle a good distance from the first suspect building, and the four policemen sprinted ahead of us to reach it before the usual Chinese child watchers could give warning, and alert the law-breakers in time to make their escape. Several squalid houses were raided but somehow news of our approach had preceded us, and we arrived to find empty tiers of bug-ridden blackened wooden bunks, the air down the dark passageways reeking with the sweet smell of opium, but no sign of the smokers. The police hacked at the rotten wooden framework of the bunks with machetes, exposing hidden spaces behind the boards, in which little packets of opium were found, and in one a small pipe, but of the addicts there was no sign, and when questioned, any nearby potential witnesses would only disclaim all knowledge, and stare at us with impassive faces.

We moved on, and drove further out of the city to a marshy area, where narrow mud dikes criss-crossed the swamp; again the vehicle was abandoned, and the team of four searchers ran ahead silently, doubled up to be less noticeable in the failing light. They reached a little hut in the middle of the marsh, and this time they were lucky, for inside, although there had been four smokers and two had got away, there was one man lying on the dirt floor, with a smile of bliss on his face, oblivious to all around him; he was skeletal and pale, his face gaunt and emaciated, and he gave no trouble when charged and removed by the police; the fourth man was a tall handsome Chinese, a burly man, grizzle-haired, who greeted Richard:

'Thank God you have found me, Sir, now I know I will be cured and then able to work again!' He was pathetic in his gratitude.

The cause of much of the opium addiction was tuberculosis. When a man was diagnosed as tubercular, he lost his job, and was no longer employable. Unable to support himself or his family, he would become addicted to opium, to forget his troubles, and under its influence all his worries and anxieties would evaporate into euphoric bliss. An effect of opium is to reduce the appetite, and many addicts eventually starved to death. However, if found in time, they would be cured, for the penalty of opium addiction was one year in prison, and the addict would be sent to St John's Island, which was a police hospital for the treatment of addiction and tuberculosis. If they were not too far gone when apprehended, they would be fit again after a year, and able once more to find employment. The big Chinese we found had been a seaman, and was not too seriously affected, and so there was an excellent chance that he would be rehabilitated and able to work again.

Unfortunately on that evening's raids, no drug trafficker had been picked up; by Singapore law they were treated very severely indeed, with the result that nowadays there is very little drug trading in the island, and the death sentence is still mandatory without mercy on all who are caught pushing drugs.

Richard was also responsible for catching smugglers of other contraband goods, such as tobacco and cigarettes. I asked him one day what happened to any that were found and seized.

'They are burned,' he said, 'we have regular incinerating days every month.'

I thought about this; it seemed such a waste of cigarettes which the sick sailors in BMH would so enjoy. They were entitled to duty-free tobacco on board their ships, anyway, but lost that right when ashore in hospital. I asked Richard if there was any way I could be allowed to have some of the seized cigarettes to distribute in hospital, and he contacted the relevant government department, so that after that, I was allowed a weekly allotment for each man while he was in hospital; all I had to do was submit a monthly list of naval patients, and go down to the government contraband godown (warehouse), to collect each month's supply. It was a wonderful concession, and very much appreciated by the sailors.

The children and I were ill quite a bit in Singapore; they had much bronchial trouble, and I spent periods in the British Military hospital before and after a major abdominal operation, which was complicated by uncontrollable internal haemorrhaging. Eventually the Army surgeons called in a local consultant on Christmas Eve, and I was told Professor Shears was coming to sort me out. Just as I was being wheeled into the theatre once more, I was electrified when a smiling Chinese face looked down at me and introduced himself.

'I am Professor Shears; I hope to be able to help you.' Because of his English-sounding name, I had not realised that he was Chinese. Several years later, he became the President of the State of Singapore.

After my recovery, Michael and I were invited to go to Kuala Lumpur, and on up to Fraser's Hill for a convalescent holiday. We stayed with Bruce Wood, who had been head of ICI in Singapore and had recently moved up to Kuala Lumpur. He lived in a luxurious bachelor house, and drove us up to the cool heights of Fraser's Hill for several days. It was wonderful to have a fire in the evenings there, and to need a blanket on one's bed. Waking early, we would listen to the bands of gibbon monkeys leaping through the jungle tree-tops on the hill-sides below us, their whooping cries echoing round the hills as they called to each other, till gradually the sound faded as they moved on to other feeding-grounds.

I was offered another trip to Hong Kong just before we left Singapore. This time I flew up, again courtesy of the RAF, and returned a week later in a spare cabin aboard the troopship *Dunera*.

By this time we had many friends in Hong Kong, and I had come to know well the wife of the American Naval Attaché, Captain Billings. Winni and I decided to visit Macao together, the small Portuguese colony and free port down the China coast to the west.

We were offered accommodation there in the house used by a subsidiary of Jardine Mathesons, the big Far Eastern trading organisation based in Hong Kong.

We set off in the regular daily ferry from Hong Kong, steaming close to the coast, between a hundred small islands. In all the bays and inlets were junks and sampans fishing. The other ferry passengers were all Chinese, and we aroused much interest, which was entirely mutual.

Winni was an enjoyable companion; she was a very determined person, deep-voiced and matter-of-fact, with a strong sense of humour and loud laugh, who, like me, was not going to miss any opportunity that arose of seeing as much of the East as possible.

The ferry trip took about five hours, and we arrived at 5.00 pm to be met by Chang, the Chinese house-boy of the house where we were to stay. He had a taxi waiting, and we went off through the little town, and then turned up the coast road along the peninsula which the town fills. This residential road is lined with banyan trees, and all the houses have thick walls, high cool rooms, elegant wrought iron balconies, and arched verandas, and all look across the road to the sea. The Portuguese architectural influence was very strong; the houses were colour-washed in soft pastel shades, lemon yellow, pale green, rose pink, with the elegant plaster mouldings on the walls and over windows picked out in white.

Macao had an extraordinary atmosphere of intrigue and mystery; everyone seemed to know where we were staying, and we were met with smiles and friendly remarks wherever we went. The little town was a centre of gold trading, and illicit gold and opium smuggling, and we gathered that the house where we were staying belonged to a company that dealt only in gold. Only breakfast was provided there, so we went out to a restaurant where we had such a good dinner that we sent compliments to the chef, who came out to see us, a plump little dark-eyed Portuguese. He gave us the recipe for the dish we particularly liked, and he promised us two jars of his special sauce which was the making of it.

'You are staying at No. 17, I expect? I will have them sent round,' he said. We wondered how he knew we came from No. 17. There were three hotels there, yet he seemed to know who we were and where we were from, and so did the pedi-cab drivers whom we hired.

There were many Intelligence agents of all nationalities there: as Macao is so near the Red China border, it made a good listening-post, and the atmosphere of undercover activities was almost palpable.

I only experienced one disquieting moment: I took my camera everywhere, and I wanted to photograph some fishermen unloading large barrels of fish from a sampan, which made a picturesque scene. Luckily something made me approach them to ask their permission first, pointing my camera at them questioningly. They were furious, and gestured menacingly at me, so I hastily retreated. Chang told me later that they were Communist soldiers who brought in the fish caught by Red Chinese fishermen, and as soon as they returned across the bay to their own territory, they would don their uniform again. He said there had recently been an unpleasant incident when a tourist had taken a photograph without asking, and the camera had been seized, trampled, and flung into the sea.

After dinner Winni and I went round to the casino to see if we could play Fan-Tan there. It was early in the evening, and little was going on on the third floor where the élite usually gamble, so we walked down to the second, but found that floor was obviously used for other purposes than gambling, for there were curtained cubicles, red plush settees and pretty girls giggling and turning away when they saw us. On the first floor we joined the coolies who were playing Fan-Tan, and much to their amusement, sat down with them, and were shown with courtesy and smiles, how to place our stakes. We won, or were permitted to win, two or three dollars each, and then tried our hand at a dice game. We stayed a half-hour or so, and then took a pedi-cab back to No. 17.

The next morning, Winni refused to have breakfast before 8.30 am, so I left the house at 7.00 am, and went for a walk with my camera. I met a few Portuguese going to work or school, and all smiled broadly, and wished me Good Morning. I decided to climb up to the Bishop's palace on the hill in the centre of the town. It was a steep climb up winding cobbled streets, between old houses with arched verandas and pillared porches. Some had eaves curling up in the oriental style, and some were inside small walled gardens glimpsed through wrought iron gates. The road became narrower, and turned into shallow cobbled steps, and finally I came out into an open square in front of the palace. Round it were gardens, and from it a steep ramp curved up round the bastion of the palace itself, a beautiful austere white stone building, with a tall conically roofed tower.

I wandered round the public gardens, which I had to myself, and was evidently spotted by the Bishop, who was out on the ramparts above me, for he sent a message down, inviting me to go up the ramp and into his private gardens, where I would get better views to photograph; he had gone by the time I had climbed up, so I was not able to thank him.

After breakfast, Chang took us out by car to the Chinese border, although he was very nervous indeed, and would not approach it too closely, and would not allow me to take any photographs.

We had tried to get in touch with someone called Sydney, as we had been instructed in Hong Kong, by asking at a certain hotel for him, but had been unsuccessful. However, while we were eating lunch in a restaurant, having told no-one where we were going, Sydney turned up at our table, asking if we were the ladies from

No. 17. He was Chinese, a tall man, and he spoke faultless English. He said:

'I've just seen my aircraft off safely, so now I have no more work for today.' He insisted on paying for our lunch, and although we had been warned not to ask his full name, or what his occupation was, we gleaned a little from his conversation, and we thought he was responsible for the buying and despatching of the gold on behalf of the company which owned No. 17. He saw us off on the 3.00 pm ferry, putting us in the charge of the captain, a hard-bitten Scottish sea-dog, who seemed to be subservient to, and quite in awe of, Sydney. It was all quite an intriguing experience.

We left Singapore in July 1960, in the troopship *Oxfordshire*. Emma had bronchitis when we sailed, and it was hoped that the sea air would help her recover. The Singapore climate had not really suited the children, who had both had frequent minor illnesses and much bronchitic trouble.

Oxfordshire was carrying an infantry battalion home to UK, as well as many service families from Hong Kong and Singapore. The regimental band played on deck each Sunday morning, where officers and their families enjoyed drinks before lunch; this was a troopship custom, and a pleasant social occasion.

On the Sunday after a brief call at Colombo, we were all listening to the army band, and James was perched on top of the upright piano, at one end of a row of little boys; another child climbed up on the other end, calling out:

'Budge up, everyone!' They did, and James was pushed off the other end. He fell on his head, hitting a ring-bolt in the deck just behind his ear. He was unconscious for two days in the sick-bay, and I stayed with him there, talking and singing to him in the hopes that he might hear me, and be comforted. Although there was an RAF surgeon among the passengers who had experience of skull injuries from aircraft crashes, there was no equipment in the ship to enable a proper diagnosis to be made. It was therefore decided that Michael and James would be disembarked at Aden, where James could be admitted to the well equipped RAF hospital there, but that Emma and I should remain onboard to continue the voyage to England, as Aden in July/August is hot, dry and dusty, and it was not thought advisable for Emma to stay there so soon after her recent bout of bronchitis. She had been diagnosed just before we left Singapore as having some form of congenital heart condition, possibly a 'hole in the heart', so we were anxious to get her home and into the care of a heart specialist as soon as possible.

Shore leave was not given at Aden, and it seemed that everyone on board was leaning over the side to watch James being carried, still unconscious and strapped into a stretcher, down the gangway and into the waiting launch to be taken ashore. At that point we did not know if he might be paralysed or mentally affected by the apparent skull or brain damage. The ship sailed that afternoon, and I will never forget watching Aden gradually fade into the dust and heat haze, feeling so helpless, and torn in two between the children's needs.

Michael was able to send radio messages to *Oxfordshire* and I heard within forty-eight hours that James had recovered consciousness, and was able to move his toes. A day or two later I had a message to say he had spoken a few words, and then that after x-ray and tests, it was thought he had fractured his skull, split his right ear-drum, and severed the aural nerve, but that there appeared to be no other lasting injury. He has been totally deaf in that ear ever since.

He and Michael were able to travel on to Southampton a few weeks later.

CHAPTER 8

Bahrain, 1962

MICHAEL'S NEXT APPOINTMENT was to the Imperial Defence
College in London, to do the senior officers' staff course there.

We found a flat in Wimbledon, which was the large ground floor of
a big Victorian house, in which the owners lived on the upper floors.
We also had half of the quite big garden, and were able to buy a seven
year lease. This became an ideal base, which we sub-let a year later
when we went to Bahrain, and to which we returned for the period
when Michael was on the Intelligence staff at the Admiralty.

James was sufficiently recovered from his accident to start at his
preparatory school after a term's delay, and Emma went to a small
private day school in Wimbledon. James was very happy at his prep
school, Rose Hill, in Gloucestershire; we had chosen it because of its
proximity to Michael's parents at Much Marcle in Herefordshire, who
would act *in loco parentis* during our possible absences abroad.

Early in 1962, Michael's great-uncle Cecil Money-Kyrle died, aged
ninety-three. He was a retired country parson, and had lived at
Homme, the family home in Much Marcle, since his wife (who pre-
deceased him) bought it from a cousin in 1922. She had left it to my
father-in-law, and he and my mother-in-law lived there after the
Second World War, during which it had been used as a military
convalescent hospital. Uncle Cis lived there during the war, and stayed
on with my in-laws when they moved in, and so we saw a lot of him,
as we spent most of Michael's leaves at Homme; he was the last
survivor of the family Victorians, much loved by all the many cousins
of several generations. Second and third marriages in late Victorian
years had produced literally dozens of near and distant relations, and
Uncle Cis knew and loved them all. His death was a happy release, for
he had suffered both physical and mental debility in his later years, and
many relations attended his funeral in Much Marcle, on an icy day in
March. After the service, all were invited to Homme for tea, and it was
a memorable and happy family gathering. It was on a Friday, and the

entire family of four sons of Roger and Minora Money-Kyrle all came
from London and elsewhere by train, meeting their parents at the
church, who were to take them back to Calne for the week-end.
Eventually after tea, Cousin Minora called the boys together and told
them that their grey flannel trousers and jerseys were all in the boot of
the old family Bentley in the drive, so they could change out of their
morning-coats before the sixty-mile drive home. They went out to
the car, and the next thing I saw was all four of the young men
stripping off in the snow, down to underpants and socks.

'Wouldn't you like to come in and change in the house where it is a
bit warmer?' I called. They looked surprised at the suggestion, and one
of them replied:

'No, why? We're fine out here!' It was a very funny sight, but
entirely in keeping with that delightfully eccentric family. They then
all piled into the car, five large men, and generously proportioned
Minora, and drove off.

The occasion was a very happy farewell to Uncle Cis, a party which
he would have enjoyed enormously.

Soon after Uncle Cis' funeral, we went out to Bahrain, where Michael
had been appointed as Senior Naval Officer, Persian Gulf: SNOPG,
commonly called 'SNOPJI'.

When I first heard of this, I cried:

'We can't take Emma out there! It's known as the White Man's
grave!' Such was my ignorance, and little did I know that in December
and January there we would be glad of jerseys, coats, blankets and
electric fires.

Michael was to take over the Jufair naval head-quarters, in which
we lived in Navy House, an old low, thick mud-walled house, built
originally in the local style, a single storey, the rooms with ceilings of
woven *barasti* (palm leaves) supported by mangrove poles brought up
from Zanzibar and East Africa. It had a later pitched roof, and a very
fine veranda facing onto a small lawn leading straight to the sea. This
view, to the east, across a large almost enclosed bay, showed many
small islands, and, about two miles away, the larger island of Muharraq,
on which was the airfield, both RAF and civilian, and also a large old
Arab/Persian/Portuguese fort, and a small town occupied mainly by
fishermen and builders of dhows.

We had a household staff of Goan stewards. They were naval ratings, members of the RN Goan Division, who were recruited from the Portuguese colony in South India, and who formed the cook and steward personnel for the Gulf frigates and other ships based at Bahrain.

We had an excellent cook, Coelho, a splendid Petty Officer Steward called Veigas, and three other junior stewards under them. Veigas became a friend to us all, almost part of the family, and later he was able to come to England to be with us for Emma's wedding in 1976. We still keep in regular touch with him. However, he and I had a few initial difficulties to surmount.

We had to do much official entertaining in Bahrain, and before lunch and dinner-parties I would go into the dining-room to see that the table was arranged to my liking, and to put the name-cards at the relevant places. The first time I did this, I found that Veigas had laid the dessert-spoons and forks across the top of each place-mat, so I moved them to the inside of the rest of the cutlery on each side. Veigas came into the room.

'No, Mem, that is not right! They should go across the top,' and he started to move them back.

'Veigas, I like the table set with all the cutlery at the sides of the places, please.'

'No, Mem, that is absolutely incorrect. I know, Mem, for I have been trained by the Royal Navy and the Royal Navy is always right!'

'I am sorry, Veigas, but I insist on it being done my way. This is not a ship, but my home, and I am afraid you must do as I say, even though you know my way is incorrect!' and I managed to get him to laugh. After that he conceded the reins of running the household to me more happily, and we became firm allies and friends. He was loyal and hard-working, and together we waged war against the cockroaches which permeated the walls and ceilings of the pantry in the old house; they were not seen by day, but emerged by night, and when we returned late from a dinner-party and went to get a cold drink from the fridge before going to bed, as we opened the pantry door, there would be a rustle, and myriads of the huge insects scurried back to their holes and cracks to escape the light. They were the largest cockroaches I have ever seen (and I have world-wide experience of them!) and were up to two inches long, with glossy chestnut brown backs, and four inch long feelers: I thought them beautiful creatures, but few people agreed with me!

The Royal Navy's presence in the Arabian Gulf began in the nineteenth century, when there had been a strong British political presence which mainly centred on Bushire. Royal Naval ships operated increasingly in the Gulf from 1815 onwards to prevent and stop the piracy and slave trade which formed a livelihood for many Arab groups and clans living in the small inlets of the Ras al Khaima area, and along the coast of what is now the United Arab Emirates, and Qatar to the south of Bahrain.

Gradually the British diplomatic presence moved from Bushire, with the establishment of Political Agents in Kuwait, Bahrain, Qatar, Abu Dhabi and Dubai, and a Consul-General in Muscat. A senior post of Political Resident, Arabian Gulf was set up at Jufair, in Bahrain, to provide overall co-ordination. This made it convenient for naval matters also to be centralised and administered from Bahrain, and thus HMS *Jufair* was created.

Kuwait declared its independence in 1961, retaining a defensive treaty with Britain, and Iraq tried immediately to annex it. Britain reacted at once, and landed a substantial military force, with strong air support, and the Iraqis were deterred. To maintain this deterrence, we set up a large stockpile of tanks, arms and munitions in Kuwait, and arranged a military mission to enlarge and train the Kuwaiti army.

We also increased our ability to reinforce and defend the RAF force in Bahrain and at Sharjah, establishing a parachute battalion in Bahrain, and reinforcing the naval commitment in the Gulf, to comprise three small frigates and an amphibious warfare squadron with landing-craft, as well as several regularly visiting ships such as HMS *Bulwark*, the ex-aircraft carrier, and large Tribal frigates such as *Ashanti*, *Gurkha* and *Eskimo*, which came to the Gulf for exercises, being based on Bahrain for a few months at a time.

Ships on entering the Gulf came under Michael's command, all being part of Middle East Command, under Rear Admiral Fitzroy Talbot, based at Aden.

The Commander of the Land forces in the Gulf, also based in Bahrain, was Brigadier Dick Bryers; we had known Dick and Phyllis very well indeed in Washington ten years previously, and it was really marvellous to find them already well-established when we first arrived.

There were several Army units in the island, including armoured squadrons which served in turn to exercise with the naval amphibious warfare squadron, and they were from the 17th/21st Lancers, the Scots Greys and the 16th/5th Queen's Royal Lancers.

Bahrain was still comparatively unsophisticated and unspoilt at that time; there was little development outside Manama, the main town, except for the American oil refinery residential area of Awali.

The island is shaped like an elongated or Conference pear, and the northern or wide end is the siting of all urban development. The middle to southern part of the island, which is about thirty-six miles long, is barren rock and sand, with one central hilly area of volcanic rock, a wonderful place for multi-family picnics in the cooler months, with realistic games of cowboys and Indians. To go to the lovely sandy beaches at the southern tip of the island required the permission of Shaikh Isa, the Ruler, but a pass was easily obtained through the police, given enough notice.

Sir William Luce was the Political Resident, known colloquially as the PR. He was a senior ambassador with quite a large staff; he had a wide understanding of the Arab Middle East, and was much respected, admired and even loved by all who met and worked with him. His daughter Diana, at that time in her late teens, was, like her father, an accomplished pianist, and she undertook to give Emma piano lessons. When I asked Emma how her first lesson had gone, she replied:

'It was great fun, Mummy, Diana said before I began to learn to play I had better see how a piano works, and made me climb up on top to look inside and see,' which seemed both highly imaginative and practical to me.

Our arrival in Bahrain coincided with the three-day holiday at the end of Ramadan, the Id al Fitr, when it was customary for the PR, the PA (Political Agent) and the heads of the three services, to pay courtesy calls on the Ruler, Shaikh Isa bin Sulman al Khalifa, and for their wives to call on his wife, Shaikha Hassa. Accordingly, Rosemary Tripp, the wife of the PA, picked me up at 09.30 am, and with an interpreter, Mrs Al Umran, whom Rosemary knew well, we set off to the Shaikha's palace at Rifa'a, where all the ruling family had their palaces of varying size and grandeur, in the desert to the south of Manama.

Shaikha Hassa's palace was adjacent to Shaikh Isa's private one, but he was 'sitting' in his *majlis*, or audience chamber, in his large formal palace, where any of his subjects, of high or low degree, were free to call on him on the days when he regularly 'sat'. Outside the Shaikha's palace we found a group of Arab men doing a staid shuffling dance in the sand, to music played on weird instruments, with skin drums and tambourines to maintain the rhythm. They made a path for us to pass through and under an archway leading into a courtyard, from where we entered the reception room of the palace. It was a spacious audience chamber, startlingly decorated with two walls painted mauve, and two cream; the furniture was upholstered in scarlet and sulphur yellow moquette, the carpets were of bright turquoise and electric blue. From the centre of the high ceiling hung an exquisite crystal chandelier, and above it were bars of strip neon lighting fixed to the ceiling. On one small table I noticed a pair of magnificent Venetian glass flamingoes, almost life-size. The contrast of tastes and culture was bewildering.

We were beckoned to approach the young Shaikha, who rose to greet us. At twenty-eight, she had just had her seventh child. She wore a brilliant apricot gold-embroidered robe under the usual all-enveloping gold-bordered black *abba*, but her face was exposed, which it would not have been in public. We sat down, and other Arab ladies arrived, were greeted and sat round the room until all the seats were occupied. Then a negress servant entered bearing a tray, and we were offered tumblers of orange juice or tomato juice; after five minutes these were collected, whether consumed or not, and two trolleys were wheeled in, laden with fruit, nuts and sweetmeats; we were given plates, and had to take something from each proffered dish. Next, after plates and trolleys had been removed, came Arab coffee, poured into little handleless bowls like egg-cups. That first time I tasted it, I could hardly get it down, but later on I came to love it: it is thin, pale brown, and strongly flavoured with cardamom and spices. After the cups had been collected, rose-water from an elegant long-necked silver ewer was sprinkled on our hands.

'Keep your hands well clear of your skirt,' whispered Rosemary, 'it stains dreadfully.'

This was followed by another servant with an incense burner, and the smoke was wafted into our faces: it was delicious. This was the signal that the audience was over; we rose, and after saying good-bye to the Shaikha, we left.

I had been interested that there was almost complete silence in the *majlis*. Mrs Al Umran translated some polite remarks between Rosemary and me and the Shaikha, but the Bahraini ladies mostly just sat, smiling and bowing to each other across the room. I determined then that I would learn enough Arabic to be able to talk to them.

We then went on to call on Shaikha Khalifa, who had been the favourite wife of the late Ruler, who had had four wives. She was elderly, lined of face, with twinkling eyes, and she had great charm and wit; with her, through our interpreter, we had lively conversation.

The servants to the ruling family are mostly descended from the original negro slaves brought from East Africa. Their children appeared to be brought up with the Ruler's and all were playing happily together in the courtyard of Shaikha Hassa's palace.

The Ruler (later to be known as the Emir) of Bahrain, was the eldest of three brothers; he had succeeded his father, Shaikh Sulman, only a few months prior to our arrival. The second brother, Shaikh Khalifa, was a charming unreliable womaniser, who later caused a complication for Michael when he seduced and took over the wife of a naval Leading Radio Mechanic and, having presented him with a very handsome sports car, the Shaikh wanted Michael to get her husband transferred elsewhere. She did later marry him, against all our repeated advice and warnings, and of course she found life in purdah very different to when she was being extravagantly courted, and it all ended in much unhappiness.

The youngest brother, Mohammed, a very devout Muslim, found it difficult to accept the changes in the Arab world, and was a potential source of trouble in Shaikh Isa's first years as Ruler, although he was always friendly to meet.

Shaikh Isa was quite different; he showed great wisdom and maturity on becoming Ruler and has always been a strong constitutional and moderate leader of his people, by whom he is now much loved. I remember discussing with him the emancipation of Bahraini women, and possible education of his daughters in Europe.

'Yes, it must come, but slowly, slowly; we would wish to adopt that which we admire in Western culture, but not the things we deplore,' and he added:

'I would not send my daughters to school in England, there is not enough discipline there any more: possibly to Switzerland, yes.'

The Koran forbids the drinking of alcohol, and at formal parties, Arabs abide by this strict law. However, some are more devout Moslems than others. At one formal dinner in an English household which we attended, an elderly uncle of the Ruler was very circumspect over his drinks until after dinner, when the formality relaxed, the Shaikh's will weakened and he accepted a glass of champagne, followed by a pint tankard of beer; he pointed to the latter when it was set in front of him, and said with a twinkle in his eye:

'Extraordinary colour, the water in Bahrain, isn't it?'

Shaikh Isa had a fine stud of Arab horses, which were raced very informally each Friday afternoon, on a course laid in the desert south of Rifa'a; anyone was free to go and watch, and there was usually quite a crowd of onlookers. The Ruler sat on a high-backed stone seat, on a cement platform; the seat also had high sides to screen him from the public. The platform was carpeted with Turkish rugs, and sitting cross-legged facing him, each holding one of his hunting falcons, were four or five Arabs; in turn, a man would be beckoned to bring his falcon to the Ruler's knee, where it would be stroked and caressed until another was summoned to take its place.

The whole desert area of the southern two thirds of the island was the Ruler's private hunting preserve, where the falcons were used to hunt buzzards, gazelle and the pale desert hare. Most wealthy Arabs were very keen on this sport, and they would travel as far as India and Pakistan to select and buy a good hunting bird.

I once met a very entertaining Arab lady, who spoke English fluently, and she told me her husband had recently acquired a superb hawk, and had taken it to America on a hunting trip; when he and his entourage arrived at their New York hotel, he had insisted on going into the hotel kitchens to prepare the bird's food (chopped raw steak and scrambled egg). Later, on the hunting trip when the hawk was released it had not returned with its prey, and was lost, much to the owner's fury.

Although the Ruler's horses were exercised most evenings on the race-track, on Fridays his Omani camels were also raced, so this was the day when the largest crowd gathered to watch. Omani camels are the fleetest and the most beautiful, and the Ruler's were well looked after and groomed, each having its own rider/groom, who wore a bright orange wool head-cloth wound turban-wise around his head. The camels were ridden bareback (as were the horses), with one black cord rein from the left corner of their mouths. The camels raced with their long necks stretched out horizontally, some roaring, and the

riders waved yard-long canes in the air, yelling wildly to encourage
their beasts to win. It was thrilling to watch as they pounded past, a
few feet away from us.

If one knew the Ruler it was possible to ask his devoted negro
servant Fahan, who was always in attendance, if it would be acceptable
to go up to greet him. There would be a pause, and then a message
would be brought inviting one to go and sit with him to watch the
racing. Arab coffee would appear while we chatted. Michael and I
often did this, and took James and Emma, and any guests who might
be staying with us. Shaikh Isa was always most friendly and relaxed,
and it was a memorable and picturesque scene as the evening light
softened and the sun sank over the desert.

Soon after our arrival in Bahrain, we had to have the Admiral and his
wife to stay from Aden, where the Middle East Command was based. I
had known Fitzroy Talbot as a lieutenant in Malta before the war, and
had always thought him rather overpleased with himself; with renewed
acquaintance twenty-four years later, my opinion did not change.
However, Joyce, his wife, was charming and beautiful too, and it was a
great pleasure to entertain her.

At a dinner party we gave for them, at which the Admiral sat on my
right, I was not impressed when I heard him ask our chief steward,
sotto voce, who was serving the Admiral's vegetables:

'How are you getting on under the new regime, Veigas? Are you
quite happy?'

As Veigas was also valetting him, I thought the enquiry could have
more fittingly been made in the privacy of the Admiral's dressing room.

Fitzroy Talbot was relieved a few months later by Rear Admiral
John Scotland, who was very different, and we got on well with him
and his wife, Anne.

We came to know very well the captains of the frigates, mine-
sweepers and ships of the amphibious warfare squadron which were
permanently based in Bahrain, and would entertain and be entertained
by them on board their ships regularly.

The three frigates *Loch Lomond*, *Loch Ruthven* and *Loch Fyne* were
very old indeed, and subject to various mishaps and engine-room
breakdowns, and all were due to return to UK at the end of the year
to be scrapped. In July they took part in a naval exercise code-named
FOMEX in the southern part of the Gulf, and Michael went to sea

with them for it. The three ships then split up to go on visits to Muscat, Abadan and Karachi, and when they parted company after the exercise the following series of signals was sent:

Signal 1: From HMS *Loch Ruthven* (Captain Peter Beale).

> We three frigates of Orient are;
> From the UK we've travelled afar.
> FOMEX was our rendezvous,
> And we went to Yas for a barbecue.
> When shall we three meet again?
> In sand, *Shemal*, or in Bahrain?
> Or will it be, as we suspect
> On a chemist's shelf, marked 'Blades, Gillette'?

Note: *Shemal* is a local sharp storm.
> Yas and Das are two islands in the south of the Gulf often used in exercises as assault areas.

Signal 2: From HMS *Loch Lomond* (Captain David Smith).

> Ashes to ashes, dust to dust;
> If Gillette don't get us,
> Then Wilkinson must.
> R.I.P.

> The signals were addressed to Michael, as SNOPG, and I was shown them and invited to compose a reply:

Signal 3: From SNOPG, To   *Loch Ruthven*
                           Loch Lomond
                           Loch Fyne.

> While SNOPG watched the Lochs by night,
> And anxiously by day,
> They laboured long with all their might
> Their boilers not to flay.
> At Yas, and Das, and Muscat too,
> They strove to keep in trim,

With Sellotape and tubes of glue,
Good Beale and Smith and Kimm
So SNOPG's mind is now at rest,
The frigates' homeward sail.
In all the Gulf they were the best,
Though elderly and frail!

Because Bahraini ladies were still in purdah, Michael was never invited to parties by the Ruler's wife, for she, like the other ladies in the ruling family, was not allowed to see or be seen by any man other than her husband, father, sons or brothers. On the other hand, I attended the Ruler's dinners at Rifa'a palace with Michael on several occasions. Invitations were printed in Arabic on gold embossed cards, and sent usually at very short notice, and had to be considered as royal commands; thus it happened sometimes that one was unable to be present at one's own dinner party for a visiting VIP, planned in advance, which entailed arranging a stand-in host at short notice to take one's place.

The Ruler's dinners were more like feasts, and began early at 7.00 pm, and were usually over by 9.00 pm. They were very formal, one wore evening dresses, and they were opportunities to wear any good jewellery one possessed. On arrival at the palace, one entered the main *majlis* chamber, and was greeted by His Highness, who invariably wore a gold-edged *abba* over his white *dish-dasha*, with a wide gold cummerbund, which would hold a gorgeous curved gold *khunja*, (dagger) with jewel-encrusted scabbard. His head-rope, or *agal*, holding his white *keffiah* (head cloth) in place, would be triple width of three ropes of gold. Although short in stature, he made a most dignified and magnificent figure.

After fruit juice had been taken round, we would leave the *majlis*, being offered an enamel bowl, soap and towel held by a servant, the water being poured over our hands from an aluminium kettle, on our way to the dining-room. This was a long narrow room, with one table which could seat forty to fifty guests, who could sit where they liked, the Ruler only indicating to the guests of honour that they should sit by him.

On the table would be ten whole sheep, lying on their sides on huge round dishes, heads and tails intact; they would be steaming hot, and stuffed with spicy rice and quail's eggs. By each place would be a whole cold chicken, and between two people would be a small cold turkey. In addition there would be many side dishes and salads, and one would be helped to generous portions of the sheep by servants standing behind the guests, who reached over and tore off succulent pieces of meat with their hands and put them on one's plate. The tongue was considered the greatest delicacy, and the wide tail, consisting entirely of fat, was also much prized. Luckily we were not offered that.

Everyone rose from the table when he had eaten enough, and we were all glad to rinse the grease from our hands in the same hand-washing ritual on our way back to the *majlis*. Arab coffee was then served, and immediately the rose-water would be brought in to sprinkle on our hands, and then the incense burners, which I was interested to see the men wafted not only into their face and beards, but also under their *abbas* into their armpits: prosaic and sensible I thought. We then rose, made our farewells, and left.

Shaikha Hassa's dinners were very similar at her palace, but no men would be present, and there were always bowls and baskets of most superb fruit to follow the main course of mutton, and afterwards both the television and a juke-box would be switched on, and we would be invited to dance. At the first party of the Shaikha's which I attended, I was the first to be asked to get up and dance; I was appalled, and had no idea whether I was meant to dance a polka, flamenco, or rock. So I asked one of the Arab ladies present to dance with me, pulling her to her feet, and together we rolled about waggling our stomachs and bottoms, which caused much hilarity, and all inhibitions quickly disappeared.

Salwa Al Umran, who was usually asked to act as interpreter for the British ladies, was a charming Lebanese lady of about my own age, wife of Ahmad Al Umran, the Bahraini Minister for Education. She was a very gentle, modest person, with the usual lovely olive complexion of the Lebanese, and with a sweet expression and smile. She most kindly undertook to try to teach me to speak a little Arabic, and to understand it. I was particularly anxious to be able to communicate a little with the Bahrainis we met, especially the ladies, and eventually I was able to do so in the most elementary fashion, on such feminine subjects as children, fashion and cooking; although my efforts caused much amusement, I am sure more doors opened to me in consequence of making the effort.

I used to very much enjoy going into Manama, the large commercial town of Bahrain, parking the car on the sea-front and then going off deep into the *suq*, away from the offices and shops catering for expatriate trade. In the early 1960s some western women were nervous of wandering alone in these quarters, but I found it far more rewarding to do so on my own than accompanied, and that the local people would react to friendly advances with warmth and interest. As I walked further and further away from the developed commercial area, the roads became unmetalled lanes, became alleys, became narrow walkways, threading through facing rows of small shops, which were little more than holes in the wall, or rough *barasti* shacks leaning back to back, and side to side on their neighbours. The alleys teemed with people and donkeys, with baskets and bundles piled on their heads or their animals' backs, shouting and calling their wares. In some lanes were fabric shops, in others were filthy shacks full of scrap metal, old tins, bicycle wheels, nails and bits of iron; in one dark narrow walkway, to which I was drawn by the sound of hammering on metal, I found coppersmiths hammering out water pots, dishes, pans and other domestic utensils. Some of these were being tinned by sheets of tin being heated and smeared over the surface rather like spreading butter. It was fascinating to watch, and I would stand for minutes at a time, smiling and gesticulating at the artisan, who would sometimes stop his work to try to communicate with me and show me more items which he had made.

One market day, near the horrendously noisome open meat market, I came across a large pen, surrounded by a wall four or five feet high, full of tethered donkeys; this was the equivalent, I imagined, of our municipal carparks of the Western world. Bahraini donkeys are beautiful animals, being quite pale in colour, some almost white, with a dark line running down the back from mane to tail. They are highly valued as work animals and for family transport between the villages and Manama, and are well-fed and looked after; I never saw a thin or badly treated beast in all the years we were to spend in Bahrain.

I tried to talk to any shop or stall-holders, and made many friends in the *suq*, but the men who worked in the iron smithy were far too busy to stop. They worked in pairs under a high roof of corrugated iron, standing in waist-high pits facing each other, the raised area between them serving as their anvil; to one side was their fire and bellows, which one man operated with his knee. They hammered alternately

and very fast, bringing down massive sledge-hammers on to the iron
they were working. The din from twenty pairs was deafening; their
faces were blackened by the smoke which rose to waft in blue clouds
under the tin roof. This again would hold me spell-bound for long
periods, while I watched the heaps of nails, stacks of iron bars, piles of
sheet metal cut to measure and hammered thickness, grow higher
beside them.

As I completed my circle of wandering, I would slowly re-enter the
area of more prosperous shops, and outside one there always was a
Bahraini standing, his hands clasped behind his back under his *abba*, his
head-cloth spotless white under the black *agal*. He was a big man, tall
and of imposing stature, and he would beam at me each time I passed.
One day I stopped to speak to him, and he invited me into his shop
for coffee.

'You prefer Nescafé, I expect?' he asked, with a polite smile.

'Oh no, thank you, not if you have Arab coffee available,' I replied.
He looked surprised, and also pleased, and soon a tray was brought,
and we sat in an inner part of the shop, curtained off from the front.
Nothing was on show for sale, and I wondered what his business was.

'I am Mohammed Almudaifah,' he introduced himself, 'I deal in
pearls; would you like to see some?' and he reached into his flowing
abba and white *dish-dasha* beneath, and brought out a little screw of
cloth, which he untied, spilling out some pearls on to the velvet
topped table between us. They were not very big, and I didn't know
enough then to comment on their quality, but then he produced
another little bundle, and poured out some black pearls. I was
interested, having only read of such gems in stories by Sapper or
Dorothy Sayers, and I thought them very unattractive, and politely said
so.

'Ah,' said Mohammed, 'I agree with you, but the Americans, they
like them very much!'

After that first encounter, I always ended my regular walks through
the *suq* at Mohammed Almudaifah's shop, and we would sit and drink
coffee, while he opened his safes and showed me his most prized
pearls. He had nearly completed an order for a triple choker necklace
of perfectly matched huge lustrous gems, which had taken him over
three years to collect.

He greeted me one morning with the words:

'Ah, here you are! You have been a long time in the *suq* this morning. I wondered if you had forgotten your friend!' I asked him how he knew I was in Manama, and he replied enigmatically:

'I always know when you are in the *suq*, and I look forward to your call,' but he would not tell me how he knew.

Bahrain used at one time to be the most important trading centre for pearls, which have been found in the Arabian Gulf for hundreds of years, but the advent of Japanese cultured pearls has practically killed the natural pearling industry. There were still a small number of pearling dhows operating from Bahrain, Kuwait and Qatar, and Michael visited a group early in 1963, which were working together over a bank in about eighty feet of water. Each dhow had twelve or fourteen divers, working six or seven to each side, each with his diver's mate on board. The diver lay in the water about four feet from the side of the dhow, attached by a cord to a wooden beam. He wore a shirt and a loin cloth, and had a net bag round his waist for the shells. When he was ready, his mate passed him a heavy stone on a rope, he took a deep breath, let go of the cord attached to the beam, and the stone took him to the bottom. He had a clip over his nose to prevent air escaping, and he wore rudimentary goggles made of slips of wood with a narrow slit in front of each eye; his hands were protected by leather gloves. When he had collected a dozen or so oysters, he tugged on his rope, and his mate hauled him and his stone to the surface. The oysters were then piled on the deck and were opened in the evening, when the pearls were stowed in a locked chest by the *nahkudar* (captain), and some of the oyster meat was cooked and eaten. The pearl fishermen stayed at sea for several weeks, and because there are so many sweet water springs they could collect their drinking water by holding skins to fill over the bubbling heads of the springs on the sea-bed. I have seen this done under the sea just off Bahrain, and in fact have done so myself on boat picnics.

CHAPTER 9

Overland to Muscat via
Buraimi and Sohar, 1962

DICK BRYERS, as Land Forces Commander in the Gulf, had to carry out an annual inspection of the administration of the Sultan of Muscat's armed forces which were British trained and led. In the autumn of 1962 he made this into a more general tour to include Sharjah and the Trucial Oman Scouts. Phyllis was also going on the tour, and he invited Michael and me to join them.

We flew by RAF to Sharjah in a small six-seater Pembroke aircraft, which, with our luggage, the four of us filled. Flying low over the Gulf, we could enjoy the colours of the varying sea depths from clear pale green, through which we could see the ripples of the sandy sea-bed, through deeper green and light blue to deep aquamarine. It took two hours to reach Sharjah where we landed on the sandy air-strip and were met by Colonel Bartholomew, known hereafter as 'Bart', who commanded the Trucial Oman Scouts. In these outposts, all work seemed to stop when a new face came through, and we were taken to the officers' mess for coffee, where five or six young officers were gathered to meet us.

Phyllis and I did a quick change into the trousers we had been told to wear, found our army khaki jungle hats, and then we all embarked in three long-wheel-based Land Rovers on the first lap of the journey. Dick and I went in the leading vehicle with Bart driving, Phyllis and Michael were in the second with an Arab TOS driver, and we both had an armed soldier in the back, perched on the mountains of baggage. The third was a W/T vehicle so we could keep in touch with any incoming signals for Dick or Michael, and this vehicle accompanied us, with the W/T operator, all the way to Muscat.

Our first stop was to be at Buraimi oasis, staying in an old fort occupied by a troop of the Trucial Oman Scouts. Buraimi was the largest of nine villages clustered round the oasis, and at that time it was thought that there might be oil in the vicinity; the oasis was at a point where the unmarked borders of Abu Dhabi and Muscat rather vaguely

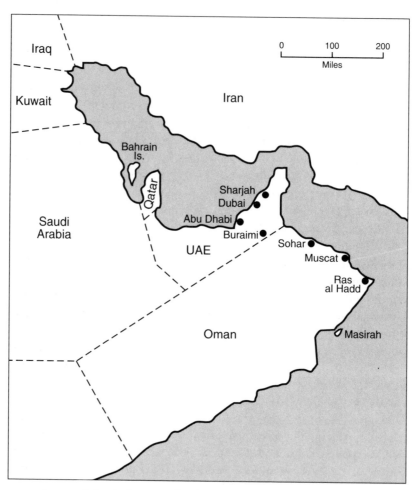

A map of the Arabian Gulf – formerly known as the Persian Gulf.

could be said to meet, and because of the possibility of oil being discovered, the whole area was in a state of unrest and potential dispute.

There were no roads as such, nor recognisable marking of any kind of the safe tracks across the desert avoiding treacherous patches of soft sand and other hazards; our TOS drivers knew the route to follow and we twisted and turned, moving from one well to the next, stopping to inquire of any other travellers we met, the state and level of the next well.

There was an etiquette to observe *vis-à-vis* other travellers in the desert. The lowliest were those on foot; next came those riding donkeys; then camels; and finally those in motor vehicles (we only saw one other vehicle: more of that later). On meeting someone, the lower in rank gave the first greeting; we always stopped to ensure other travellers had water. Water-bottles in wet canvas bags were hung round the outside of our Land Rovers, to cool by condensation as we travelled, and the vehicles had canvas roofs but no sides, so we were as cool as possible and shaded.

There was no visible road as we left the camp behind us and turned south, inland, just a feeble track in the sand, packed down by other vehicles' use. The drivers had to watch this and stick to it, or we'd be in soft sand and get stuck at once. It wasn't all soft sand; much of the route was over rock, uneven and bumpy. The desert stretched ahead, yellow dust colour, dotted with low grey bushes of camel thorn. We drove on and on, and the land rose and fell in larger or smaller dunes around us. Some mountains appeared on the horizon, and we headed towards them.

We saw few other people, but once we passed a camel train of about six men each riding a camel which was leading two more, walking in single file along the top of a dune, running parallel to our track, the men shouting to one another. Bearded and dark, roughly turbaned with large Omani head-cloths in various bright or sombre colours, each carrying a beautiful beaten silver curved *khunja* in his full cartridge belt, and with rifles slung across their backs, they looked real brigands. They waved and shouted greetings as we passed, which we returned, and we stopped to allow them to come up and pass us, and then we overtook them again with much waving and flashing of white teeth through their black flowing beards.

Occasionally, under a camel thorn tree, we saw a small nomad Bedu camp; their tents had just a piece of black material acting as a shelter, attached to poles like a veranda. The women ran away in terror from us, and the children followed, leaving only their goats and camels to gaze at us as we passed. We saw none of their men-folk.

It became very hot, with not a breath of wind except where a 'sand-devil' whirled up the sand in a vertical funnel seventy or eighty feet high, visible for miles; these occur constantly in the heat of midday.

We reached the mountains, high, steep and entirely barren, and we entered them, leaving the sand behind, and drove through a pass, all rocks and boulders; the previous rough going had been billowy compared with this! The purple mountain-sides were streaked with orange, brown and the vivid green of verdigris, and the peaks were jagged and cruel.

A fourth Land Rover of the TOS met us, to escort us on the final stretch to Buraimi; it had anti-mine plating under it, and preceded the convoy to set off any mines laid by the rebels. We had sand-bags filled and put under our feet and seats.

'Very good ambush country!' said Bart, eyeing the mountains round us as we drove on.

We stopped when we emerged into open desert again, and found here that the sand was red. Bart's quartermaster had gone ahead that morning with lunch, and we found a trestle table under a tree, white cloth and napkins, wineglasses and porcelain, and 150 yards away what we were all longing for, a screened hole in the ground, with wash-stand, basin, jug of water, soap and towel provided: it was delightfully incongruous.

On then, hotter than ever, for another two hours, into more mountains, this time through a narrow rocky defile, the convoy closing up, the soldiers with loaded rifles ready. The route was winding and tortuous, and very bumpy indeed, with sudden drops of a foot or more into the bed of the *wadi* (dry water course); we climbed up the other side as best we could. It was an amazing exhibition of what a beating Land Rovers (and we!) could take.

As darkness fell, we entered a wide open flat basin surrounded by mountains, and a stream flowed to one side of our track. We stopped for the Muslim soldiers to say their sunset prayers, and we left the vehicles to stretch our legs. Beside the stream were one or two palm trees, silhouetted against the last green streak of sunset between the mountain peaks, black now, and jagged against the sky; the full moon suddenly rose behind them, and frogs began to croak; it was a magic moment.

We drove on across more desert until the lights appeared of the first of the Buraimi villages, glowing dimly through *barasti* huts and the doorways of houses built of mud bricks, and at last we came to the fort where we were to spend the night.

Fort Jahili was like an illustration from a *Beau Geste* Foreign Legion story, and it looked in the moonlight when we first arrived, standing alone in the desert, like a film set.

Fort Jahili, Buraimi.

It was enclosed in a square of high white crenellated wall, and one entered through an impressive arch, leading into the parade-ground. There were round towers at each of three corners, the officers' mess occupying the three-tier circular fort in the fourth. This had slit windows in each tier, which decreased in diameter with height. It looked just like a large wedding-cake.

The soldiers' quarters were in the furthest corner from the officers' mess, and the camel-lines down one side of the parade-ground.

Michael and I were allocated the top tier of the fort to ourselves, which we reached by several flights of steep stone outside steps; Dick and Phyllis were in the middle storey and next to the officers' anti-room, and the officers slept in the largest ground level area.

There was no electricity, running water or sanitation; to reach the latrines outside the compound, you had to pass through a locked door in the wall, and cross a hundred yards of desert to the latrine block. I found this quite daunting in the night, with the howling of jackals not far away.

In the morning we were woken by the Reveille bugle call, and as the sun rose, the Scouts mustered on the parade-ground to do PT in vests and shorts, their long black locks bushing out on to their shoulders from under their white cotton skull-caps.

At 7.30 am we were summoned to 'Ablutions'. Phyllis and I wore swim-suits under our dressing-gowns, and Bart, Michael and Dick wore swimming-trunks only; we went in a Land Rover to an irrigation tank a quarter of a mile away, which was 60 feet long by 20 feet, and 3 feet deep, and which had filled overnight direct from an underground fresh warm spring. We wallowed in it, washing off the dust of the previous day's travel, enjoying the fresh morning air and sunshine. As is always the way in the desert, several Arabs sprang out of nowhere and came to watch us; we exchanged greetings and hand-shakes, and Bart talked with them; both they and we were quite unembarrassed by their curiosity.

We returned to Fort Jahili for breakfast, and then the Land Rovers were lined up and re-stowed, to resume our journey.

Before leaving Buraimi, we were taken round two or three of the villages in the oasis. The whole area was very fertile and green, with citrus fruit, date palms and vegetable gardens. The irrigation system, called *falaj*, is hundreds of years old, entirely man-made, and copied from Persia, where it is also still in use in desert areas. Wells were dug at intervals of 20–30 yards, and between each vertical shaft, underground tunnels were constructed at water-level. This extended over the whole oasis, about forty square miles. In some places the tunnelling had been brought up to ground-level, and connected to springs, and public bathing arrangements were cemented into fern-hung bowers under acacia trees. We walked along a mossy green path, shaded by the trees and scented with acacia blossom; crimson dragon-flies alighted on floating plants in the stream flowing by the path, and butterflies danced in the sunlight filtering through the branches; it was odd to think we were in the middle of the Arabian desert.

We came to a widening of the stream where four laughing men were washing, their clothes left on the bank; they were squatting in the pool to give each other cover as we passed, but even in these circumstances, we exchanged unhurried friendly greetings!

After this deliciously cool and green interlude, we said good-bye to Bart, to continue on our way east across the desert to Sohar on the Batinah coast of the Gulf of Oman.

We met our armed escort for the next stage of the journey in the village of Buraimi, on a wide spacious area of trodden sand and dust surrounded by *barasti* and mud brick dwellings, rather as an English village is built round a green.

There was plenty of activity here. Outside one *barasti* was a man planing a beam on a long improvised trestle type of work-bench. A little further on another was drawing water from a well in the open space between huts; he had a magnificent curly black beard splaying over his bare chest, and he wore only voluminous Turkish style trousers, tucked up in folds between his legs; his skin was a dark golden-brown, with powerful shoulders gleaming with muscle, and he was swinging rhythmically as he hauled the bucket up.

Across the road toward him came a woman, heavily veiled in black, a water-pot of unglazed pottery on her head, another carried under each arm; when filled, she would probably carry two on her head, one on top of the other, and the third under one arm. The pots are made with convex bases, so as to sit one into the rim of another, for steadier balance. The woman had a small circlet of plaited palm leaves on her head in which to seat the lower pot.

A few yards further on rows and rows of these pots were stacked on the open ground, baking out in the hot sun, and in the *barasti* behind we could dimly see and hear the potter at his wheel throwing a continuing succession of them.

Further on still were stacks of mud bricks drying, and the wooden forms in which they were cast. Cement was mixed with the sand and dust of the desert, stirred together into a dryish pudding, then packed into the rectangular forms, tipped out, and left to dry. They would last a year or two provided the one or two annual rain-storms were not too heavy, and huts built with them were certainly proof against the daily invasive sand-storms of the hot months of the year, against which *barastis* give little protection.

Our new armed escort were in a larger vehicle than ours, with eight soldiers of the TOS, and they preceded us through the allegedly rebel-infested mountains to the Batinah coast. These terrorists were of Arab groups centred in Iraq, who were involved in internecine feuding in a minor civil war in the area, which continued sporadically into the 1970s. All the vehicles had to have sandbags on the floors against damage from possible land-mines.

After an hour crossing the desert, we approached the foothills of Jebel Akhdar, and as we drew nearer we wondered where we'd ever cross them, they appeared to be such an impenetrable barrier of relentless jagged peaks, which rose in front of us higher and higher as we approached.

Suddenly the rocks ahead opened up to disclose a narrow entry to the Wadi Jizzi, and just as we were about to enter it, two Land Rovers drove out toward us; in one was the English doctor from Muscat, doing his rounds of Government health centres in the villages. To the fury of Phyllis and me, he had his wife with him, thus displacing us from being able to claim we were the first white women to go through the Wadi Jizzi!

We drove through the *wadi* for some hours, mostly at 10 mph; the terrain forbade faster progress. The track was narrow and rocky, the scenery breath-taking. We saw no-one until we stopped for lunch where the wadi opened out and suddenly became green and lush, with a large shallow pool to one side at the foot of the sheer mountain-side. We sat on the shady side of the track, the mountains towering all round us, watching dragon-flies and bee-eaters darting over the pool, while we ate our sandwiches.

Suddenly a camel emerged from the far end of the rocky defile, and plodded slowly toward us. It was ridden by a small gnome-like Arab; he stopped by the pool, unstrapped a leather water-skin from his saddle, and jumped off the camel on to one leg, on which he hopped down to the water and filled his skin. He hopped back and buckled it on to his saddle, and then, without making the camel kneel, he hopped up and down about ten or eleven times, jumping higher with each hop, until with a prodigious spring, he was up again and they plodded off. It was an extraordinary sight. Neither man nor beast had even glanced at us, nor acknowledged our greetings, which was quite unlike the usual courtesy of desert Arabs. The incident was somehow disturbing, full of an atmosphere of detachment, endurance, and solitariness.

The *wadi* gradually opened out as we drove on, till we emerged on to a sandy plain, dotted with thorn trees, all the branches cropped to the same height from the ground, as though with a giant's shears, although in fact by camels, whose staple food the leaves of those trees are in that area. All the trees for many square miles had this uniformly tidy and uncluttered shape, making the plain appear like a vast well-tended orchard.

We arrived in the afternoon at the Oman Gendarmerie camp in Sohar, where we were to stay, which was on the shore. I swam from the deserted sandy beach after tea, which extends 150 miles both north and south along the Gulf of Oman.

The next morning I walked along the beach to Sohar village, a large community of *barasti* huts built on the sands above the high water line. Pulled up on the beach were small fishing-boats made of scraped palm-leaf spines; they float half submerged, carrying one or two men. There were also a few bigger timber long-boats, owned communally and used for heavier fishing. I watched a team in one of these, laying a net in a wide semi-circle out from the beach, round and back to the shore two hundred yards further along; one man stood up and propelled the boat slowly with a large paddle, and the other eight or nine sat, chanting rhythmically, laying another corked yard of net into the sea with each accented beat.

The birds were beautiful and varied, and we saw egret, ibis, waders, wimbrells and sandpipers; oyster-catchers in sparkling black and white flocks; grey babblers; brilliant blue rollers; and many more.

On both evenings we were at Sohar, the men went out for the evening flighting of duck to a nearby creek, and shot pintail, teal and mallard, and we saw grebe and other varieties.

I went to wander in the *suq* in the village on our last day; it was a warren of passages, roofed darkly with barasti thatching, the alleys so narrow you could touch the wares displayed on both sides. It was noisy and crowded, everyone shouting and cheerful, and wafts of blue incense drifting its delicate tantalising scent across one's path. Arab incense is not heavy and sweet like that used in Roman Catholic churches in Europe, but seems like a blend of delicious spices and lemon.

At Sohar we said farewell to our Trucial Scouts escort, and their place was taken by the Oman Gendarmerie. No armed escort was necessary on the last 180 mile lap to Muscat.

The Oman Gendarmerie were another local levy, under the Sultan of Muscat, and their commanding officer, a British army colonel, was Hugh Oldman, who had been at Wellington College with Michael. He and his wife had driven up to Sohar to meet us.

We started out at 10.30 am, driving to begin with along a road of hard coral rock, rough and lumpy, parallel to the sea. We passed fishing villages, some with green date gardens, and our track turned to sand, much of it soft. In turn the three Land Rovers became stuck on the rising crests of dunes, and had to be dug out, then to slither down the far side. We came to a shaded fresh water creek where we stopped for lunch; as the cans of beer were levered open, we were drenched with hot beer, but hot or not, it was nectar to our dust-parched throats. After lunch the tide was low enough to drive down on to the hard black sand, and thence we drove along just above the water-line, down the coast for three or four hours, making good time at speeds of 20–30 mph.

As the sun set and the light began to fade, a breeze got up and we were deliciously cooled. We passed between several villages and the sea, boats pulled up on the beach, and we watched fishermen hauling in their nets. One large group were wildly excited, so we stopped. In their net was a large sail-fish about six feet long. It looked like a huge mackerel, until the proud captor pulled up the dorsal fin which unfolded like a fan and, when fully extended, was two feet high and three feet long. It was a brilliant blue, with large black spots on it which were the size of a 10 pence coin. The fish use these fins literally to sail along on the surface of the sea.

We saw gigantic turtles, over a yard in diameter, which the Arabs had pulled up on to the beach and left upturned for the carrion crows and vultures to clean out the shells.

In the evening, the light almost gone and the tide very low, we came to a long pool which the receding tide had left; it was parallel to the shore, and in it a group of youths were wading, racing large home-made model dhows two or three feet long. Older men watched, chiacking and calling encouragement in an animated group on the beach. The pale *dish-dashas* of the boys and men stood out starkly against the black sand, leaden sky and purple clouds of an impending storm in the fading light.

On then again, faster now, racing against darkness and the turning tide, scattering great flocks of oyster-catchers, and herons and gulls feeding in the pools. The sands ended with rocks ahead, so we veered off abruptly into the desert once more, through rocky hills and the mountain barrier surrounding Muscat on its landward side. Darkness had fallen, and we drove too fast for comfort, the drivers anxious to get in. They were pretty tired by now; Hugh Oldman did not see a large boulder in time to avoid it. Crashing and hurtling up and down again, my head dented the steel roof (no seat-belts in those days), the roof doing likewise to my head, and I came down on one elbow in the middle of the dash-board dials, which I did not notice until on arrival I found everything sodden with blood.

'Ah well, sorry about that!' said Hugh breezily, as we drove on after the vehicle had resumed four-wheel equilibrium, 'luckily no harm was done!' with which I agreed shakily, feeling rather odd about the head! When the mess was found on our arrival, and I was cleaned up, poor Hugh got hell from his wife!

The next morning we found we were in a compound of modern houses occupied by the families of the four or five British officers of the Sultan's Armed Forces. This was outside Muscat, and we had to drive a few miles through more mountains to get down to the entrance to the town.

At this date, 1962, and for a few years more, every man carried a rifle, always: the weapons varied from the very old and probably useless to modern Lee Enfield 303s. Similarly all wore bandoliers or belts of ammunition, which was not necessarily of the kind to fit their rifle.

At the gateways of the bigger towns, such as Muscat, every man on entering had to leave his gun, hanging it up in the gate-tower. At night the gates of the city were closed, and after dark anyone out in the streets had, by law, to carry a lantern. Should a figure be seen without one, he could then be assumed to be an enemy, and could justifiably be attacked.

We were taken into the city, and while the men had official calls to make, Phyllis and I went to explore the narrow streets and alleys, admiring the beautiful heavy carved and studded doors, primitive archways and odd corners; we climbed some concealed stone steps, going through a tunnel, to emerge on a path high above the sea.

Muscat is an old walled city built round the shore of a small deep harbour; there are two mediaeval castle forts on the rocks of each headland. Barren purple rock mountains rise steeply behind the town, in which there are four small crenellated watch-towers, like castles

Muscat, 1962.

built with a child's bucket on the beach, and which sit on peaks commanding all routes of access to the city. I have not been back since, but am assured it is very different today, much developed outside the original city walls. I am glad I knew it as it was, and can remember it that way.

We met Dick and Michael again, and were taken up to one of the headland forts, occupied by a unit of the Sultan's army, and we saw cannons from British ships in the time of George III, and also of Charles II, the latter still in use as saluting guns!

Fort Jalili, on the other headland, was a prison, up whose steps one might see the occasional prisoner climbing in leg-irons and shackles. The punishment for theft was severe: one's right hand was cut off at the wrist. The law was cruel, and there was no appeal, and as the result, crime was almost negligible.

No smoking is permitted in Muscat at all, and when Sir William Luce, the PR, who was a heavy smoker, went down to pay his first official courtesy call on the Sultan, and was invited to stay in the Sultan's palace, another mediaeval fort, he thought after his first day of total abstention that it would be safe to indulge in a cigarette in the privacy of his bedroom; he flushed the butt down the lavatory, so that no trace would remain. Ten minutes later came a knock at his door, where a servant waited, bearing a copper tray on which lay one sodden cigarette end.

'This is thought to be your property, your Excellency!' said the servant. Sir William had to take it back to dispose of on his return to Bahrain!

CHAPTER 10

Bahrain Welfare Work, 1962–63

THERE WAS A CERTAIN AMOUNT of welfare work in Bahrain, as in all Forces' bases, in which I was directly concerned. I worked closely with the SSAFA nurse who had an official appointment in Bahrain, and who in turn worked under the RAMC doctor in charge of all naval and army families (the RAF had their own arrangements at their base hospital and airfield on Muharraq Island).

During the visit of a senior naval officer's wife, she found her cholera immunisation had expired, and told me to arrange for the SSAFA sister to call and give her a booster inoculation, and I was to add that she expected a new needle to be used, and not a sterilised one which might be blunted with use (this was in the days before disposable syringes). I faithfully repeated the message word for word over the telephone, knowing exactly what the brusque North Country reaction would be.

'Tell her high and mighty Ladyship that my Inoculation Clinic is on Thursdays at 0800, and I will see her there in the MI room; and for your ears only, Sue, I shall use the bluntest needle I can find!'

I did not dare ask the patient later how she had fared!

Bobbie was a splendid lass from Bolton, who stood no nonsense from lead-swingers or hypochondriacs, but who also was gentle and sympathetic toward genuine sufferers. She and I had a fair sprinkling of both to deal with.

There were sad and needy cases too, and one concerned the pregnant wife of a Petty Officer. She was in her early forties, and had already had several miscarriages. She and her husband were desperate to have a child before it became too late on account of her age. She threatened to miscarry many times during this pregnancy, and had to spend much of it in bed, but to no avail, and she aborted a foetus with spina bifida at about six months; both she and her husband were devastated. After a few months she became pregnant again, and even greater care was taken. A baby boy was born prematurely, and was christened when only twenty-four hours old, for he was frail and had breathing difficulties, and the doctors were not optimistic. The baptism was at her bedside, and there was great joy and happiness.

To start with all went well; however, within ten days he had died, having had time to become an individual and the longed-for child of the couple. I had come to know the mother very well, and visited her regularly during both her pregnancy and also the tragic period of mourning, when I called at least once each day; she told me she had been raped by her father when she was eight years old, and that he continued to abuse her violently and regularly; because of that, she had been mentally very scarred, and had married late because of her fear and loathing of any sexual contact. Her husband had been endlessly patient and full of love and understanding, but she was certain that her early history was the cause of her miscarriages and difficulties in having a child. I became very fond of the parents, and shared their loss with deep sorrow when little Adrian died; his funeral was heart-breaking, and I still remember it all with tears.

A little while later, the possibility of adoption was suggested and the British Adoption Society were contacted; they replied cursorily that both parents were too old, and that they would not help. I saw the letter, and was appalled at the unfeeling way it was written, and its bald statement of total lack of interest.

I then heard of a Swiss adoption society, of which there happened to be a representative visiting Bahrain at that time; we arranged all to meet, and on her return to Switzerland, the representative set the wheels in motion, with the result that first a little boy, and later a baby girl were adopted. So this sad story eventually had a happy ending.

There were two hospitals in Bahrain in the early 1960s, an American one at Awali, connected with the oil refinery, in which only refinery personnel were treated, and the Bahrain Government hospital in Manama, which had two or three western surgeons among its mainly Pakistani staff, and where the nursing was very elementary. The families of Arab patients would move in with their sick relative, camping in corridors outside the wards, which were open on to verandas each side to provide as much air as possible. There was no air-conditioning, although the average temperatures would be in the high 80s. The standard of cleanliness left much to be desired, and Service families were kept at home as far as possible when ill. However, sailors from HM ships, and also of the Merchant Navy, sometimes had to be admitted, and I used to visit them there. We had

David Hepworth, the captain of HMS *Ashanti*, to stay at Navy House for a fortnight during the hottest summer months when he became seriously ill with pneumonia, as we could at least provide an air-conditioned bedroom, and suitable diet and care. None of HM ships were air-conditioned then, even those operating in the hottest tropical conditions.

In the pleasant autumn of 1962, we were asked if we would have to stay for a few days the daughters of two senior Army officers serving in Cyprus. We had known both their families well in Singapore, and were delighted to have them. They were two very glamorous blondes, aged eighteen and nineteen, both of them lively and gay. They arrived courtesy of RAF Family concession arrangements, taking up vacant seats in a flight of RAF Transport Command.

Jane Cumberlege was tall, with a voluptuous figure, glorious skin and colouring, long blonde hair and big blue eyes; Melissa Pike was tiny and petite, also blonde and fair-skinned; they were a stunning pair, and news of their arrival on the island, where single girls were at a premium, circulated like wild-fire. They made a special hit with the Parachute battalion officers, and also with the Scots Greys, as well as with those in the naval ships which were in harbour. Their social life was non-stop, and we also became involved, being invited to many of the picnics, barbecues and dances which were given for them. After a fortnight we began to make inquiries about their onward travel, but were told that there were few RAF seats available, and we later discovered that the Paras, in collusion with the RAF Movements staff, had managed to ensure that the two girls stayed on considerably longer than the originally planned 'few days'. They eventually left after nearly a month with us, leaving us distinctly flagging and weary! It was the greatest fun having them, although I found it hard to keep up with which young men were in current favour, and which had been discarded. When we finally waved them off, we were left feeling very flat!

There were two mongooses in our garden, and one day we spied a baby with them. The family played riotous games on the lawn below our veranda, running up oleander branches which bent with their weight, when they fell off in a heap on the grass; this went on for hours, and was enchanting to watch.

We also had a plague of shrews in the house in one especially hot period, when we thought they came in to enjoy our air-conditioning; they became tiresome, and from being friends of the family, such as Charlie, who came into the drawing-room and amused dinner-party guests, they became vermin to be got rid of by fair means or foul, when I found them nesting in my drawers of underwear: they had discovered that the cups of my bras made excellent prefabricated maternity wards!

In all our overseas travels I have particularly enjoyed the picnics, and they were an excellent way of entertaining our many official guests, who often might be with us over weekends. In Bahrain we would go off in a launch to little islands or sand-banks, to swim in the clear water, watch fish and collect shells. Sometimes we'd look down from the boat to the sandy sea-bed, to see nothing, until the sand appeared to ripple, and a huge mantua ray, six or seven feet in diameter, lifted off the bottom to undulate gracefully away, its long wicked tail streaming out behind.

Unlike Singapore, there were no coral reefs within accessible range of our picnics, but there were other delights. We sometimes obtained permission to drive down through the Ruler's private hunting grounds to the southern tip of the island, where there was a long sandy spit to explore, and scrub areas in which to find desiccated turtle shells, skeletons of birds, or even dead sea-slugs etc., a beach-comber's paradise. In the cooler months of December and January, we would join with two or three families, and drive to the volcanic hilly area of the Jebel Dukhan in the centre of the island. This was barren and rocky, with a central dry crater in which we left the cars, then going off to play realistic games of cowboys and indians or hide-and-seek in the surrounding caves and crannies.

Of the official visitors whom we had to entertain to meals, or have to stay, some were great fun, and some were not. They arrived as strangers, and with most we soon became friends, others we were delighted to speed on their way. We once had to have a lunch-party for a group of parliamentary delegates, and I was warned that the Labour MP in the party was extremely left-wing and I might expect some sparks. When they arrived (eight of them), poor Mr Woof was white as a sheet and very silent: I asked if he was all right.

'Oh no!' he replied vehemently, obviously grateful for someone's concern, 'I'm in ever such pain and trouble, this 'ere climate don't suit me at *all*!'

I offered him the use of our guest room to lie down, and also our usual remedy for the local form of 'dog', which he accepted with alacrity, but said he would like to attend the lunch. I suggested that he should have a lightly poached egg, rather than the curry we were all having, and with an expression of relief, he actually smiled his thanks. Over lunch he brightened up a little, but all the same, I steered the conversation well clear of politics.

Another visitor was a Brigadier, Royal Marines, who came to stay three nights with us; no-one seemed to know what he had come for, for he spent his visit either sleeping on his bed, swimming or at parties. We couldn't crack a spark out of him at all. Although the dinner we gave for him was an easy and gay party, he hardly ever smiled; he was the most stolid and dull guest we ever had to endure.

On New Year's Day the Ruler paid an annual official call on the Political Resident and came to inspect a parade of the Royal Navy on Jufair parade-ground, which our house overlooked. In 1963 it was a clear and sunny day, but unseasonably cold, and we all wore every woolly we could under our best clothes.

All the male members of the ruling family attended, wearing their full ceremonial robes. The Ruler, Shaikh Isa, had on a magnificent robe of gold from neck to ground, worn under his *abba* of filmy white and gold Kashmiri wool, with his usual gold *khunja* in his cummerbund, and a white embroidered lawn *keffiah* secured on his head by a four-fold gold rope *agal*: he looked most regal and dignified.

The Foreign Office personnel also wore their full dress, plumed cocked hats and all, and naval officers were in formal white uniform with medals, and carrying swords. After the parade a reception was held in the garden of the Residency; it was a memorable occasion, both for its splendour and for the bitter cold.

In the afternoon the Navy ran a Donkey Derby, at which everyone let their hair down after the formality of the morning. There was a ladies' race in which I rode, wearing the white Stetson hat which Michael had been given at Calgary when the IDC course had visited there the previous year; thinking it might encourage my animal, I held a cane from the end of which I dangled a carrot on a string, a yard in front of its nose. I have never been able to strike an entente with four-legged beasts, and my mount had no interest in the race or the carrot,

Michael in Bahrain, 1963.

and decided to go off on a little potter, so I had to acquiesce, having no control whatever on where the animal went. However when he decided to return and resume the course, we finished such a long way last that we came in first in the following race, to loud cheers.

Michael's parents had been staying with us over Christmas, and he and his father, who was a retired Commander RN, and also had once been an amateur jockey, rode in the Brass Hats' race, but neither did much better than me.

The in-laws' visit went well; they joined in all we did and had planned for them, with unabated enthusiasm. One morning Kyrle was banished to the wardroom, and the Arab gardener was given the day off, to ensure that no men would be about to embarrass her, when I invited the Ruler's wife, Shaikha Hassa, to coffee, and suggested she brought with her the children who were nearest in age to Emma and James, who was with us for the school holidays. This apparently had never been done before and caused great excitement at the palace. Her Highness told us that the children were so excited that they would not go to bed the previous evening, and were up at 5.00 am getting dressed in their best clothes. I had hoped the eight-year-old son Rashid would come, but his father had made him to go school, whither he went in tantrum and tears, his mother told us. Eleven year-old Shaikha Noora and seven year-old Shaikha Shaikha came and also little Shaikha Mariam, aged four, who refused to be left behind; they were accompanied by their Seychelloise nanny and a negro servant, and they, with our children and Judy Ryan, who lived with us as Emma's 'minder' when we had to be out or away, sat on the veranda where we had put toys and sweet drinks, while the adults were in the drawing-room. Besides the Shaikha, Salwa Al-Umran came to help, along with Phyllis Bryers, and I had invited a young Navy lieutenant's wife who I thought would enjoy the opportunity of meeting Her Highness.

They all stayed well over the usual hour decreed by etiquette for such calls, and Shaikha Hassa was most gay and friendly; she told us her children had not met European children before, let alone been to their houses and played with them.

CHAPTER 11

Iran, 1963

'SAY, SUE, how would you like a trip to Teheran next week? Kit and I are flying up in my aircraft, and I'd drop you at Teheran airport on Monday afternoon, and pick you up there on our way back a week later. We're going on up to visit Iranian ports on the Caspian, and we can't take you there, but if you can find somewhere to stay in Teheran, the place in the aircraft is yours!'

The Americans maintained a naval presence in the Gulf, and their Admiral, B.J. Semmes, and his wife Kit were friends of ours.

At a dinner-party one evening, I was sitting next to 'BJ' as he was always known, when he suddenly made this amazing suggestion.

What an opportunity! Then I remembered that Rear Admiral and Mrs Scotland were coming up on an official visit from Aden, which would partly coincide with the visit to Iran, and so, almost weeping with disappointment, I told BJ I couldn't accept his offer, and why.

'Gee, Honey!' he exclaimed, 'You're being altogether too British about this. You may never have another chance to do it.' Here he paused, and then went on:

'I tell you what we'll do, we'll invite Mrs Scotland to come too!'

Signals flew between Bahrain and Aden, as the result of which the Scotlands refused on Anne's behalf, for she'd have had to fly up ahead of John, and was fully committed in Aden until the date of their planned trip; however it was stipulated that I was not to refuse the invitation on account of their visit, and as it would be Anne's second and she knew the ropes, as well as other people in the island, I felt cleared to go, and was urged to do so by Michael.

We took off from Muharraq early on a sunny day and flew across the Gulf at 14,000 ft. Over Persia we had a clear view below us of massive snow-covered mountains, occasional villages, and barren desert. Criss-crossing the desert were straight lines of dots, which were the shafts down to the *qanat* irrigation tunnels which I had seen when visiting Buraimi; they showed clearly in the sand, and were quite extensive; I was very pleased that I knew them for what they were, and had seen them before at ground level. (*Qanat* is the Persian term for what in Arabia is called *falaj*.)

The party consisted of BJ and Kit, the US Naval Attaché from Teheran, a US Navy wife, and me; also, invited at the last minute, was a great friend of mine, Digna Sutcliffe, the wife of a retired Commander RN, who was in charge of the Persian Gulf Lighthouse service. Little did we know then, that nine years later my husband would take over Edward Sutcliffe's place as General Manager on Edward's retirement. Digna, a South African, was independent, adventurous, and ready for anything; we found we had a lot in common.

She and I were met by the British Military Attaché at Teheran airport, and driven to his house on the north side of the city, where we spent the first night, and where we were not made to feel particularly welcome. The next day we decided to move to a hotel in the centre of town, to be independent and nearer the sights, markets, and places we wished to see.

The population then was 2½ million, and the city sprawled untidily for miles, with long boulevards, lined with half-built and abandoned houses and blocks of flats. It had been a booming city eighteen months previously, and buildings were going up everywhere, but suddenly the economy crashed, and when we saw it the city looked depressed and shabby.

After we had registered into our hotel, we visited the Gulestan Palace. The entrance hall was entirely walled and ceilinged with mosaic of one-inch square pieces of mirror; the lighting throughout the building was by huge exquisite crystal chandeliers. Fabulous Persian carpets covered the floors of vast halls, which were lined with displays of exotic porcelain, antique swords and cuirasses, the many gifts presented by foreign monarchs to former Shahs. We saw the royal marriage bed, an ornate jewel-encrusted raised gold box, with three steps to climb to get into it; it was then still used on the Shah's wedding-night. The Shahs were crowned in this palace, and we went to see the crown jewels in a vault, arranged by a firm of Paris jewellers.

We walked on from the palace to the covered *suq*, a huge underground labyrinth of passages and aisles, crossing and recrossing, with cathedral-like arched roof, steps up and down, and sudden open wells and streams. It was all in half-light, and teeming with people. We walked down alleys of jewel-workers, of silver-smiths, of shoe-makers, of spice-sellers, and of carpet-sellers. Some carpets outside the *suq* were spread flat on the road, to be driven over by cars and lorries to compact the pile; they would then be washed and spread on roofs, or hung over the branches of road-side trees, to dry.

That night we were invited to dine with the local head of Gray MacKenzie, the Middle East subsidiary of Inchape Ltd, whom Digna knew. Also there was Charles Noble, their local General Manager from Bahrain, whom we both knew well, and who was paying a business visit to Teheran. He suggested that he should take a day off during his visit, and take us up into the Elburz mountains north of the city, to see the new Karaj dam, which had just been completed and opened by the Shah the previous year.

Charles lived a lonely bachelor life in his large Company house in Bahrain, his wife preferring to remain at their home in Scotland. We met several of these lonely senior business executives in both Bahrain and Singapore, who were unaccompanied by their wives, and I was always sorry for them, and was sometimes invited to act as their hostess when they had to have formal dinner-parties for visiting business colleagues, when I was a temporary grass-widow during Michael's many absences on naval duties. I enjoyed Charles' parties, for he often would serve large bowls of iced caviar, which was sent in 1 lb tins from Teheran, which even in those days was a very expensive delicacy. Ten years later, Michael was in a similar situation when he was General Manager of Middle East Navigation Aids Service for seven years, based in Bahrain, and I remained mainly in England, but he did not have the facilities, either administrative or financial, to serve Persian caviar at his parties, although I am sure there were always many available grass-widows willing to act as his hostess!

We set off early in the morning in a comfortable Gray MacKenzie car, and headed north into wild barren mountains, climbing into deep snow. There was little traffic, and the road was good, so we made good time up to the impressive dam, and the lake still building up behind it. We had hoped we might get further north to see the Caspian Sea, and we did just catch a glimpse of it when we reached the highest point of our route. The road wound through the mountains following the side of a long valley, also slowly flooding with brilliant turquoise blue water. As the valley rose, we were winding beside a river banked with rounded stones and boulders of rose and green, mingled together like beads. We passed occasional charcoal burners, their kilns cut out of the sheer rock on the higher side of the road, and we passed two villages built in terraces high up on ridges looking like those in Tibet.

Cheerful Persians were working at the kilns, or driving donkeys carrying large packs of charcoal. All the people we saw were dark with bright rosy cheeks; men, women and children all had gorgeous colouring, and were friendly and very amused at my efforts to greet them in their own language.

We stopped for lunch at what must have been a caravanserai; it was very primitive indeed, and the food we were served was neither palatable nor recognisable! I noted in my journal that the soup 'was thick, orange coloured, streaked with sour cream or milk, and tasted of rhubarb, onion, and dried limes'. The meat stew which followed was also orange, and very stringy: camel, we wondered?

Our homeward route south followed a different gentle valley: we saw many high-walled gardens, built beside the river, and were able to look down on to cypress-lined paths, rose-beds, weeping willows, pergolas, pools and water-falls. There were no houses, just the lovely gardens which were owned by townspeople in Teheran, to visit for pleasure in spring and summer: real 'Persian Gardens', and in that mountain setting absolutely enchanting.

Digna and I were anxious to visit Isfahan, but were told by embassy officials that no British personnel were permitted to fly by Iran Airways, which was the only airline flying there, as their standard of aircraft maintenance was not considered reliable at that time.

'All right!' I said defiantly, 'we'll go by train!'

'You'll be clever if you do,' I was told, with a maddening smile of supercilious authority, 'there is no rail connection with Isfahan!'

'Then we'll go by bus!' I triumphantly declared.

'You can't possibly do that!' was the horrified rejoinder, 'nobody travels by bus in Persia, except Persians!'

'Well, we do,' I said firmly, at which the embassy washed their hands of us.

'You must be mad!' exclaimed a British commercial representative whom we'd been told to look up, 'no-one goes anywhere in Persian buses. The journey is over 250 miles, over snow-covered mountains, it will be hell!' we were told.

'Well, it'll be a different kind of hell from any we've experienced before,' we said, and we nearly added that we wanted to see the real

Persia, and meet Persians, and not just join in the cosmopolitan social round of the capital city.

Charles Noble was able to make a hotel reservation through his office, and Digna and I set off in the darkness of early morning to catch the 6.30 am bus from the bus station in the purlieus of Teheran. When we reached it, and found our bus, it was swarming with yelling Persians inside and out. We found the numbered seats we'd booked the previous day, turned two other would-be passengers out of them, midst much laughter all round, and as the driver started the engine, 60 per cent of the shouting citizens dropped off, and miraculously we started with one passenger per seat, no-one standing, no pigs or chickens or other (apparent) livestock, although plenty of parcels, boxes and bundles filling every inch of space.

It was a surprisingly comfortable coach; all of the seats were occupied by Persians, who eyed us with friendly curiosity; we soon got to know each other, as dates, pistachio nuts and any other nourishment were handed round; it was difficult not to accept the sticky fly-blown sweets, and then to avoid being seen disposing of them under our seats. For the return journey we provided ourselves with paper bags for this purpose.

The journey took seven hours, across the plain in which Teheran lies and into the mountains, through snow and blizzards, out into the sun, and higher through more mountains and snow, and out again on to a sunny plateau covered with almond orchards in profuse blossom, and so to Isfahan. We had one 'comfort' stop, when everyone disembarked to squat in orderly rows, men and women together, round the edge of a road-side field. There was no embarrassment or false modesty about this, and thankfully we joined the intent-faced pre-occupied line, an old crone making a space for me beside her, a man on my other side rising and bowing to me, before moving back to the bus.

We were all firm friends by this time; we had even managed to get our window open half an inch, though this was not popular; as it was the only fresh air admitted, I'm afraid I remained deaf and uncomprehending to all requests to shut it.

Isfahan was the capital in the time of the great Shah Abbas, who was contemporary of our Queen Elizabeth I, and much of the city still survives from this time. There is the Maidan, or main square, with the huge turquoise domed Shah's Mosque, and the Ali Qapu, the pavilion

from which Shah Abbas watched polo played on the Maidan below;
also the beautiful delicate Lotfollah, or Ladies' Mosque, with its dome
of creamy yellow tiles. The patterns decorating the exquisite tile-work
of mosques, gateways, arches and walls, are not representational, and
quotations from the Koran are largely incorporated into the designs.

Copper shop, Isfahan.

The main avenue, said to have inspired the Champs Elysées in Paris,
is lined with little shops like Aladdin's caves, full of lovely craft-work
made in Isfahan; beaten silver and copper; filigree silver jewellery;
carvings; rugs; enamel-work; bright turquoise blue pottery, with
designs drawn on it in black; and also the exquisite miniatures which
are so famous. You could watch these being painted in the shops, or
even on the streets, the painters using one hand as a palette on which
to mix the colours. I bought two of these, painted on camel-bone (I
could not afford those on ivory, and rejected cheaper ones on plastic);
one is of a hunting scene, measuring 5" x 2", and the other is of a
game of polo, roughly the same size; they are in mosaic frames made
from bunched canes of coloured wood, each less than a quarter the
thickness of a match-stick, so arranged that when glued together, and
then cut in cross sections, they resemble little formalised flowers,
which were inlaid round the frames.

We stayed at the old-fashioned rather dark Hotel Isfahan, a partly Victorian and partly Oriental building, and although ugly, it was clean and quite comfortable, with lines of smiling servants outside the door of our room, all day and part of the night it seemed, to do our bidding. Wherever we walked we were followed by smiling groups who wanted to show us places of beauty or interest, and air their English, but no-one asked us for tips or alms, and we saw no beggars.

One well-dressed prosperous man who took us round the Shah's Mosque, into which we would not have been allowed by ourselves as it was Ramadan and the mosque was full of men worshipping, told us that his English was really at its best when he talked of love, but it was said in an amusing and harmless way, and without innuendo. All our many escorts were delightful, and we enjoyed our encounters with much mutual fun and laughter. We saw no other Western people, it not being the tourist season, yet wherever we went we felt welcome and at ease, and never for a moment felt nervous or at risk. I doubt if that would be the case today.

We wandered without rest for every hour of daylight, gazing at vast tiled domes and minarets gleaming in the sunshine, into courtyards with pools and fountains, gardens planted with cypress trees, rosemary, jasmine and roses.

The return journey took nearly nine hours, our driver being very slow and enjoying long conversations with his passengers, looking back over his shoulder for this, regardless of the snow and icy narrow road through the mountains. This bus had a radio, which was tuned very loudly for the entire journey to a *mullah* (Moslem priest), reading from the Koran in a high nasal voice, to which no-one paid the slightest attention.

We were picked up by the American Admiral's aircraft at Teheran airport after six wonderful days. I took back to Bahrain pieces of antique chased copper; a pair of Bristol blue coloured glass tear-bottles, into which harem ladies used to weep during the absence of their lords and masters, to prove their devotion and faithfulness; carnations, caviar and antique tiles, as well as my two miniatures. The Semmes had bought many Persian rugs, but the little aircraft safely lifted off, and delivered us back to Bahrain.

CHAPTER 12

Bahrain, 1963

THE COMMANDER-IN-CHIEF Middle East, Air Marshal Sir Sam Elworthy, was about to be relieved, and came up to bid farewell to those in the Gulf command. His wife Audrey accompanied him, and also the Flag Officer, Middle East, Rear Admiral Scotland and his wife Anne. They all flew up from Aden, and there ensued four days of formal socialising, including a farewell dinner in our house, attended by the other Forces' commanders in the Gulf, Dick and Phyllis Bryers, and Air Commodore Bill Tacon.

I was distinctly nervous lest our generally good, but sometimes erratic, Goan cook would have one of his fits of temperament on the night, but he rose to the occasion with confidence and artistry, and the C-in-C even sent for him after the meal to congratulate him; this was the menu:

> Smoked salmon with caviar garnish.
> Iced gazpacho soup.
> Roast fillet of beef, various vegetables.
> Meringue baskets, filled with ice-
> cream, garnished with marrons glacés.

It was a successful and relaxed evening; it helped that we knew the Elworthys well, as Sam had commanded the RAF staff college at Bracknell when Michael was on its directing staff in 1956, and he also had been the Air Officer in command at Aden at the time of James' accident during our return voyage from Singapore in 1960, and Michael had stayed with him and Audrey while James was recovering in the RAF hospital there.

The Elworthys left Bahrain the next day, but the Scotlands stayed on. They were staying in Khor Cottage, an old house next to ours in Jufair, which had been refurbished for their comfort during their visits to the Gulf. They had their meals with us, but Anne had had the sitting-room in Khor Cottage redecorated, with new carpet, loose covers and curtains so that she could use it and be independent of us during the day. However, each day she was down in our drawing-room by 10.00 am in the morning; she was unable to go swimming or shopping because of her allergy to the sun, nor did she appear to do any sewing, letter-writing or reading. My mornings were usually fully occupied with household shopping, attending meetings or visiting SSAFA cases, so I was unable to entertain her all of every morning.

There was one splendid evening's entertainment during the Scotlands' visit, at least for Anne and me. At very short notice, as was usual with Arab invitations, I was invited to the wedding of the daughter of one of the Shaikhs of the Ruling family, whose mother I knew quite well, and I was able to arrange to take Anne with me.

We had to be at the house of the bride's parents at 8.30 pm, to join in the bridal ceremony; this was attended only by women, the bridegroom having his own party at his father's house, for men only.

The bride's house was large, and stood in the corner of a big high-walled enclosure; the wedding party took place in the open L-shaped compound round two sides of the house. In one arm of the L there were rows of chairs, flanking a central carpeted path leading from the house to an ornate canopied dais, on which stood a gilt and pink brocade sofa. We were lucky and were shown to two upholstered chairs in the centre of the front row looking across the carpeted aisle to Shaikha Hassa sitting opposite. More and more ladies arrived, many with their servants who, with the bridal family retainers and villagers, filled the other arm of the compound, where there was no seating, and where nut and sweetmeat vendors had laid out their wares around them on cloths on the ground.

The Bahraini ruling family and aristocracy were all seated round us, some in Arab dress, many in the latest fashions from Paris, Rome and Beirut, but all were wearing over these their enveloping black *abbas*, and all also wore gorgeous jewellery of gold, pearls and precious stones, which slowly were revealed during the evening, as their *abbas* slipped further back off their heads and shoulders.

Her Highness arrived at 9.30 pm, and by that time there must have been 1,500–2,000 women there, all still wearing their black *abbas* drawn over their heads; I only saw about twenty European women among them, and the only men were four or five professional drummers and one dancer; these entertainers were known always to be homosexual, and so were considered to be no threat to the women present.

The dancing then began: a negress mimed a shy virgin, shuffling up and down the carpet in front of us, preceded by a negress drummer, who shimmied backwards in front of her, followed by a male drummer with a large tambourine drum; the drummers chanted, while the dancer made great play with a gauzy veil, and shook her head of thick snake-like plaits, which were braided tight to her scalp and had tied to their ends either gold ornaments or little bunches of tuber-rose blossoms.

As the drums beat out the erotic rhythm, the whole gathering of guests set up a high ululating sound, a continuous eoo-eoo-eoo-eoo which was most eerie. After an hour, there was a hush, and the bride emerged from the house on the arm of her bridegroom, who had by this time arrived from his father's house. He would visit the bride each night for the first fortnight of marriage in her own home, and then if they pleased each other, she would leave her parents' roof, and the couple would set up their own home. This was the first night that the bridegroom had come.

The bride was resplendent in a white satin western-style dress, voluminously hooped and panniered and embroidered all over with pearls and diamante; she was preceded by thirteen little child bridesmaids wearing short blue western-style party frocks, holding bunches of roses, and they were followed by five teenage girls in long white dresses, who had their hair dressed high on their heads in knots held in place by circlets of tuber-roses, who gracefully strewed fresh rose petals on to the path ahead of the bridal pair.

The procession moved slowly to the dais, where the bride and groom sat on the sofa, eyes downcast and not speaking, and the retinue sat at their feet. After twenty minutes or so, they rose, and slowly retraced their steps to the house, where, after they had entered, the windows of the bridal suite were shut, and the curtains drawn in a suggestive way, and we did not see them again.

The gathering then noticeably relaxed, people started talking to their friends, and dishes of various nuts and sweets were passed up and down the rows of chairs where the more exalted guests sat; Arab coffee was served, and then four male drummers appeared and moved to the foot of the dais, where they squatted to play for a male dancer who entered. He was wearing the usual long white *dish-dasha*, which was tied tightly round his hips with a chiffon scarf, and had another which he twisted provocatively between his upstretched arms; he began to gyrate, and did a most erotic belly-rolling, hip-jerking dance; the Arab women all became very excited, and the high ululating began again. Anne leaned toward me, and without taking her eyes off the dancer, said:

'I don't think this is quite nice, Sue, do you?' to which I replied:

'I'm quite sure it's not, but isn't it fun?'

After this was over, Shaikha Hassa rose to leave, and we followed through the excited crowd.

The bridegroom was twenty-four years old, and good looking, a cousin of the bride; they knew each other, and wished to marry. In many marriages arranged by the parents, the bride and groom have never met nor seen each other before their wedding night. I attended one such wedding, in which the bride was a pretty girl in her late teens and the groom a sour-faced elderly man, taking a fourth wife. He snatched off the bride's veil when they reached the dais, to see her face; it was quite shocking the unfeeling way in which it was done, and I shall never forget the expression of horror on the poor girl's face when she saw him for the first time. However, I heard later that she pleased him very much, and that they settled into a happy marriage.

It was quite a problem thinking up entertainment for the school-children during the long summer holidays, which coincided with the hottest months when the temperature could reach 105° for long periods; although there was swimming, the beaches along the north of the island were mostly of mud, and the number of swimming-pools was limited.

There was no children's library in the island; the US Awali club had an adult library, and a few British families were permitted to use it, but no children's books were available. I therefore thought I would start one; we had a spare store room in the narrow single-storey extension of the house leading to the ward-room garden, which was easily turned out and furnished with enough shelving and a table and chair for the librarian, but the greatest difficulty was in obtaining books, and the money to buy them.

I let it be known what I was proposing, and asked for volunteers from among the other Service and Foreign Office mothers to help organise and run it; when I had a few names, a meeting was called, and we discussed how to obtain books. Obviously we could ask for cast-offs to be given, and those formed a nucleus, for which we charged a nominal sum to each borrower. We also had a fund-raising children's fete in our garden, at which I arranged for some swarthy fearsome pirates to be present (sailors love dressing up on these occasions!). We asked for donations from everyone we could think of, and meanwhile I wrote to one or two publishers and wholesalers in UK, and several offered us preferential terms, as the library was to be primarily for Service children. They were able to send out our orders through the Forces mail, that is at UK inland postage rates, also ensuring there was no duty or import tax to pay at our end, which was an enormous help.

It got off to a flying start, and was very popular; we opened for two hours on three mornings each week, and we soon found that there needed to be a small working-party of mothers to come fortnightly to effect repairs; for any badly damaged, torn or stained books, we instituted a fine, which initially was another fund-raiser, until the children learned to take greater care of the books. By the time I left Bahrain a year later, we had accumulated several hundred books, and when the Forces finally left Bahrain in 1971, the library was handed over to the English school, which was run in conjunction with the Christian interdenominational church in Manama.

Having been told how much the Ruler's children had enjoyed visiting us earlier, we invited them to tea one day. Shaikha Noora (eleven) and Shaikha Shaikha (seven) came, wearing their best party dresses, and also little Shaikh Rashid, aged eight, who was wearing a white *dish-dasha*, and *keffiah*, with a gold *agal* as befitted a shaikh of the ruling family. He was golden-skinned and plump, with huge liquid dark eyes, an enchanting child, just like a butter-ball.

We took them onboard a mine-sweeper, and they were allowed to sit in the seat behind the gun and operate the direction controls, which caused much excitement. The same Seychelloise nursemaid accompanied them who had done so last time they came; she spoke good English, and told us how excited the children had been, Shaikh Rashid determined not to be left behind this time.

By this time Dick and Phyllis Bryers had left Bahrain; their successors were a couple with whom we could find little in common.

I was drawn on one side one day, to be told I should not have

invited Shaikha Hassa, the children and other members of the ruling
family to our house.

'It is simply not done, and is certainly not your position to do such
a thing,' said Mrs Brigadier; I replied that over our period in the island
we had made many Bahraini friends, including the ruling family, and
we would continue to invite those friends we wished to our house.
We were both amused at this attitude and interference from such
recent new arrivals on the island.

A contrasting opinion was obviously held by the Kanoos, the
Bahraini family who owned and ran the greater part of the
commercial concerns in the island at that time, as will be seen.

We had been friendly with Philip and Pam Higham ever since Philip
and Michael had served together in HMS *Vanguard* for the royal cruise
to South Africa in 1947, and Philip was now our Naval Attaché in
Beirut. They had invited us to fly over for a break from the heat of the
Gulf. Michael was unable to get away, but I had gratefully accepted
the chance to take Emma for a holiday in September 1963, and I
booked the flight through Kanoo's, who were the only travel agents in
Bahrain.

Soon after the arrangements had been made, I was asked to look in
at their offices in Manama, to see Mohammed and Ahmed, the two
cousins who then were the joint heads of the firm. I did so one
morning, and was offered Arab coffee, to which by then all our
Bahraini friends knew we were addicted, and then Ahmed said:

'Sue, we want to give you a present in recognition of all you have
done for your Bahraini friends while you have been here, and we
would like to fly you to Jerusalem for a visit to the Christian shrines
during your visit to Beirut. Can you leave Emma with your friends
there for forty-eight hours?'

My breath was completely taken away.

' But I've done nothing. We have enjoyed enormously making so
many friends here, and have been deeply rewarded by being so warmly
accepted. I really feel overwhelmed by your offer, and I don't know
what to say . . .' They were both laughing, and Ahmed went on:

'If you can leave Emma, you will be driven to the airport, and will
fly first-class to Jerusalem. There you will be met by David, who is the
best guide available, and you will have the car and his services
exclusively for two days. You will stay at the King David Hotel, and

after your visit, I am going to Beirut on business, and I will take you out to lunch to hear all about it.'

Luckily Judy was also going to Beirut at the same time, and it was no problem for her to look after Emma, and so it all took place as Ahmed and Mohammed had planned.

David was a charming Palestinian, sympathetic and quiet, and also extremely knowledgeable of Biblical history. However, on the whole, although it was a wonderful experience which I would not have missed for anything, I was disappointed, and sometimes shocked, by the commercialism and greed at the various Christian shrines, particularly in the church of the Holy Sepulchre, where there were priests of each of the sects that had side-chapels and altars, who thrust alms plates at one in a quite unpleasant and aggressive manner, which totally destroyed any atmosphere of holiness or worship.

The same was the case at Bethlehem and Calvary; in fact the only place where I felt a real sense of authentic history and an atmosphere of prayer throughout the centuries, and of quietness and peace, was in the Garden of Gethsamane. It was marvellous though, to walk the Via Dolorosa from where I was taken aside by a nun to see the original Roman pavement where Christ had walked, now several feet under the present ground-level; and also to see the site of the guard-room and soldiers' quarters of Pilate's palace, where there were circles and squares cut roughly in the stone where they had played a type of board game resembling draughts.

David also took me to the house which had been the Virgin Mary's, which was also underground. We had to walk down a narrow tunnel to enter it, it was little more than a blackened cell, with a shelved alcove along one wall, where she had slept; I felt a presence here very strongly, and was moved almost to tears; David said nothing, until we were rudely interrupted by a party of young Americans wearing 'fun' hats, who came screaming and shouting down the entrance passage, and into the shrine.

'SILENCE!' he roared, and told them to respect the beliefs and feelings of others even if they had none themselves. They stopped as if pole-axed, and gaped at him, and we quietly left. I remember that visit to Jerusalem in every detail, and remain deeply grateful to the Kanoos for their generosity and friendship.

While in Beirut, Emma and I were driven over the hills into Syria to visit Damascus. We walked down the Street called Straight, and

visited Ananias' house (another now below ground level, owing to the
silting up of the earth over the centuries); it was exactly as when he
had lived there, a small hovel, lined with blackened roughly-hewn
stones, with nothing there of modern origin, full of the atmosphere of
mystical holiness.

Ahmed Kanoo took me out to lunch in Beirut, and also picked me
up one evening together with a friend of his, to go out to dinner. We
ate the most delicious Lebanese food on both occasions, both of which
I enjoyed enormously.

Beirut at that time was the pleasure-ground of all Middle East
wealthy Arabs, a beautiful city in a glorious setting, with hills rising
behind, covered with green cedars of Lebanon. It was rife with
corruption and undertones of violence even then, and most British
expatriates who had to live there by reason of their employment did
not enjoy it.

During our stay, Emma and I were collected one day by Salwa Al-
Umran, the charming Lebanese who was teaching me Arabic in
Bahrain, and she drove us out of the city up into the surrounding
mountains for tea at a restaurant; among the cedars in the hills were
luxury villas, hotels and restaurants, where in the hot summer months
the wealthy Beirutis and rich Middle Eastern Arabs went for holidays,
and in winter would visit again for skiing. The scenery was
magnificent, and as we drove down to the coast again, darkness had
fallen, and we saw Beirut laid out below us with a million lights, and
the hills above strung together by necklaces of lights along the
mountain roads. It is sad to think of Beirut and the Lebanon today; I
wonder how much of what we saw remains after the bitter fighting
through recent years.

In Bahrain we had become friendly with an Arab merchant called
Abdulmohsin Algosaibi and his vivacious wife, Lulu. We were
delighted when we were invited to go shark-fishing one Sunday in
Abdulmohsin's converted dhow, which had no mast or sails, but a
powerful engine. The forward half of the dhow was decked in as a
raised platform, leaving a catwalk each side to reach the wheelhouse
and anchor cable. This raised deck was covered with Persian rugs,
which I would have loved to have in my drawing-room, and many
long plastic-covered cushions were lying about. Further aft were three
large deep-freezes, bolted to the deck, and then a hatch leading down

to a cabin and a boxed-in lavatory. Under the decked-in area was another huge deep-freeze, and aft of that the engine-room. All these freezers were run on oil, and were used for shipping frozen food down to the marine oil-field at Das Island, our host's business being the cold storage firm which supplied the oil company.

The previous day a *shamal* had been blowing, and we thought the fishing expedition might be called off. On Sunday morning the wind had moderated slightly, and the sea in the bay was calmer; even so, four of the male Bahraini guests had cried off, wise in their decision as it transpired, but at the time we thought them poor sports, and the rest of the party met on the jetty at 6.45 am as planned, and cast off.

The party comprised our host, Abdulmohsin, his wife Lulu, and two of her cousins; a Bahraini friend of Abdulmohsin's; Michael and me; and Ian Jamieson, the captain of HMS *Eskimo*, and his wife Pat, who were staying with us. There was a Bahraini crew of about six.

As soon as we sailed we were served a delicious breakfast of curry puffs, hunks of new bread and cheese, hard-boiled eggs and crackers, and Arab coffee. Before we had left the lee of the bay, the dhow was beginning to move about a bit, but outside in the open sea it was very rough, and one by one the party succumbed to sea-sickness, and spent the next eight hours lying green-faced on the cushions, convenient bowls and buckets to hand. Poor Pat Jamieson, who hadn't been feeling well anyway but didn't want to miss the trip, collapsed first, swiftly followed by the two lady cousins: they staggered in turn and with difficulty to the cabin below, returning, pale and wan, to recline on the rugs and cushions, uncaring whether or not they were soaked with spray from the mountainous waves, and there they remained for the rest of the day.

Lulu looked at me and said:

'You all right, Sue? You not sea-sick?' almost hopeful, I thought, that I too, might join the other ladies, and realising that her husband was going back for no-one, and that it was going to be extremely rough the further we sailed out into the Gulf. I replied cautiously:

'I'm not sea-sick *usually*.'

'I never sea-sick,' said Lulu gaily, '*nevaire! nevaire!*'

On we went, the sea deep blue in brilliant sunshine, the clear pale blue sky looking so innocent, but the waves large and lumpy. Half an hour later, Lulu suddenly dashed aft, and emerged after ten minutes, her face green and bathed in sweat.

'I *nevaire* before sea-sick!' she exclaimed, still laughing gaily, 'it must be because I am so constipated: five days, Sue, in spite of pills every night . . .' and then I was given a graphic description of her internal economy, doctors and medicines.

Abdulmohsin was resplendent in primrose yellow swimming-trunks which had to be of a large size to encircle his embonpoint, so that they hung loosely round his knees flapping in the wind, for he was short in stature; above this he wore an elegant shirt in primrose and white one-inch stripes: he looked like an over-grown seven-year-old boy, with his short curly black hair, and his face alive with pleasure and laughter all day long. He came across the deck to see if Lulu was all right, and then turned to me to ask curiously:

'Are you *sure* you're not feeling ill, Sue?' By that time I was the only woman still vertical. The Bahrainis were all chatting merrily in spite of their sea-sickness, laughing at themselves and at the antics of the boat. By this time Abdulmohsin's friend had also succumbed, and Ian Jamieson was palely swaying, and a little later also collapsed, leaving Abdulmohsin, Michael and me to fish.

A young three-foot shark was caught by Abdulmohsin.

'Mmm; good! A good supper tonight!' he cried with satisfaction. There were no other bites, so we moved to another fishing-ground, out of sight of land now, the sea rougher and dull leaden grey, reflecting the now stormy sky, the wind rising. We three had to hang on with one hand to some part of the dhow, and control our rod with the other; there was no rail, for we were on the cat-walk, with only a low gunwale a few inches high between us and the sea.

I then began to catch fish, and pulled in six or seven loathsome remora, the sucker-fish three to four feet long, which clamp the suction pads on their heads on to the bellies of sharks, to catch the morsels which drop from their hosts' mouths when feeding. They are revolting looking fish, and no good to eat. I also caught cat-fish, some quite large, but these are not edible either, although were good sport to catch.

At about 2.30 pm we turned for home, and when we neared the shelter of the Bahraini coast, we were given lunch of rich curry and rice with baskets of melons and other fruit, to which only Abdulmohsin, Michael and I did full justice. We tied up at about 5.00 pm, Ian and Pat thankful to reach *terra firma*, and we three soaked with spray and 'green' seas. The three sickly Bahraini ladies were still gay and chattering as they stepped ashore; Abdulmohsin was very apologetic that we had found no shark, but obviously delighted that Michael and I had enjoyed the day so much. At times the rough seas had been a bit alarming, but these old dhows, large and solidly built of teak, are wonderful craft, and inspire one with complete confidence.

There was a sudden very trying spell of hot weather in September that year; it only lasted a week or two, but the temperature reached 105° in the shade. Everyone thought that summer was over and the cooler weather had arrived when we were hit by this discomfort. It coincided with, or caused, a spate of unpleasant viral infections, and I succumbed to a heavy cold. I was at my nadir the evening we held a large formal cocktail-party which, judging by the noise level, was very successful. The guests had all left by 8.40 pm when Michael and I sank back with a drink while awaiting Veigas to tell us supper was ready.

Suddenly, horror of horrors! The front doorbell rang; we held our breath while Veigas answered it, and then announced the arrival of an elderly shaikh of the ruling family, who had not turned up at the cocktail-party. He flourished his invitation, and said:

'But where is the party? You said 8.30, didn't you?' as indeed I had, as the time it should end, not begin! So we had him to supper instead.

'We call this "Old Men's Food",' said Shaikh Rashid, pushing his omelette to one side with his fork. In spite of that, he must have enjoyed himself, for he stayed until 11.30 pm, by which time my eyes and ears, as well as my nose, were bunged up and aching, and I was almost crying for mercy.

'I talk to you from the heart, Sue, not from my head,' he said, 'I feel for you and Michael like my own brother and sister, and that this is my home.' Although very flattered, and also fond of him, I only longed at that moment to go to bed, and for him to return home to his! He was a delightful old man, very pro-British, and with a lively sense of humour.

That winter he invited us to dinner at his house in Rifa'a, where we sat on the floor and ate with our fingers. It was a bitterly cold night, and was the day of an almost unheard of twenty-four hour steady downpour. Old Arab houses are not built to withstand such heavy rain, and we sat round a table-cloth laid on the floor, with buckets, bowls, dishes and tins all round us catching the steady drips and trickles from the leaking roof. Besides us, there was one other guest,

Christopher Burne, who was the First Lieutenant of HMS *Jufair*, and acted as Michael's flag lieutenant on formal occasions.

For the four of us the front half of a sheep was served, with the usual many side dishes. Shaikh Rashid, of course, sat comfortably with his legs crossed in the Arab fashion, a position which is agony for an unaccustomed Westerner to maintain for more than a few minutes, so we three sat on one buttock, our legs tucked away from the dinner setting, and we all enjoyed the tender succulent meat and spicy rice, which we managed fairly well, using only our right hands to manipulate. That is, until I developed excruciating cramp in my legs and thighs, when I absolutely had to change position. One may only eat with one's right hand, for in the Moslem world the left hand is used for intimate bodily purposes, which are considered unclean. I could not therefore settle down again on my other buttock, and so I could only kneel, and lean forward to help myself to mouthfuls of food.

'Good Heavens!' exclaimed Shaikh Rashid, 'whatever is the matter with you, woman?'

'It's all right, pay no attention to me,' I said, 'I've only got cramp . . . OW!' which he thought a great joke, and I was able after that to move about without embarrassment, as the wretched cramp came and went.

The most succulent morsel of an Arab meal used to be the sheep's eye, but by this time it was realised that this treat had little appeal to Western palates, and so the tongue would be offered instead to the guest of honour. This titbit was wrenched from the sheep's throat and offered to Michael; it seemed about a foot long, and he grasped it as one would a banana, and took a large bite. He then craftily passed it to me, saying:

'This is delicious, Shaikh Rashid, I simply must share it with Sue!' It was delicious, too, but very rich, and I had already eaten my fill; after one mouthful I was wondering what to do with the rest, when I saw Shaikh Rashid eyeing it hopefully, I thought, so I said:

'Shaikh Rashid, it would be too greedy to eat all this myself, I hope you will share it with us?' and I passed it to his ready hand.

It was a period of bitterly cold weather, and caused much hardship among the poorer Bahrainis who lived in palm-leaf *barasti* dwellings. There was such a strong cold gale that pipes froze out at the Parachute Battalion camp in the desert, and up in Awali, the hilltop oil town, when someone accidentally left their lawn-sprinkler on all night, they woke up to find a tree in their garden entirely encased in ice, with foot-long icicles hanging from every branch. Bahrainis from the nearby villages hurried to see the spectacle, and photographs were in the local newspaper, causing much wonder and amazement at the phenomenon of the 'Dry Water' at Awali.

During that cold month fish were dying in the sea; at Zallaq, a narrow sandy beach down the west coast of the island, there was a bank over a foot high of dead sea-snakes of all colours and sizes, which had been washed up in the gales and high tides; it was a loathsome sight.

At Christmas we held a children's fancy-dress party, which was nearly a fiasco, as there was a power-cut in the naval base just as the first of the thirty-four guests were arriving; other than a Disney film I had no alternative entertainment prepared, after the judging of the fancy-dress. However, after frantic SOSs to everyone I could think of, power was restored, and all was well. Supper followed the film, and the party ended with a visit from Father Christmas, who terrified the young Arab guests to begin with, until they got the hang of the idea; four of the Ruler's children were among the guests and it was four-year-old Shaikha Mariam who overcame her fear first and then went up to her eleven and eight year-old sisters and upbraided them for being cowards, which greatly amused their Seychelloise nursemaid.

CHAPTER 13

Sharjah and Abu Dhabi, 1963

JUST BEFORE CHRISTMAS we were invited to the Trucial Oman Scouts' annual ball in Sharjah. The Army and RAF commanders in Bahrain were also invited, and we flew down together in a small RAF aircraft in which there was just room for us all. We were invited to stay in the house of the Scouts' commanding officer, who was still Colonel Bartholomew, who had escorted us to Buraimi twelve months previously; three other couples were staying there too. The house was like a large army hut, and we learned the following day that Bart and his wife had given up their own bedroom, and in fact, had not gone to bed at all.

As many of the TOS officers as possible came in from their desert squadron areas for the dance. They were seconded from their British Army regiments, having volunteered for TOS service, for the adventure and solitariness of desert life: all of them were young men of guts and character, some a bit cranky.

The dance was in the new officers' mess, a luxurious type of Nissen hut, and there were fabulous tents surrounding it, lined with silk and brocades, lent by the shaikhs of the various Trucial states for the occasion.

Girls had been gathered from Bahrain and Aden, including SSAFA sisters and hospital nurses, oil company and Foreign Office secretaries, filling all the spare seats in the Commander-in-Chief's aircraft from Aden, and any others flying in official guests, and it was a splendid all-night 'thrash'. The Scouts lived a tough life, and seldom saw a girl from one year's end to the next, but this was their one big party of the year, and among expatriate girls in the Middle East invitations were much sought after.

The next morning the camp was very quiet, and one by one aircraft took off from the sandy air-strip to take guests home. Michael left with the Bahrain party at 9.15 am, but I stayed on, so as to fly later in the day to Abu Dhabi, some hundred miles along the coast to the west.

During that morning I thought my absence would be more
appreciated than my presence by our hosts, so I went off with my
camera to walk across the sand to the village of Sharjah (which today is
a thriving town with its own airport). On the way I headed for a
cluster of *barasti* huts, and came upon a group of women squatting on
the sand, two old crones sharing a hubble-bubble pipe, and a younger
woman doing some sort of pillow lace, as I thought. I approached
them slowly, stopping for them to look at me and register that I had
friendly intentions, until I eventually came right up and said my
greetings; they all shook hands in turn with me, and I was invited to
join them, whereupon two or three others came over to the group. A
man also came out of a hovel and reclined on the sand a little distance
apart, obviously to keep an eye on the proceedings. I talked haltingly
with them about their clothes, and the silver and white braid which
was being woven on the pillow, which I had thought was lace; we
talked also of our children, and where I came from, and then I asked if
I might take a photograph.

'*La! La!*' (No! No!), they all exclaimed, and the man sat up at once,
and burst into animated objections; so then I said but I didn't want to
photograph *them*, it was the pillow braid work in which I was
interested, which we didn't know in England.

'Oh, yes,' they said, I could photograph that! However, in the time
it took me to set my camera, the two smoking crones had sidled off,
and others had also vanished, so I only managed to catch two in the
photograph.

I walked on into the village, and watched a group of Bedu with
rifles slung on their backs, being greeted by the ruling Shaikh outside
his palace and ushered in; there were some falconers holding birds on
their wrists, who entered with them. I found my way back to camp by
a different and less interesting route, and then Bart's wife suggested
taking me the ten miles west along the coast to Dubai, where she was
to take home some of the overnight guests.

Dubai, known then as the Venice of Arabia, was an attractive old
town built along two sides of a lagoon, the water passing right through
the *suq*. Many of the buildings were old, with tall elegant wind-towers
to draw cooling breezes down into the houses below, which were
quite effective, I was told, but they are seldom seen today.

I flew off from Sharjah after lunch, in a RAF Twin Pioneer which
was taking two Arab soldiers back to their squadron at Buraimi, and

then going on to return the squadron commander to a distant outlying area after the dance. At Buraimi, where we landed on the sand, for there was no prepared air-strip, our erstwhile passengers jumped out and started walking off into the blue, and we took off again to fly to Abu Dhabi. We flew quite low, so I was able to see clearly the contours and colours of the desert: huge sweeping dunes, cleanly arc-ed and curved by the wind, with no-one in sight for mile after mile, and no habitation, tree or animal; I found the space and emptiness exhilarating to the point of intoxication, and when suddenly the colour of the sand changed to bright brick red, as though drawn by a sweeping celestial paint-brush, it was magical.

Abu Dhabi from the air, 1963. Shaikh Shakhbut's Palace is in the centre background.

At Abu Dhabi we again landed on the barren flat sand, but a Land Rover was driving across it toward us, and as soon as I had alighted, the aircraft door was slammed, and it flew off again.

I was met by a TOS officer and driven into Abu Dhabi, a little primitive town on a promontory, with dirt roads, bordered by *barasti* huts, leading to the ruling Shaikh's fabulous white *Beau Geste* type of palace standing out starkly near the sea. He was then the notorious Shaikh Shakhbut, a tall figure of piratical appearance, hawk-eyed, with beaked nose, and full black beard. He was only too conscious of the enormous oil revenues about to accrue from the recently discovered marine fields in his state, but he was reputed to keep all his wealth in coffers under his bed: an apocryphal story, but true in so far that he spent none of it on roads, hospitals, schools or other development for the benefit of his people. He was also of uncertain temper and unstable mentality, and thus difficult to deal or reason with. The only person he respected and would listen to, and who could handle him at all, was Colonel Hugh Boustead, the British Political Agent in Abu Dhabi, with whom I was to stay. Hugh was eventually able to persuade Shakhbut to move his money into the local branch of a British bank, but the Shaikh insisted on the cash being stored in trunks, and he would visit the bank regularly to count it, to ensure it was all still in safe custody!

Hugh, nearing seventy years old, was a legend, having spent most of his life with Arabs, in the Sudan, Yemen, the Hadramaut and then Abu Dhabi. He had been in the Royal Navy at the start of the First World War, but deserted so as to join the Army and get out to Gallipoli, to avenge his brother's death there. He was never punished for this! He was an Olympics gold medalist (pentathlon) in 1920, and took part in the 1933 Everest expedition. In Arabia he was known, revered and loved by all tribesmen, and by all who met him. We had been able to get to know him well, as he often visited Bahrain on Foreign Office affairs, to talk with the PR, Bill Luce, our neighbour in Jufair.

Staying with him was tremendous fun. His house was in the British Agency compound, and was right on the beach; behind it was Shaikh Shakhbut's palace. The household was run by four servants who were devoted to Hugh (who was a bachelor), and whom he summoned either by blasts on a referee's whistle, or by shouts of:

'Bakhri! Where are you, you bloody old bastard!' and the servant called would come running, a huge grin all over his face. Hugh always carried a camel-stick wherever he went, that is, a thin bamboo cane, hooked at one end.

The old house was rectangular, the whole first floor being one large room divided by sliding doors into dining and drawing-rooms, with wide verandas running the full length of each side and Hugh's bedroom and bathroom across the seaward end. Downstairs were four guest-rooms, each with its own bathroom, all opening on to verandas and thence straight on to the sands of desert and beach. Hugh preferred to work in his dining-room than in his office across the compound, because he so loved the views across the desert and out to sea, so all his visitors, Bedu, villagers and the Shaikh's secretary and messengers all came to the house, and my bedroom on the ground floor was several times invaded by bearded brigands looking for 'Colonel-Sahib'.

There was another guest staying the weekend, a young trainee of one of the oil companies called Philip Royston, who was learning the oil business before going into his company's London office. He was engaged to one of the daughters of the Comte de Paris. Philip was going for an audience with Shaikh Shakhbut during my visit, and he suggested he should take with him a postcard portrait of the Shaikh which I had bought in the *suq*, to ask the Shaikh to sign it for me to send to James at prep. school. Shakhbut looked at it, and said:

'This not flattering, I not like; I send you a better one!' and he put my postcard, which had cost me the outrageous sum of 3s.0d., on his chair, and sat on it! and that was that, and he never sent me another: I was quite affronted!

Hugh had a Jordanian judge to lunch while I was there, who was a member of the Jordanian senate, an erudite and interesting man, whose son was at Rugby School in England. Somehow conversation over coffee developed into a discussion of capital and corporal punishment, which became quite heated, we three English being strongly in favour of both, and the Jordanian disagreeing with us. I, not knowing that his son was at a British public school, said:

'You asked me just now why I send my son to a private, rather than a state school; this is one reason why: so that he shall be properly disciplined, which means probably being beaten when necessary!'

The Judge was horrified, and entirely incredulous, and told us that if he thought his son was being beaten, he'd take him away from Rugby at once. We all assured him it was probably too late, and that the boy had most likely been beaten many times already! I think he thought we were teasing him, for he then invited us all to lunch with him at the plush new hotel in the town the next day, so he presumably bore us no ill-will.

I was supposed to have returned to Bahrain the following day, but Hugh made it very difficult; he was very obstinate, and also eccentric, and was used always to having his own way. I told him I had to get

back for the Goan naval ratings' dance, which Michael would be very
cross with me if I missed.

'To Hell with the ratings' dance!' shouted Hugh, 'you can dance
here with my cook, he's a Goan! And anyway, there's no transport to
get you to the air-strip tomorrow. You'd far better stay here and help
me entertain some shipping fellers who are coming to dinner
tomorrow, and fly up with me to Bahrain on Tuesday.' There was no
more to be said.

That evening the three of us went for a walk through the little town
and out along the beach to the eastward. We started at sunset, and got
back in the dark with a full moon well risen. Coming back,
silhouetted against the scarlet and black streaked sky of the sunset's
after-glow, we watched camels being milked on the beach, dhows
gently rocking at anchor on the sea behind them.

The following day two Trucial Scouts officers came to stay, to enjoy a
comfortable bed and bath between one desert patrol and the next; they
were a pleasant pair of young men, who took me off that evening to a
little fishing village up the coast, which was entirely undeveloped and
unspoilt, with no buildings other than *barasti* huts, no electricity or
sanitation. We walked through the village and along the beach,
watching the sunset, and while doing so, a long canoe was poled in
from the horizon by a crew of eight men, all standing up, using their
twelve-foot long poles as though punting, but vigorously and fast. As
they poled, they chanted, and to hear this gradually approaching across
the silk-smooth sea out of the glorious sunset, with no other sound
except the low murmurs behind us of women tending the fires outside
their *barastis*, while preparing the evening meal, and the regular soft lap
of the sea rippling on to the sand, was deeply moving in a primitive
way.

As the boat drew nearer the shore, a few men and boys came down
to join us, to watch it beach at our feet; the crew, excited and
laughing, jumped ashore and started throwing plump fish up on to the
beach, where the women collected them and took them to cook over
the waiting fires.

The light by then had almost gone, and we walked on, seeing the
crimson after-glow light up the western sky, dhows and the outer
islands silhouetted black against the vivid colour reflected in the sea. At
length we stopped, to sit on the beach and watch without speaking.

We were joined by two Arabs, who sat down with us, in silence also, after first exchanging quiet greetings. When the after-glow had faded into darkness, we rose to retrace our steps, but were invited into a hut to have coffee; I was ushered through the doorway first, and luckily remembered to leave my shoes outside. The hut was about fifteen feet long, eight or nine feet wide, and roughly seven feet high. It was well built with a wooden framework of beams lashed one to another, and with palm matting hanging in two layers over the frame, forming an inner and outer wall; palm matting covered the floor, and on one side was a colourful Turkoman tribal rug hanging, with cushions along its lower edge to lean against when sitting on the floor. Across one end of the hut was built a wide box-like platform bed, with a gay blanket covering it, which looked comfortable. On the walls hung large round woven straw mats, which would be laid on rigid palm-leaf trays for serving food. The only light was a hurricane lantern hanging high from the roof, which cast a soft gold light and gentle shadow.

By this time a third villager had joined us, and also our TOS driver: we four guests were invited to sit, leaning against the cushions, our feet tucked under us, for it is a gross insult to show the soles of one's feet to an Arab; our hosts squatted or sat cross-legged, one of them first bringing a large straw tray to put on the floor in front of me, on which was set a dish of apples, one of tangerines, and one rather primitive knife. I peeled a tangerine, and almost separated the segments before offering it to our hosts in turn, which seemed to amuse and please them. After fruit, coffee was produced from a small charcoal fire in a stone brazier in one corner: there were only two cups, so Tom Walcot and I had them first, and a refill each, and then Archie and the driver were served, after which our hosts had some. Meanwhile there was general conversation, Tom and Archie being fluent Arab speakers; the newly discovered oil-field under the sea was under discussion, and which of the Trucial states owned it, or should share it.

'How can you share or divide what is in the sea?' asked our host, 'The sea and all that is in it belongs to Allah!'

Sweet clear tea was then produced, and the same cups, unwashed, were used again. I was then asked if I would like to visit the women's quarters in neighbouring huts, but our host, who was unmarried and the Headman of the village, sent for his mother, so I never met the younger women. She was a sweet-faced woman, wearing a heavily embroidered bright coloured garment under her black *abba*; she seemed over-awed by me (this village had never before been visited by western people), and she took one of my arms with both her hands, and drew me out into the darkness, gently stroking my arm and murmuring to me while I was led away between the huts in total darkness. I must confess to a moment's anxiety, but thought Tom and Archie would rescue me if necessary. The old lady took me to another immaculate hut, much like the first, and she indicated that I was to spend the night there with her, which somewhat surprised me, and I wondered what that might entail. We sat on the floor and discussed our children at length, and I asked how the fish were cooked that we had seen brought in. I eventually persuaded her to take me back to Tom and Archie whom I told of my invitation to stay the night, which they vetoed at once, in a tactful way, but quite firmly. I was very touched to have been asked, and would have been willing to stay, but it might have been embarrassing if I had got into difficulties. After protracted farewells, we left. It was a delightful experience; the people were so gentle, dignified and hospitable; the simplicity of their life, and the beauty of their world I found deeply enviable.

The following day I flew back to Bahrain with Hugh.

Before the spate of farewell parties prior to our departure in April 1964, I thought it would be fun to invite Shaikha Hassa to dinner as a way of saying good-bye. The suggestion was made to her by Salwa Al Umran, and there was pleasure and much enthusiasm shown for the idea.

We could comfortably seat fourteen in our dining-room, and I thought I would invite four or five English guests, and ask Her Highness if she would like to suggest ten friends whom I would also invite. Her list numbered fifteen, all of whom accepted; I am not sure now how we all fitted in.

The Bahraini ladies much enjoyed the dinner, and all gasped when the dessert was brought in: Coelho, our Goan cook, had excelled himself, and somehow, despite the very hot day, had managed to make spun sugar baskets, with plaited sugar handles decorated with flowers of coloured icing; the baskets were filled with ice-cream and peeled segments of fresh oranges, and looked very pretty indeed.

After dinner I showed the photographs which I had taken in Bahrain, which I projected on to a large screen. Many were of places and scenes which Shaikha Hassa had never seen or visited, such as the *suq*, including the 'donkey park'; the coppersmiths at work, and the inferno of the blacksmiths' compound; also scenes of horse and camel racing, with her husband sitting watching, and his falcons nearby. Those of the *suq* particularly interested her, including the ones of the dhow jetty, where cargoes of timber, sheep, jute, fruit and other commodities were loaded and unloaded for shipment along the Gulf coasts, and I was constantly asked to go back and show the slides a second time. I led up to the final slide by saying:

'Your Highness, I have told my husband so much about you, and he is so sad that he has not, and cannot meet you, but at least you can see him, even though you cannot exchange greetings!' and I flashed up a full-length photograph of Michael in his full dress white uniform, with sword and medals, on the occasion of the Queen's birthday parade, when Shaikh Isa came to inspect the naval force and take the salute at their march-past. Michael was smiling into the camera, and certainly looked very handsome, and the Arab ladies all clapped, and made a long indrawn hiss through their teeth, of pleasure and admiration, followed by much giggling; it was a delightful moment.

The next day I was in the town and called on my friend the pearl merchant, Mohammed Almudaifah; he had heard all about the previous evening, and told me it was the talk of the *suq*. I was so glad the ladies all enjoyed it so much; our cook and Goan staff had all worked very hard to ensure its success, and I too had been so anxious that they should enjoy themselves.

One of our last official visitors before we left was the naval Medical Inspector-General, Vice-Admiral Steele-Perkins. Both Michael and I were particularly anxious to impress on him the very poor standard of medical services for naval personnel and families on the island, but we had no need to say much; he toured extensively all the medical facilities and was horrified and shocked. He left vowing immediate action, which was satisfactory, but as we left only a fortnight later, we never saw what improvements transpired.

We were so fortunate to have lived in the Arabian Gulf then, when what are now cities of concrete sky-scrapers were simple fishing villages and small coastal trading towns. We were really able to get to know and become sincere friends of many of the Bahraini people, who warmly welcomed us into their circles. Returning eight years later, life was greatly changed, and spoiled by so-called modern progress.

In December 1997, the Amir, Shaikh Isa, very kindly invited us to visit Bahrain again.

On our arrival we were met, then looked after during our visit, by His Highness' personal private secretary of many years, Major Gerald Green, whom we knew well from the Jufair days.

We were amazed and impressed by the amount of land reclamation and building development in the island in the last twenty five years or more since we had left; I even found it hard to discover some of my old haunts.

The happiest moments of our stay were the reunions with old friends: Michael's audience with His Highness, and my call on Shaikha Hassa with Salwa Alumran, where I also saw Shaikha Lulua and Mariam Kanoo and many other old friends. We also looked in on Hussain Yateem, whose lovely rose gardens we used to visit in the 1960s.

It was truly heart-warming to find our old friends as unchanged as ever. The holiday was a feast of friendship, long to be remembered and discussed.

CHAPTER 14

London, 1964–67

'GOOD MORNING, MADAM. How may I help you?' I asked, as I stepped out from behind my desk in Selfridges furniture department one spring day in 1965.

We had settled back into our Wimbledon flat on our return from the Persian Gulf, when Michael was appointed to the Admiralty. The daughter of one of our friends earned her living in temporary jobs demonstrating commercial products at exhibitions and big stores. That March, as she was already committed to working elsewhere, she passed on to me an offer of a job demonstrating 'Cintique' chairs at Selfridges, during a promotion to last three weeks; I was required to work three days a week, from 10.00 am to 4.00 pm with an hour off for lunch, which I was entitled to buy in the excellent employees' canteen, where a good three-course meal cost 1s.6d. I worked ostensibly under the manager of the furniture department, a Mr Gomme, who was a fierce disciplinarian of whom the staff were rather in awe; I was also, however, employed by Mr Glover, Cintique's representative in the London area. Mr Glover and I struck up an excellent rapport, and he several times arrived to check on my sales successes (or otherwise) at midday, and would take me out to a lengthy lunch at a Viennese restaurant in Bond Street; we would split a bottle of Hungarian Bull's Blood, and I would return to my duties in a rosy aura of contentment in time to do an hour's work before knocking off for the day.

There was a surprising amount to learn about the product I was selling, and I was expected to know the answers to any questions I might be asked by potential customers: details of the exact measurements and construction of the chairs, the materials and woods used, and comparative prices with other makes; it was great fun luring hesitant customers into definite purchases, and persuading determined ones into buying models of better quality than they had planned. Mr Glover seemed pleased with my sales totals, and I was invited back to work at the regular autumn and spring promotions for as long as we lived in London. It was fascinating seeing from the inside a little of how the huge store was run, and I enjoyed getting to know the regular sales staff 'on the floor', and also the boozy lunches with Mr Glover.

Michael's parents, Kyrle and Agnes Pope, lived in the large family house called Homme, at Much Marcle, in Herefordshire. It was convenient for James' prep school near Badminton, and for Emma too, when she went to St Mary's Calne; James moved on to Bradfield in 1966, so I was regularly driving from one school to the other and on to Homme for half-terms and exeat weekends. We went to Homme often, and all kept our holiday clothes, boots and raincoats there. There was plenty of room in the rambling old house, and the park, woods and large ponds were ideal for picnics, barbecues and walks; James learned to shoot pigeon and rabbits. My in-laws loved to have us all, particularly the grandchildren, and Michael was able to help his father in the estate work and management of the woods, which he was encouraged to think would be his one day.

In Much Marcle was another big house, largely of Tudor origin, called Hellens, which belonged to the Munthe family. Malcolm was the elder son of Axel Munthe, the Swedish doctor who had written the best-seller, *The Story of San Michele*, in the 1930s. Malcolm and Anne had two sons, and a daughter of Emma's age; the two girls became friends, and were able to see a great deal of each other, for although the Munthes, like us, only used the Much Marcle house for holidays, their main home was also at Wimbledon; this was an old house in a considerable state of dilapidation, with constantly falling ceilings, holes in the floors, and very ancient electric wiring. The family was very unconventional and Malcolm a most amusing and imaginative raconteur: one never quite knew what to believe of the amazing stories he would tell of his exploits.

Living in London, after so many years abroad in different parts of the world, enabled us to catch up with many of our friends and relations once more, and in particular, Ginny was able to rejoin our family again. She was training as a nursery nurse at St Christopher's in Kent, and was able to come up often for her days and weekends off. It was the greatest joy getting to know her, and perhaps because I had seen so little of her in her childhood, she now felt more like a younger sister than a daughter. When she qualified, she got a job as a nanny with a delightful practising Jewish family who lived in Notting Hill

Gate, where she learned the strict customs of having separate dishes, pans and cutlery for milk foods and meat etc., which were new and strange to her, and of much interest to us all. Although she liked the family, she found the job very lonely, and so she applied to join the nursing staff in the maternity department at Guy's Hospital, which she loved. This was nearer to us and more accessible, and so we saw more of her, and when Shaikh Isa of Bahrain visited London with his family in the summer, I was able to take both Emma and Ginny to call on Shaikha Hassa.

By then the Shaikha had a large number of children; in Bahrain she had told me she did not want any more (she always had much difficulty in labour), so I was amazed to see that she was once more pregnant.

'But, Your Highness,' I exclaimed, after we had exchanged warm greetings, 'I thought you had decided that your family was large enough!'

'Yes, I know,' she agreed, and then, cradling her arms and looking wistfully down, she added, 'But my arms, they were so empty.'

That autumn of 1964, we sent Emma to Rookesbury Park, a girls' preparatory school at Wickham, in Hampshire, which was not far from where my mother lived, at Winchester. Before we had gone to Bahrain, two years earlier, she had been at an excellent dame school in Wimbledon, where she had progressed well ahead of her peers; in Bahrain, the schooling left much to be desired, and on returning home to her old school, she was found to be two years behind her expected academic standard. We were anxious for her to go to St Mary's Calne when she was eleven, but to do so, she would have to pass their quite stiff entrance exam. In Bahrain she had been the centre of much attention from the officers of visiting ships, who were missing their own children, or in the midshipmen's case, their younger sisters, who all played with her in the wardroom swimming-pool and gardens. Her old dame school took children only up to nine years old, which Emma had reached, and there was no other in Wimbledon that would have been suitable at that time, so poor Emma was sent to Rookesbury. She hated it, and I felt I was a cruel and hard-hearted parent, added to which I missed her companionship enormously.

Michael had gone to Paris just before the school terms began, to do the NATO Defence College staff course of six months, and my father died a week later, after a brief illness. I cannot say I mourned him, but had many regrets that he and I had not had a happier relationship. I hold only bitter memories of him, for the way he treated both me and my mother. She survived him for another eight years, which I think were some of the happiest of her life. She died aged ninety, after two days of 'just feeling a little seedy, darling'. The morning of the day she died, she said to my sister, Winifred, who was sitting by her bed:

'Don't worry about me, darling, I know I'm dying, and I have no fear. I'm just lying here thinking how lucky I am to have had so much happiness from you three wonderful daughters.' She died in her sleep a few hours later.

During the summer holidays that year, we went camping in France. Judy Ryan came with us, who had been Emma's 'minder' in Bahrain, and also Ruth Pruen, an old friend who had been part of the family for the first two difficult years of Emma's life.

We hired a Dormobile which would sleep four, and bought a tent with an inner floored compartment in which Judy and Ruth slept on camp-beds in snug comfort. We four had hard bench bunks in the Dormobile, which rocked in the icy gales we encountered on the western Brittany coast. Michael decided we should spend the first few days in the Loire valley, so as to improve our education by visiting as many chateaux as possible. We parked in a good camping site at Amboise, from where the children and I were taken to see three chateaux every day, in a fierce heat-wave. Judy and Ruth wisely refused to accompany us, and spent the days lazing in the sun, enjoying wine and delicious French bread and cheeses, to my considerable envy. We four returned to the camp-site in the evenings, hot and tired, when I had to transform the Dormobile from our day's transport into a kitchen, and cook the supper; then the stove had to be re-stowed, the bunks lowered and made up, when we could go to bed. In the morning the reverse process was necessary, to cook breakfast, and then prepare the vehicle to drive off again on the next culture tour. After four days, the only site in which I was interested was the camp, and I'd have given anything to stay there for a quiet day in the sun: this was not permitted. I never wish to see another chateau, nor have we ever been camping again!

Our continued progress westward to the sea coincided with the end of the heat-wave, and an onset of sustained gales and rain. We camped in an obliging farmer's field outside Vannes, where of course there were no latrine arrangements; James was appointed Chief Lavatory Man, and had to dig a pit, over which was rigged the brand new small latrine tent we had especially bought: it even had a pocket on the inside wall to hold the loo-paper. Michael had made a very efficient folding throne from a spare mahogany lavatory seat he happened to have lying about in his work-shop, and the frame of an old camp-stool; so we were in business, and there is a photograph of me at the initial enthronement. This proved to be the most successful aspect of the holiday.

Many years later, long after Michael's retirement, the loo-tent came into its own again. I had become the Tory representative in our small village, where, at general elections, our village hall becomes the Polling Station. The constituency head-quarters asked me to organise a rota of tellers, so the loo-tent was erected near the village hall, and there was just space in it for a small card-table and chair, and the loo-paper pocket held pens and paper. The visiting candidate, on his rounds, was delighted when told the history of the booth, but our hopes of a photograph in the local press came to nought, although the candidate was duly elected. The loo-tent has not seen the light of day for some years now, and I no longer work for any political party. Anyone going camping this summer?

After six months in Paris, Michael was appointed to the Admiralty as Deputy Director of Naval Intelligence under Rear Admiral Bill Graham who was the Director. A little later the administration of the three services was merged into the Ministry of Defence (MoD), and the Admiralty ceased to exist. The service Intelligence divisions also amalgamated, and Michael became the head of the naval branch, still under Bill Graham, who was appointed overall Director of the Defence Intelligence staff. In this capacity, besides being concerned in many other aspects, Michael was directly responsible for the large number of Naval Attachés, both ours posted abroad around the world, and also the foreign Naval Attachés in London, whose job it was to glean as much information as possible about all defence matters in this country, particularly relating to our Navy, and report back to their governments. Their first point of reference was to Michael's office, which gave them regular briefings of the information which we were willing to impart, but of course they did all in their power to find out more.

The Cold War was pretty icy at that time, and the Russians and other countries of the Eastern block were limited in their movements to a narrow radius around London, thus preventing them snooping round our Army and RAF bases, naval ports and dockyards. Of course any Attaché worth his salt tried to evade these proscriptions and escape the following watchers when information-gathering or on holiday tours with his family.

They were a friendly and delightful group, whom I also got to know well through the constant round of parties which we had to attend and give. These took the form of the inevitable cocktail-parties, dinners and receptions, the last held in the various embassies to celebrate the Emperor of Japan's birthday, American Independence Day, Russian Armed Forces' Day, the French 14th July, etc., and of course our own Queen's birthday.

The dining-room in our Wimbledon flat was small, but we had a spacious hall and large drawing-room; I was determined that our dinners should be different from the usual formal ones generally held, and more relaxed and fun. The cheese and wine parties, which later became so routinely dull and ordinary, had not then been thought of, and I like to think ours were among the first. We put up three card-tables in the hall, attractively set with red and white Arab *keffihas* as table-cloths, with candles and on each table three different bottles of claret; I served good home-made soup in cups while guests finished their pre-dinner drinks, then they were invited to help themselves in the dining-room to a wide selection of English cheeses, breads and rolls, with celery and large bowls of salad. Finally there would be a choice of puddings, and of course, coffee. Sometimes I made three or four big terrines of different patés instead of cheese. These parties were always successful, and became talked about, so that we seldom had any refusals.

Among the Naval Attachés we became particularly friendly with the Greek Captain Spiros Mourikis and his elegant and vivacious wife, Lilika; with the tall, attractive French Admiral Marcel Noel, and his witty wife Gilda; also with the Portuguese Lionel Cardoso, and his friend Felipe Gonzales, the Spaniard, whose wife had their eleventh child while they were in London.

It interested me always to watch the Japanese at the social events. Although it was twenty years since the war had ended, they were still mistrusted and disliked, and few people talked to them, so that they stood together in a group on the fringe at most parties. We had to entertain their Naval Attaché and his wife, and they came to one of our cocktail-parties, at which she wore an exquisite kimono and brocade obi, but she was a sad faced little woman, and when I gave her a black rectangular Japanese dish for flowers, she was pathetically grateful. I had taken a course in the Sogetsu school of flower-arranging in Singapore, but the sparse placing of three, five or seven blooms, each of regulation length, looked out of place and self-consciously affected back in England, so I was glad to find someone to whom to pass on the shallow containers. (I was awarded a diploma by the Sogetsu school, which I came across the other day: it is printed in Japanese, so could be a Christmas card for all I know!)

Perhaps our most amusing contacts among the Attachés were with the Soviets. Their senior Defence Attaché was a tough communist Army General (KGB); the senior Naval Attaché under him was Captain Boris Polikarpov, who had a sweet-faced rather homely wife who spoke no English. Under Boris there was a Commander Lebedev: he and his wife looked archetypal spies: he was tall and slim, with sparse ash-blonde hair brushed straight back, grease-glued to his scalp above a palid glistening brow and face, and pale protruding eyes; he had a thin cruel mouth, and it was not difficult to imagine him conducting brutal interrogations in the Lubianka. His wife, also tall, was a brassy bosmatic blonde, her face always immaculately enamelled with plenty of make-up, her eyes steely above high cheek-bones; her ample curves were usually encased in clinging black, her corseted cleavage deeply alluring. Both Lebedevs were obvious members of the KGB and were like caricatures of James Bond baddies. It always amused me to watch them at parties, but I kept well clear of them.

Boris Polikarpov, on the other hand, appeared to be a simple sailor, and we all became quite fond of him. He invited Emma and me to a concert in the Albert Hall given by the visiting Red Army Choir, which was a splendid occasion of rousing military choruses and nostalgic love-songs; Boris was charming to Emma, then aged eleven, and sent her Soviet stamps, and it was his encouragement that lead to her learning Russian, which was later to be one of her 'A' level subjects. We never knew, but feared what became of Boris, for he became involved with our police, in a way which, though amusing to us, cannot have gone down well with his masters. He and Felipe Gonzales were close friends, and just before the Spaniard left London, the two men met for a final farewell; it must have been a very bibulous lunch, and when it broke up, the rush-hour had begun. Boris was driving home, rather the worse for wear, and, failing to see a red traffic light ahead, drove into the back of the waiting car in front; he reversed smartly, straight into the car which had drawn up behind him; swearing, he once more shot forward into the car in front for the second time! The police arrived, and failing to spot Boris' CD plates, whisked him away to cool off in the cells overnight; it wasn't until the following morning that Boris was coherent enough to summon help from his embassy. He was not immediately sent home, but was relieved of his post early, not long after that, and we still wonder what became of him, and if he ended up in the Siberian salt-mines.

I much enjoyed watching the guests at the diplomatic parties: the men would gather in knots, exchanging gossip and information, and the women were left to themselves. Michael always maintained that in his several Intelligence appointments, he did a great part of his work at these gatherings.

During the school holidays when the children were at home, I tried to cut down on our entertaining, and also on the parties to which we were invited, except for purely family affairs in which the children were included; among these was the annual visit to the Royal Military Tournament in the summer, to which all the foreign Attachés and their families were invited, and we filled a large block of seats.

We spent Christmas 1965 at Homme. The house was full, as Michael's brother Ernle and his wife Pam, with their five boys, were all there too. A cousin of the family, Robin Harvey, was then the vicar of Much Marcle; he was a strange man, pale and prosy, with a permanently glistening countenance and a mincing walk; he would stand, eyes downcast, hands clasped limply over his waistcoat, and I am afraid that, behind his back, we used to enjoy a good deal of ribaldry at his expense. The family all walked across the park for the midnight service on Christmas Eve; it was a crisp and starry night, and the church was candle-lit and decorated with holly. We took our places, filling two pews, and sat awaiting Robin. The church was full, and we all nodded and smiled to each other as we waited. Eventually, after three-quarters of an hour, my father-in-law, Kyrle, went out to see where Robin was; after a few minutes he returned, looking harassed and upset, and took Michael out into the churchyard: Robin was lying

Michael saying goodbye to General Sir Michael Carver, Singapore, 1969.

under the old hollow yew-tree, having celebrated Christmas early and a little too freely. He was carried back to the Vicarage, and we walked back across the park in a state of some hilarity. Poor Robin thereafter fought a losing battle against the demon alcohol, and died a few years later. This story is told and retold throughout the family, and continues to be enjoyed by young and old.

Michael had for many years been a member of the International Co-operative Wine Society, and while we lived in London, we joined the dining off-shoot, attending their quarterly dinners in the hall of the Royal College of Surgeons, and sometimes in the summer at the zoo. It was fun pitting one's taste-buds against those of the experts, in marking out of seven points the seven wines served at each dinner, and afterwards wandering round the cases of the surgeons' grisly exhibits in glass bottles, or in summer-time, the animals in the zoo.

Ernle, Michael's brother, also in the Navy, had been appointed to the NATO staff in Oslo, where Pam accompanied him, their boys joining them for school holidays. Pam returned home rather abruptly, and shortly afterwards, we were introduced to the wife of a Group Captain in the RAF who was also stationed in Oslo. The advent of this determined little woman soon had Ernle's marriage on the rocks. I well remember her coming to our Wimbledon flat, and saying to me:

'I love that man, and I'm going to have him!'

Neither Michael nor I liked her, and both we and my in-laws were shocked by the change she wrought in Ernle. His marriage ended, and he married her, which brought nothing but sadness to the whole family, including his five sons, which persists to this day.

While in London, with the children at school, I began to learn a little about antiques, and became a 'runner': that is, I searched for, and bought from junk shops, auctions and markets outside London, items which I then sold on to London dealers at a profit. If the grandly accommodated antique shops in Wimbledon village or Putney were not interested, I took them to the Caledonian Market. It was great fun, and I learned a lot. There was a junk-yard at East Challow which was on our route to Homme, and we never passed it without stopping; James became involved as well, and we nearly always were able to pick up a bargain of some kind, but alas, it has gone now.

To the delight of the family, Michael was promoted to Rear Admiral early in 1967. My mother, then aged eighty-five, proudly boasted of having for her three sons-in-law, a general (General Sir Ian

Riches, Royal Marines), a bishop (Bishop John Armstrong, Bishop of Bermuda, late Chaplain-of-the-Fleet), and now an admiral, Michael. His promotion brought a new appointment, as Chief of Staff to the Commander-in-Chief, Combined Forces, Far East, so we began to pack up once more, to return to Singapore.

CHAPTER 15

Singapore, 1967

'COOKIE DEAD! Cookie lie on his bed, I sure he DEAD!' cried Siew Fong hysterically, when she returned from finding out why Cookie had not materialised one morning to cook Michael's breakfast.

The Chinese are extremely superstitious about death, and will not stay on in any house in which death has recently occurred. They move their dying relatives out of their homes and into Death Houses, a few days before death actually takes place, where they are looked after until the end. We were therefore anxious that Cookie should not have died under our roof, for we foresaw that we might lose our entire household staff, just as the busy Christmas season of entertaining was about to begin.

Siew Fong, who had not entered Cookie's room in the servants' quarters, was calmed and Michael told me to keep the servants busy in our part of the house, while he quickly rang the BMH (British Military Hospital) for an ambulance, and Cookie was borne away, having had a 'heart attack', the servants were told. A little later they were informed that he had very sadly died on the way to hospital. I think they knew perfectly well, as we did, that he was indeed dead in his room, but faces were saved, and Good Joss was maintained on the house.

On our return to Singapore, we had inherited a lovely house from Michael's predecessor, together with the household staff, in which we had to make some changes, as the butler, or No. 1 Boy, was due to retire. Soon, the eldest of his family, was promoted to the post, which left those of Nos. 2 and 3 Boys vacant, for which there was no-one available through the army department which was responsible for the domestic staffing of senior officers' quarters. Amah, as the wash-*amah* was known, then took a hand. Why must we have house *boys*, she asked (talking through Soon, her son), why not *girls*? She had two well brought-up daughters who would work well, she promised, and what was more important, would take orders from Soon, their elder brother, whose authority over men we rather doubted, for he was a shy and diffident young man. So Siew Fong and Siew Wah arrived, and the household settled down happily, and was run very efficiently: that is, except for Cookie (who was not a member of Soon's family), whom we had also inherited from our predecessors, and who was temperamental, an indifferent cook and over-fond of the bottle. After his untimely death, we were left with no cook, with an awesome programme of entertaining about to begin. For a few hours I panicked, for once more the relevant army department could provide no-one. Then Soon approached me, with Amah just behind.

'Mem, my mother say she know someone. You like she ask him? She say he velly good cookie, and a good man she know long time.'

I could have hugged him, and Amah too, who went off down the drive to find this paragon (which he proved to be). That afternoon he was installed, and stayed with us until we left Singapore two years later. We were a very happy household, and our family became increasingly fond of the Soons, with whom we kept in touch for several years after we returned to England.

It was great fun renewing contact with old friends such as Charles Letts, and Tan Chin Tuan and his wife Helene; once again we were lucky in that Michael's office was in Phoenix Park, and Nelson House, where we lived nearby, was also in the Tanglin area of the city. Michael was Chief-of-Staff to the C-in-C, General Sir Michael Carver, and later to Admiral Sir Peter Hill-Norton, two very different men, both brilliantly clever but neither of them easy; each of them destined to become Chief of the Defence Staff in overall command of Britain's defence, and later to be ennobled into the peerage.

Michael Carver was tall, thin and gaunt of face; I have a letter I wrote to my mother describing the first time I met him, when I sat next to him at a dinner-party: 'He has a long thin nose, and thin lips, and was never still of feature for an instant. I hardly had to open my mouth throughout dinner, for he never shut his!' I did not find him an easy dinner companion either then or when I knew him better, although I always enjoyed observing him from a distance: his personality radiated cold dynamism and calculating purpose.

Peter Hill-Norton, another vibrant character, could be ruthlessly determined too, but he also had charm and a sense of humour, which gave him a warmer personality.

After dinner at a Chinese restaurant in China-town one evening, Michael and I were picking our way up a street to our car, over refuse and drains, when we heard a tremendous cacophony from a side-street where we could see crowds of people and myriads of lights. We went to investigate, and found a *wayang* in progress, that is, a Chinese mandarin theatre; it was taking place on an improvised stage built across the street on bamboo scaffolding, the stage being quite small, with an open area behind it acting as green-room and scenery store; the cast applied their make-up there, or waited to go on stage, chatting together the while (I saw one man enjoyably picking his feet!). This was all clearly visible from the street beyond the raised stage, on which from the front, the play was being watched by a large crowd squatting on the road, or standing leaning against the footlights, causing the bamboo structure to sway alarmingly. Two musicians stood to one side, one playing a two-stringed type of violin, the other a form of bamboo xylophone. The actors and actresses were heavily made up, with whitened faces, rouge and eyepaint superimposed on to the white masks. They semi-chanted, and semi-spoke their parts in nasal twanging voices; stylised battles were fought with wooden swords, and the villain's face was painted horribly green, black and white. The audience momentarily transferred their attention to us when we appeared, and seemed amused by our interest. We watched for a while, and would seek out *wayangs* after that, enjoying the crude spectacle and noise, and the total thrall in which the audience was always held.

We had to have many 'visiting firemen' to stay, that is, service or government personnel on working visits for meetings or conferences, and although they were entertained at many formal dinner-parties, I think they much preferred the informal nights of sight-seeing in the city, when we took them to *wayangs* or night markets. These were held in different areas on set evenings in the week, when stalls were set up lining the streets, brilliantly lit by naptha flares or hissing acetylene lamps, the vendors shouting their wares. You could buy anything, from rattan furniture to orchids, from T-shirts to knives, and we bartered for all we were worth. We might stop to eat at one of the food stalls, perched on high wooden stools, selecting the raw ingredients for our supper and watching them being cooked in a wok over a calor-gas flame or charcoal brazier; we would eat from coolie-bowls with chopsticks, and a youth would be sent to another stall to fetch us cans of Tiger beer or 7–Up. These open-air entertainments in the cool of the tropical nights were always noisy and friendly, without threat or thought of possible violence lurking; the streets would be full of happy people of all nationalities enjoying themselves. It was a feature of our life in Singapore at that time which we all enjoyed, as did our delighted official guests.

James and Emma came out for the summer holidays, and were very happy to be back in Singapore. However, their travels to and from school were not without incident during the next two years. On returning to England in September 1967 their aircraft was delayed for several days; to begin with we were told there was no trace of our children, who were supposed to have been in the care of the airline BOAC, as unaccompanied minors. I was beside myself with anxiety, until after forty-eight hours we were told that they had been found safely lodged in a hotel in Delhi, from which they were not allowed to stray while awaiting the fitting of a new engine to their aircraft. This had to be flown out from England, and the first to arrive was found to be faulty, so a second one had to be sent for. Communications were slower in those days, and both children arrived late back at school that term. On their flight out for Christmas, they were once again delayed, this time at Beirut, where once more they were put into a hotel for the thirty-six hour delay. James simply slept through the long waits for onward transport, on beds, benches or floors, whatever was available (he was then fourteen). Emma, at thirteen, was more nervous, and adventurous. When they eventually arrived at Singapore, Emma was strained and unwell, so I kept her in bed for twenty-four hours. During that day she asked me to get something from her small attaché-case, in which, on opening it, I found two paper-back books with lurid covers depicting semi-nude women. I heard a gasp from the bed. Emma had forgotten what I would find, and she awaited my reaction with some anxiety.

'Oh, are they good?' I asked, 'May I borrow them when you've read them? I've always wondered what stories by that author are like. Where did you get them?'

Heaving a sigh of relief at my apparent equanimity, Emma replied:

'A black man gave them to me at the Beirut hotel, Mummy; he was awfully nice, and I had dinner with him.'

My maternal fears flared, and I visualised my innocent little girl being propositioned, or even kidnapped into white slavery, but carefully I asked:

'Oh yes, what was he like? Did you find out anything about him?'

'He was something to do with rubber, he was going back to Kuala Lumpur, he said,' Emma replied, without much further interest, so I dropped the conversation.

Our children were flown out for two of the three school holidays each year, so I applied to the RAF for an 'Indulgence' passage to UK to return to Homme for Easter, where we could all be together with my in-laws. In due course I was summoned to Changi to board an aircraft of Transport Command to Brize Norton. As I handed my passport over the desk to be stamped, a head peered over my shoulder, and a voice asked:

'Is that name Kyrle-Pope? Are you by any chance Emma's mother? She and I spent a day together at Beirut last December during one of BOAC's inevitable flight delays.'

He turned out to be Sir Claude Fenner, a tall, good-looking and most charming man, who was sun-tanned to a deep bronze, which presumably accounted for Emma's description of him as a 'black man'. He told me he was the Chairman of the Rubber Institute of Malaya. We travelled together, spending a most entertaining day which included a fuelling stop at Gan in the Maldive Islands, where we had lunch in the RAF mess after a glorious swim in the clear turquoise sea. We stopped again at Akrotiri in Cyprus, where I was able to buy a large basket of oranges to take home.

As Michael was on the staff of the overall C-in-C of all three services, I had no particular wifely duties concerning the Navy or the other two services. I have never partaken in coffee mornings if they could be avoided, and so, in termtime anyway, I found myself often unoccupied in the mornings. I had long wanted to try my hand at painting in oils, and began to make inquiries about taking lessons. There were certainly classes that I could attend, but I found that the students were already experienced, and I hesitated to join in, remembering my total lack of artistic ability in water-colours from my schooldays. I mentioned it to some of my closer friends, suggesting that the only requirements to join the class I was planning was that we should all be roughly the same age, and that none should have worked in oils before. I found several friends all avid to try, and at the same time heard of a qualified Chinese teacher who, on being approached, showed considerable enthusiasm and amusement at the project.

Mr Sim gave us a list of the equipment we would need, and suggested we buy large sheets of hardboard, have them cut into eight rectangles, and then paint the rough sides with white undercoat, and these would be our 'canvases'.

We met in each other's houses in turn, the first lesson being at ours, at which we were told we were to spend the morning learning to mix colours. We were told to mix any we pleased, and to paint small patches on our canvases, not trying to produce a picture or design, but just haphazardly, and Mr Sim would come round to see what we were doing. It was extraordinarily daunting having no subject, pattern or precepts to follow, but we all puddled about on our palettes, and after a couple of hours when we were told to stop and look at each other's efforts, it was extremely depressing to see the patchwork of muddy daubs we had all produced. All, that is, except for Ann Hibbert (wife of Reg, who a few years later became our ambassador in Paris), who had painted the same patches of different blends as we had, but her colours were clear shades, and somehow there was a pleasing design to her arrangement of blocks.

'Ah!' said Mr Sim, when he looked at Ann's canvas, 'now this lady can paint! We will see in future lessons how she will develop and express herself!' and how right he was, for she was even selling some of her pictures within six months.

It was the greatest fun, and we all progressed in various forms and at different speeds; we tried still life, perspective, landscapes, flowers, glass and silver arranged on a table, and finally, at my request, during the last few weeks before I left Singapore, we attempted portraits. I had always wanted to do this, and I think if I had been able to study properly, I might have achieved some ability. We began by trying to do self-portraits.

'Who is that very old, sick-looking Red Indian woman you have painted, Sue?' I was asked by one of my so-called friends!

We went on to paint our Malay *kabun* (gardener), who was notoriously lazy, fat and amiable. His physical structure was all in curves, and his skin-tones were a glorious blend of cadmium greens and ochres, all the greens and golds of the spectrum, in fact. We subsequently painted someone's wash-*amah*, and the difference between Chinese and the Malay colouring was fascinating to break down and study, and try to reproduce.

Mr Sim spoke English well, but retained typical Chinese inscrutability; he never criticised our efforts unkindly and always tried to find something encouraging to say, and he never laughed at us, although I am sure our daubs must have given him much amusement.

CHAPTER 16

Bangkok, Chiang-Mai and Penang, 1967

I HAD ALWAYS WANTED to see Bangkok and also Borneo; the latter had to wait another year, but the opportunity to visit Thailand arose in December, when Michael had to attend a meeting of SEATO (South East Asian Treaty Organisation) in Bangkok. He took a few days leave at the same time, so that we could fly up to Chiang-Mai, then an unspoilt small town in north-west Thailand encircled by little villages each specialising in various crafts.

In Bangkok, Charles Letts had arranged for us to stay with a charming young couple, Richard and Valerie Evans; Richard worked for Jardine Waugh, with which Charles had business connections. I had flown up a day ahead of Michael, and was met off the aircraft by a dapper little Thai wearing a pale blue silk suit with a toning darker collar, who told me his name was Woudhjira Picmontri, but that he was always known as Woudh. I was to learn that he was the prop and mainstay of Jardine's Bangkok office. While Woudh retrieved my baggage, I was taken to the office, where I was introduced to Phensei Nivatgong, a pretty Thai girl who had worked for two years in London, so she spoke English well, and it was arranged that she should take me to see the temple of the Reclining Buddha.

This was in a large enclosed area containing several small *stubas* which were entirely covered in gold leaf, each one containing large or smaller effigies of Buddha. Trees grew around the courtyard, and saffron-robed monks sat or lounged on seats, rocks or on the ground. The temples were roofed with glistening red, yellow and green curved tiles, like fish scales, and the entrances and gable-ends were of heavily gilded carving, the latter upturned with dragons' heads and tails pointing skyward. Wind, or prayer, bells hung round the eaves, with brass plates pendant from the clappers, and as these caught the breeze, every bell sounded a different clear sweet note, filling the air with enchanting sound.

The Reclining Buddha was a huge grotesque statue, lying on his side with his head raised and supported on one hand. He was covered with flaking gold leaf, and was not inspiring, at least not to an unbeliever, although of enormous size.

The next morning I was up early to be taken to the Floating Market. At a jetty on the main river, I was handed over to my guide, and handed into a boat. Near the banks were bamboo rafts, roughly lashed, carrying teak logs which were being floated down-stream from the forests in the north; the huge logs had large holes through one end, to take the chains by which elephants had dragged and pushed them down from the hills to the river. A precarious game of badminton was being played between a plump mother and her eleven or twelve year-old son, each balanced on a different floating log, with much barracking by other younger members of the family who retrieved the shuttledore when necessary.

Timber-yards and boat-building slips lined the banks, and rough teak houses on stilts were built out into the river, each with steps down to the water from its veranda. Women were washing clothes in the filthy river, children swam in it; buckets of refuse were thrown in and refilled with the day's supply of washing water; the drinking water was sold from a boat manned by two women who called at the steps of those who hailed them, ladling water into the big Ali Baba type pottery jars which stood on every veranda, together with pot plants, and orchids, arching out gracefully over the river.

After a while, we turned into a narrow side-stream, which at once narrowed again, and became leafy and purely residential; here each house had its patch of garden round it, and tucked into the bank a bamboo raft smothered with mauve and purple morning glory, which my guide told me was a culinary herb.

Traffic became purely domestic. A narrow boat, piled with charcoal, was poled by a man standing aft, clad in black shirt and loose black cotton trousers and wearing a wide straw hat, who called his wares to the river-bank housewives. As we neared the market, the river narrowed and traffic became congested, other boats joining us, so that bumps and collisions were unavoidable, causing much laughter and ribald backchat. Naked babies played on verandas, and waved to us as we passed.

More and more boats were moving in both directions now, mostly paddled by a woman standing in the stern; they were laden with vegetables and fruit, limes, durian, bananas and papaya; some with herbs, and others with noodles and delicious smelling mixtures cooking on glowing charcoal braziers. They stopped when hailed, when often a purchase was paid for in kind, some flowers bought, and a basket of cucumbers or a few eggs given in exchange. Eventually the crush of boats was such that the banks and verandas had become long arcades of marketing, and we were hemmed in and unable to move . . . But Ah! we are rescued, the Law is at hand, in the form of a policeman, standing on the roof of a small sampan, directing the traffic with the aid of a piercing whistle and his large white gloves!

In the market centre, I was invited to go ashore to see a silk-weaving factory; I stepped from boat to boat to reach the bank, hoping I would somehow find my own boat again, and was led into a large wooden barn-like building, where the clack of looms echoed among the teak rafters. There was everything on sale here to delight the tourist, from postcards to carved teak elephants. However I was glad of one facility provided, and lest he should give me up for lost in the throng, I modestly said to my guide that I'd rejoin him in a moment.

'Toilet?' he asked, 'I come with you.'

Horrors! Is he coming to protect me from dragons, or to offer his company in a friendly two-seater, I wondered. In fact he must have been expecting my requirement, and led me to the two available 'Ladies' cubicles; the door of one would not shut, so the resulting queue for the second was somewhat lengthy, with the interval between bolting in, and relieved emergence of each desperate tourist, of considerable duration. Such a wait for me was not a pleasing or practical prospect, so I headed for the draughty cubicle, my guide hot-foot behind me, to the amazement of the ladies in the other queue. However, just as I dived in, the guide withdrew a little, and as I began to battle to get the door anyway partly closed, there came a slight tentative pressure from the outside, and very discreetly, the door almost shut, and remained so, without springing wide again. Blessings on my tactful guide, preserving for me some semblance of privacy, from the other waiting ladies anyway, if not from him!

We then started back, and passed a group of little girls, squatting on a raft, opening a pile of large mussel-like fish, with shells of a brilliant turquoise colour. Further on I saw an old grey-haired man, dressed in the peasants' black cotton, sitting resignedly in a small sampan moored to the bank, while his wife, standing over him, cut his hair. She too was old and lined of face, intent on her task.

We emerged at length into the main river, and went upstream to see the royal gilded barges in their sheds. The King uses them to go in procession once every two or three years, to present new robes to the Buddhist monks at the Royal temple of the Emerald Buddha. The King's barge is manned by sixty oarsmen in scarlet livery.

Phensei met us when we landed, and took me by car to see the Temple of the Emerald Buddha, standing in large ornate grounds surrounded by many *stubas*. Some of these were built in Cambodian style, and there was a model in stone of the temples at Angkor Wat; I asked Phensei if she had been there.

'No,' she said, 'and Thai people cannot go now. There is no friendship left with Cambodia any more.' A charming description of a break in diplomatic relations, I thought.

Inside the Royal Temple, the Emerald Buddha sits on a pedestal twenty feet high, in a golden bower, which was cleverly lit to show up the gleaming jewel and gold robes. The emerald must be 18"–24" high, and came originally from India. The King changes the garments of the Buddha himself, for each of the four seasons; when I saw him, he was wearing an enveloping robe of gold, covering his shoulders, for winter.

After lunch, Phensei and I drove out to 'Timland', which was (and perhaps still is) a tourist centre outside the city, where in two hours or so one can watch a number of typical Thai pursuits. On the way we called at the house being built for Phensei and the Army officer whom she was to marry a month later. Richard and Valerie had told me that she came from a very wealthy family, and that a girl from such a background would expect a solitaire diamond engagement ring of from five to eight carats. Her house was quite large with a big veranda.

'Far too big!' said Woudh, 'it will need seven servants to keep it clean.' But I gathered such a financial commitment would be no problem for Phensei.

Timland proved to be a large country estate; it had a zoo, gardens, and examples of local agriculture. The programme began with a pair of elephants working with teak logs, in a clear piece of ground between two ponds; each beast had a mahout kneeling on its neck and, working together, they pulled logs out of one pond, and moved them over to roll into the other. It was a fairly superficial display for the benefit of tourists, but it was interesting to watch how they used their trunks and tusks as a form of three-pronged tongs to lift and manoeuvre the tree trunks.

We watched Thai dancing next, which illustrated a story from Rama, of a Goddess who stole a precious stone from the Heavens; the wicked God of Thunder was sent to retrieve the gem, but each time he nearly snatched it from the hand of the Goddess of Lightning, she tossed it into the air, and dazzled him, and finally she escaped.

There was then an exhibition of Thai boxing, in which anything is permissible, including biting and the laying out of one's opponent with a sharp clock under one ear with one's heel. The audience much enjoyed the fun, and shouted encouragement from the ring-side.

The cock-fight which followed was not so enjoyable, but then another form of human conflict was staged with swords in both hands; this was most entertaining, as the two contestants, agile young men, actually lost their tempers, so the blows which should have been pulled or faked became vicious, and one man finally crept out of the arena looking decidedly sorry for himself.

We then wandered off, and found ourselves looking over a low rail into a snake-pit, where a man was feeding and handling cobras; there must have been at least a dozen of them, writhing and nestling cosily round the man's legs. A shuddersome sight, I thought, and was glad to move on.

Michael flew up from Singapore that evening, and the next morning we took an early flight to Chiang-Mai, which was then still an unspoilt pretty little town, with unmetalled roads, and only one modern hotel, the Susi Wongse, where we stayed. It was a two-hour flight, and we flew at only 4,000 ft, and so had clear views of the countryside below. The rice harvest was in full swing, and we could see the cutting and threshing going on.

At Chiang-Mai we were met by our guide, an enchantingly pretty girl called Amphai who we found very knowledgeable and with a delightful sense of humour; she spoke English well, and had a pleasing soft speaking voice. After lunch, we set off by car for the temple at Doi Suthep, which is in the hills about sixty kilometres from Chiang-Mai.

Like Bangkok, Chiang-Mai lies in the centre of a flat plain, which is given over almost entirely to growing rice, and which is encircled by hills. We drove through the agricultural land and small villages, and were able to watch the harvesting. The rice padi dries out as the grain matures and ripens, and then is reflooded when replanted. The fields are divided up by narrow raised paths, called *bunds* which at planting time, being higher, remain dry when the fields are flooded. Everyone possible works in the fields then and at harvest, and both operations are done in a co-operative method, each land-owner rewarding his neighbours for their labour with a party. The resulting crop remains in sole possession of its owner, and is not shared out. Reaping is done by hand with a slightly curved knife, the rice being tied into quite small sheaves, which are left to dry for a day or two on top of the long stubble. When dry, it is threshed by beating each sheaf into an enormous shallow plaited basket about 6 ft in diameter, and 2 ft deep. The grain is then winnowed by being tossed in the air with basket shovels, and then dried on large mats in the sun.

The road wound up the steep hillside, through densely wooded jungle, many of the trees of tremendous height, others heavily in flower. Among the latter were many with a cloud of feathery blossom smothering the foliage, some white, some pink and some dark red. Amphai told us that these were lacquer trees, which have resinous sap similar to rubber trees, which is collected in the same way as latex by tappers, to be used to make the lacquer articles for which Chiang-Mai is well-known. We stopped to look more closely, but as I reached up to pick a spray of flowers, Amphai and our driver, with one voice, yelled:

'DON'T TOUCH THEM!' Apparently if you touch the plant, you absorb a toxin which causes vomiting, and also a rash and irritation of the skin; the lacquer workers suffered from this a good deal, and never really became immune.

On and up we went, eventually reaching the end of the road, where we had to leave the car and climb 348 steps up to the temple. The steps are flanked by protective dragons called *Naga*, their heads at the foot, and their long scaled bodies of coloured tiles rippling up each side of the flights of steps. As we climbed, we were haunted by a weird melody being played by a crippled boy at the foot of the steps, on a bamboo set of pipes. Nearer the top, the sound of his playing having faded, instead, we heard a gay lilting little tune played by an old man on a bamboo xylophone, as a reward for the long climb, I felt. From the walls of the temple were breath-taking views for miles, the hills dropped away steeply, and were covered with vegetation on which we looked down; we watched humming-birds hovering over clusters of flowers, and many butterflies. Amphai encouraged me to ring the enormous bronze temple bell, but it was all I could do to move its heavy teak clapper; the sound was deep and resonant, and echoed down the hill-side.

We crossed from the temple to a neighbouring peak, 8,000 ft above sea-level, to see a forest research station, where tea, coffee, roses and eucalyptus were being grown experimentally; the ground was terraced round the contours of the hill; the eucalyptus trees had glassy smooth bark, streaked in purple, cobalt blue and acid green.

Amphai collected us the next morning to go to see the small cottage industries in villages round Chiang-Mai. We started at a wood-carving

Naga Steps, Doi Suthep, Chiang-Mai.

factory; most articles were of teak, some of monkey-pod, a dark beautifully grained wood, which was more expensive. We watched youths drawing the intricate pattern freehand on Buddhist 'sermon-chairs' and tables, later to be carved; young boys and girls sanding down completed carvings; women lacquering and applying gold leaf; all were busy together, of all ages. The shed was open on all sides, admitting light and air, and the scent of fresh timber filled our nostrils.

From there we visited the silversmiths' village. We were told that to make the silverware, old silver coins of pure metal are melted down. A woman was hammering a design on to a silver bowl from the inside, she used a log as an anvil, with a thick pad on it of some thick gum-like substance, which held the bowl firm, and acted as a cushion as the design was worked. When finished, it was passed to a young woman who immersed it in a tub of water and scrubbed it with tamarind, to bring the silver to a brilliant white polish. I bought here, not silver, but a pair of small antique opium weights, shaped like ducks. Reproductions of these are made today, but I think mine are genuine old ones, for their surface and moulding are very worn and rounded; modern ones are sharper and more easily recognised as the frogs, monkeys etc. which they represent.

There was time before lunch to visit one of the lacquer factories. This was in a compound with several sheds in which the various processes took place. Under the owner's house, among the wooden stilts which supported it, sat two old women, cross-legged, weaving the basic forms of the articles to be lacquered out of finely split lengths of bamboo; plates, bowls, trays, boxes, model ducks, owls and fish, all were first woven in bamboo, and then painted with a mixture of clay and lacquer to fill the cracks and interstices. Next each item was scraped or shaven, to remove any roughness, so as to ensure a smooth surface on which to build up the lacquer in many layers; when seven or eight have been applied, the ornamental design, to be left ungilded, is painted on free-hand with an ink of vinegar and wood-ash. We watched this being done by a boy of thirteen. The article is then covered with gold leaf, after which it is washed, when the gold leaf adheres to the lacquer but is lifted from the vinegar/ash barrier, so that the decoration shows black through the gold. Needless to say, the water in which the item has been washed is very carefully strained, and the resulting gold leaf sediment sent for recycling. We bought here

A parasol being painted in Bosang – the umbrella village – near Chiang-Mai.

many enchanting little gold lacquer boxes in the shape of ducks and owls, the feathers, eyes and expressions all outlined in black where they had been drawn. They made ideal little presents, unusual, and entirely characteristic of Chiang-Mai.

Amphai allowed us little time for lunch before whisking us off to Bosang, the umbrella village, where everyone of all ages is involved in making parasols of silk or paper. In the middle of the first compound was a small girl of three of four sitting on a log, solemn and unsmiling; she had another log in front of her on which was a mess of pulp, the bark of the paper tree, which she was beating with two wooden mallets. Her pulped fibre was then boiled in water, and transferred into a large stone sink of cold water. A woman was dipping a screen of nylon gauze into this, and when she lifted it horizontally from the water, which streamed through it, a gelatinous film was left, trapping some fibre on the screen; this was put in full sunlight to dry. The resulting fibrous tissue could be peeled off the screen, and it was this we saw being slapped on to the bamboo spokes and frame of umbrellas with a lacquer paint and gum mixture; two layers of paper were applied, which when dry, were painted free-hand by boys and girls aged ten to twelve in brilliant colours and attractive designs of flowers, birds and butterflies. Everyone in the village was working, and in all the compounds were dozens of finished open umbrellas, standing out to dry. I expect that this is all much more sophisticated now, with metalled roads and modern production methods, for Chiang-Mai has become a tourist boom town, thereby losing much of the charm which we found so delightful.

Our next call was to Shinawatra's, the renowned silk factory, where we watched the silk being woven on huge old teak looms, in many vivid colours. From floor to ceiling in the shop, the shelves were filled with every colour, in checks, stripes and prints. It was like an Aladdin's cave of jewels, and it proved to be an expensive afternoon.

We then headed for a hill village in the Lampoon district where a White Karen tribe had settled, having come over the border from nearby Burma, where they were continually being harassed. We turned off the main road to climb a laterite track into the woods, where the Karens had built their wooden houses on stilts under the trees. Before we could climb out of the car, several urchins were running up, demanding:

'Cigar-ette! CIGAR-ETTE!'

Then little girls followed, several already smoking small clay pipes fitted to a bamboo stem; the children start to smoke from their earliest years.

The women and girls were shy of being photographed, but the children were keen, once they had established a modelling fee of one cigarette. A grey-haired man in a black shirt and sarong was holding his naked baby, and clustering round him were several naked lads, slim young striplings of eight to twelve years; I asked if I could photograph the group, and did so, duly handing out the payment in cigarettes. The father looked scornfully at the single cigarette in his hand, and demanded fair rates, i.e. one for the baby too (it was eleven months old).

The people were small and quite dark skinned; there were few old people. Buffalo, families of black pigs, hens and dogs all scratched about between the houses, which were scruffy, the ground littered with rubbish. The houses all had an open platform built out from the main floor level, and it was out here that the cooking of the evening meal was beginning, and on one we saw a heap of raw cotton.

The women of the tribe wear identical dress, which they spin, dye, weave and make up themselves: a blouse of coarse black cloth embroidered with red thread and bands of white seeds was worn above a long skirt or sarong dyed red, with borders of similar embroidery. They wore heavy dull silver ear-rings, and bangles round their ankles; they were barefoot. The unmarried girls wore long white sack-like dresses, with a sash of red braid high under their arm-pits; there was no variation from these two styles of women's dress.

'Well,' said Michael's brother Ernle, to whom I was describing this later, 'at least you know where you are!'

The younger children, up to eleven or twelve years, wore nothing at all, so you knew where you were there, too!

We had taken some small coins with us, and when the cigarettes ran out we offered a coin for each photograph; this brought a mob of fighting, scrambling children about us. I had become separated from Michael and our guide, and when I produced a coin to give to a pretty girl, my arm was seized, my hand pulled down and my fingers prised open by a crowd of urchins who completely surrounded me, all shrieking at the tops of their voices:

'One baht! One cigarette! One baht! One baht!' I had to use all my strength to wrench myself free, and although they were only children, it was not a moment I would care to repeat.

We returned to the car, and as we lurched down the track, we were followed by the filthy urchins, still yelling for cigarettes or coins. They were really extremely unwashed, very different from the fastidiously clean Thais.

The next day Michael flew back to Bangkok to resume his business meetings, and Amphai accompanied me back to Shinawatra's to choose more silks, undisturbed by masculine impatience!

On our way through the streets of Chiang-Mai, I saw two youths on the crowded pavement; they were slim, with oriental features but rosy cheeks, and they wore black satin quartered skull-caps, topped by a scarlet button, short black bolero jackets over white shirts, and baggy low-crotched blue trousers; Amphai told me that they were of the Meo tribe, who originated in China and have lived for generations from growing opium. They had then been settled in Chiang-Mai province. Each boy carried a wooden frame, like a large scythe in shape; at each arc or corner, tethered by one foot, was a bright green parakeet with a crimson head, which was obviously being hawked around to sell. They made a most exotic sight.

I flew back to Bangkok and the next day the Evans' and we met our Naval Attaché John, and Molly Sayers, for lunch in the Oriental hotel. The restaurant was on the tenth floor, so we all stepped into the lift, the lift-boy pressed a button, and with an imperceptible hesitation, we slowly began to rise. Jokes were made about faulty lifts, getting trapped, suffocated etc. At the tenth floor the lift stopped; the doors did not open.

The boy pressed the door opening button.

Nothing happened.

He tried again. Still nothing.

'Try moving to another floor,' John suggested.

No. 9 was pressed. No effect.

Other buttons were pushed, including the alarm. Nothing happened.

We were debating what to do next, when suddenly, without warning, the lift started to descend. It stopped after a few feet.

There were eight people in the lift, which was stated to be safe for ten; I wondered where the other two would have fitted in, for we eight were packed in pretty tight. I began to wonder for how long the air would last.

Suddenly we began to go down again, a few more feet.

Then we stopped.

In fits and starts, and jerks and stops, we slowly descended through nine floors. At the first floor we stopped, and the doors flew open.

Eight people can move pretty fast, I discovered. Laughing and joking in our relief, we began the long climb up the stairs to the tenth floor. I was surprisingly glad of the banisters for surreptitious support. John said:

'Well, I think we all need a stiff drink after that!'

'Yes, please, a large brandy and ginger ale,' said I before the words were out of his mouth.

Molly, Valerie and I then confessed that our knees were still shaking, and neither Molly nor I could hold our glasses still!

After lunch, seven of us, no word uttered, began the long descent to the ground floor, by the stairs. When we reached the bottom, John was awaiting us derisively, having braved the lift, which had worked perfectly.

Later that afternoon Michael and I left Bangkok.

Woudh had reserved an air-conditioned compartment for us in the night train to Penang. He warned us not to touch the food on the train, and had thought to provide us with boxes of three packed meals, and we bought fruit from the platform hawkers.

Passing slowly through the purlieus of the city was a shocking eye-opener; the abject poverty and filthy living conditions were a sad contrast to that part of Bangkok which we had been shown.

It was dark by 6.00 pm but we settled with our books and drinks in our comfortable compartment, and after an early picnic supper, we went to bed. The following morning we watched the country slipping by; our speed never exceeded 30 mph for the whole twenty-seven hours journey, and we stopped at every station, so we were able to observe the *kampongs* we passed in detail. The wooden houses, thatched with either palm or teak leaves, were clustered near the railway line, often with a narrow *klong* (man-made irrigation canal) running between them and the line, with villagers washing themselves, their clothes or their vegetables in the water. There were drifts of mauve water hyacinth floating on the surface of some *klongs*, the leaves large and spade-shaped, the bell-shaped flowers thickly clustered on stems up to twelve inches high. They were beautiful, but I was told that they spread so fast, and are so thick, that they can choke and completely dam the *klongs*, which have to be constantly cleared.

We gradually climbed into a hilly area, and at one point when crossing a bridge over a wide river, we were delighted to see elephants working below us in the water, easing teak logs out from the banks into mid-stream, to speed their journey down to the coast.

We reached the border with Malaya at Pasang Besar, where we had hoped we would find a village to explore during the wait while Customs searched the train, but there was only a concrete platform, and a few hawkers of fruit and rather doubtful-looking sweets and curried meat balls; we bought a sealed bag of sugared cashew nuts, which were excellent, crisp juicy nuts, coated with crystallised brown sugar.

When everyone alighted from the train, we found we were the only westerners on board. Among the throng on the platform was a group of Malay Boy Scouts, who had been to a rally in Bangkok; one of them approached me and asked if I had any English stamps for his collection, which sadly I had not, but we had a friendly chat.

Meanwhile Michael was queuing, or rather not queuing so much as pushing and shoving, and being pushed and shoved, to get our passports stamped at a small enclosed counter in a little room leading off the platform, while the Customs Officers slowly worked their way up the train. Our car attendant had locked our compartment until we were called to go and clear our luggage. The Customs Officer questioned Michael closely and officiously as to where we had been and why, and finally asked what Michael's profession was:

'I am an officer,' said Michael, which caused a noticeable back-straightening and surreptitious adjustment of uniform jacket.

'An officer in what?'

'An English naval officer,' replied Michael.

'Yes sir, thank you, sir, sorry you've been troubled, sir; best wishes for the rest of your journey, sir!' and the little man bowed himself out backwards, in almost cowed deference.

'They have a great respect for the officer class,' said Michael, 'and quite right too!' he added smugly.

We arrived at Penang two hours late, and were met by Mr Ng, the local Jardine's manager, who took us by the ferry to Penang Island and to our hotel. The next day he kindly took us round the island including to the notorious Snake Temple. Here snakes of different kinds are free to roam or slither, or do whatever snakes do to get around, all over the temple precincts. They were coiled round chair-legs, draped from branches in huge pots round and on the altar, and hanging from chandeliers, or sliding across the floor, wherever you looked. We were told that at night eggs were put on the floor near the altar, and all the snakes came out to feed. Some Chinese who were watching us, followed us with delight; Michael said my expression of increasing horror caused them much amusement.

We drove from Penang to Kuala Lumpur, stopping at Ipoh for lunch; it was interesting to see how the terrain suddenly changed from padi to limestone rocks as we neared Ipoh, where we passed open-cast tin mines, and areas of barren yellow earth from which tin had been extracted which were waiting for the jungle to blanket them once more. At Kuala Lumpur we stayed in Chan U Seek's house in great comfort, and drove on the next day to Singapore.

Having dreamed all my life of seeing Bangkok, I was disappointed in the city, just as Charles Letts had said I would be, but the Royal Palace and barges, the Floating Market, and the fairy-like enchantment of Chiang-Mai's cottage industries were all quite unforgettable.

CHAPTER 17

Singapore and Pahang Game Reserve, 1968

'WHEREVER DO YOU GO, Sue, when you disappear between each race?' I was asked by Peggy Shaw, a Chinese friend, at one of the regular Turf Club race-meetings to which Helene, Tan Chin Tuan's wife, used often to invite me. As Chin Tuan was on the committee, we would watch from the stewards' box, an air-conditioned eyrie surrounded by smoked glass, high in the grandstand, which overlooked the whole of the race course. The seating was in raised tiers, with comfortable tip-up seats and recesses in the wide arms to hold both kinds of glasses, binoculars as well as drinks.

'Well, I can't afford the $5 tote up here,' I replied, 'so I nip down to the coolies' $2 tote on the ground floor to place my bets.' The Chinese thought this a huge joke, but Helene suggested that we should split our bets between us, to save me dashing downstairs and back again, and thereafter, as she had considerable knowledge of the local horses, my fortunes greatly improved.

It was a beautifully laid out course, encircling a large area of mown grass planted with various flowering shrubs. Behind the bank of seating in the stewards' box was a bar and a small dining-room, where we would have tea after the races, and sometimes we were invited to lunch beforehand. Michael was not able to go as often as I was, but I became a regular punter, and very much enjoyed it.

I made many friends among the Chinese ladies, mostly through Helene Tan, who introduced me to her circle of Mah-Jong players; Dolly Chan, the wife of Charles Letts' business partner, Chan U Seek, was one of the younger ones, who always wore large pieces of the most exquisite jewellery.

Helene asked me one day if there was anything I would like especially to do before our final return to England.

'I would love to come to watch one of your Mah-Jong parties one day,' I replied. 'I promise I would not utter a word or make a sound to distract anyone,' I added. Helene looked a bit doubtful, and said:

'I would have to ask the girls if they'd mind; I'll let you know.'

A week or so later, she rang me, and suggested I went one afternoon at about 3.30 pm to watch the play for a while, and then join the ladies for tea.

My parents had bought a Mah-Jong set back from China in 1933, so I learned to play, but only slowly with due thought before each move, rather like playing bridge. The Chinese play very fast, and the tiles click and flash, as the players concentrate in silence, their hands darting incessantly over the tables.

Helene had several friends for the day, making up two tables; they had started at 10.30 in the morning, and had broken briefly for lunch. I was surprised to find that they were all dressed quite casually, in jeans and shirts, with no make-up, and one even had her hair in rollers under a head-scarf; but their hands! That was quite a different matter, all had exquisitely manicured nails, and all wore several magnificent rings. I suppose that with their eyes focused only on the game, they saw nothing of each other's appearances, except for their hands. At 4.00 pm they broke off play, and tea was brought in.

'Oh really!' exclaimed Dolly Chan in disgust, 'I have no luck today at all! I think I will change my ring, perhaps my ruby will bring me better joss,' and so saying, she drew off her finger a huge sapphire surrounded by diamonds, and rooting in her handbag, she brought out an even larger cabochon ruby which she slipped on. A few minutes after resuming play, just before I left, she said cheerfully:

'Ah, this is better, now I will make some money!'

Michael's brother, Ernle, was the commander in HMS *Eagle* at that time, which was in the Far East and called often at Singapore for a week or two at a time. Ernle would come to stay, and was always a great asset at our parties, being lively, flirtatious and full of fun. We often visited his ship, much to James' and Emma's delight, and spent many hilarious days and evenings with him.

We planned a few days leave during the Christmas holidays, for which we were lent a house on the beach at Port Dickson, which was a day's drive up the west coast of Malaysia. At the last moment, Michael was unable to get away, so the children, Ernle and I set off via Muar and Malacca. The house was shaded by palm-trees, through which we walked down to the beach of white sand, which stretched for miles in each direction, with no signs of human habitation and no-one in sight. The house was staffed, and meals appeared at regular intervals, which we ate either on the veranda or outside under the trees. The swimming was heavenly, in the clear pale turquoise sea; we found the trunk of an old palm-tree washed up, and we rolled it back into the sea, where it floated sluggishly, half submerged. We all had much fun trying to ride astride it, but it was very unstable, and rolled, pitching us into the sea. It was a happy few days, and a welcome break from our incessant entertaining.

The constant hospitality was exhausting: on the one hand between the central military headquarters and the three services, to meet each other and all new arrivals in post, or at departure. We were also invited to parties on board visiting ships, British and American mostly, but sometimes from other countries. Then there was the diplomatic scene: our own and Commonwealth High Commissioners in Singapore; the local national days, and the occasions of Indonesian, Malay, Thai, Indian, Dutch, French, United States national celebrations. On top of that came an endless series of visitors from London: ministers, Chiefs-of-Staff, uniformed and civilian Directors from all the departments of the MOD. These came to sort out the Government's programme leading up to our withdrawal from the Far East theatre.

Singapore was the hub of our universe, with spokes going in all directions, and the oil or lubrication which kept the hub revolving easily was very largely the facilities for hospitality. Michael has always been a much more social animal than me; I prefer to have a few close friends rather than a wide acquaintance with many, and although I enjoyed the social whirl, I found much of it extremely wearing.

There were, of course, many occasions which were the greatest fun, particularly the launch picnics to distant beaches or the outer islands, and this was a popular form of entertaining with our formal visitors from London enjoying themselves as much as us and our children.

At a large national day reception one evening, in the grounds of one of the embassies, Tan Chin Tuan approached me and asked:

'Are you and Michael going on to dinner anywhere after this, Sue?' and when I said no, he went on:

'Well, would you like to accompany Helene and me, and go down to China-town, to eat Hokkien food? You will come in my car with us and Michael can follow in yours.'

It was a fascinating evening, which was often to be repeated. Although Singapore was well policed, there was a kidnapping risk for

Chinese millionaires, consequently the Tan Chin Tuans always travelled with armed guards (even for their grandchildren going to and from school), and on these evening occasions in Hokkien Street, we'd occupy a section of the street with armed bodyguards on either side, standing a few yards away from us, their rifles held ready.

After the reception we went to the cars, and I was told to sit in the middle at the back, with Chin Tuan and Helene on each side; Chin Tuan always sat in the left corner seat of all his cars, with his foot resting on an alarm button. Sitting in front beside the driver was a bodyguard, with his rifle between his knees. A second car followed, with two more armed men, and on this occasion, Michael brought up the rear.

In Hokkien Street, we sat out in the road, on wooden stools at a small table, where we could watch our chosen dishes being cooked at the stall alongside us. We always had the most delicious food, and it amused Chin Tuan that I enjoyed and would eat so much of the raw garlic paste which was served as a side dish, and also of the durian fruit, considered a great delicacy by local people but which most westerners would not even try, on account of the rotting smell, although the pulpy fruit inside the noisome shell is ambrosial, and I could never eat enough of it.

We drove into Malaya as often as Michael could get away. The country was still unspoilt, and the people friendly and smiling and very laid back; in Singapore the pressure to work, to make money, to succeed, never let up, but the Malays were happy and easy-going, and if a task was not completed on time, well, there was always tomorrow.

There were lovely sandy beaches up the east coast, and little off-shore islands within easy reach.

One day we took James and Emma up the coast to Jason's Bay, leaving the house early so as to have a long morning there; after glorious swimming and our picnic lunch, we drove inland to Kota Tinggi, where there was a shady pool with a waterfall. We had another swim and found the water blissfully cool, far more refreshing than the sea. A day or two later, I was talking to an army doctor at a party, and was telling him about our swim at Kota Tinggi.

'You didn't swim there, did you?' he asked, in a voice of horror. 'That pool is infected with Leptospirosis [Hepatitis B] from rats' urine! You must be mad to have taken such a risk! Whatever were you thinking of? The troops are strictly forbidden from swimming there when on Army exercises; you'll be very lucky if you get away with it!'

We had had no knowledge of the risk, and luckily we did survive unscathed.

Charles Letts invited us all to have dinner in a Chinese restaurant during the first school holidays that the children were with us. He took us to a large restaurant downtown, which was full of Chinese diners; we were the only westerners. It was brilliantly lit, with a tiled floor, and plastic chairs and tables each to seat ten people. Although Michael and I remembered the art of eating with chopsticks from our earlier years in Singapore, it was a new experience for James and Emma. James was fifteen, and already had very large strong hands; he was determined to master chopsticks and not make a fool of himself, and with teeth clenched, and an expression of fierce determination, he gripped the chopsticks so tightly that with loud reports like rifle shots, they broke, and four pieces of plastic shot across the restaurant over the heads of the other diners. There was a sudden hush, before everyone burst out laughing; poor James was mortified, and later put in some practice at home before eating Chinese-style in public again.

We became friendly with the High Commissioner for New Zealand, Jim Weir, and his attractive wife, Joy. The start of our friendship, however, was not auspicious. On Remembrance Day in November, a Cenotaph parade service was held in the city on the Padang. It took place in the early morning, before the heat and humidity rose, and we all had to be in our seats by 7.00 am. Michael was to lay a wreath, representing the C-in-C, who was absent, and so we had seats in the front row, with the heads of the three services and their wives, and the High Commissioners. It was a formal sombre occasion, and the wives were all wearing hats. I had on a wide-brimmed straw in two shades of pink, which I had bought at Dickins and Jones at least four years previously. (Although as a senior officer's wife one had to have hats, the formal occasions when they had to be worn were infrequent, so mine accompanied me from one posting to the next for several years, and being invariably wide-brimmed, they did not date.)

We were among the first to arrive, and were shown to seats at the far end of the front row, near the Cenotaph. The seats filled up, and then a tall elegant couple stepped out of a car, and I saw my hat walking towards us, and Joy Weir's face underneath it; I nudged Michael, and whispered:

'Look! Joy's wearing the same hat as mine!'

As they sat down, I was able to mouth the one word to her:

'Snap!' with a broad grin.

But Joy did not look happy, and I think she was not amused, although later, after a drink, she did soften a little, and told me she had bought hers in New York where it had cost far more than mine!

In the summer of 1968, Ginny came out to spend some months with us. She was then twenty-four, and had never had the opportunity to enjoy the fun of being a service daughter. It was lovely to have her with us, particularly for me, and when James and Emma arrived for the holidays and the family was complete, I was in seventh heaven.

One of our neighbours in Tanglin was Graham Starforth Hill, an English barrister who practised in the Singapore Law Courts; his fourteen year-old son Rupert, and nine year-old daughter Claudia also came out from school for the holidays. Graham had a swimming pool in his garden, and in the absence of their mother, he was glad of some company for his children, so we saw a lot of them, and were able often to use their pool, as well as taking them on launch picnics.

Sometimes on Sundays, we would cross the Causeway into Johore, and drive up the west coast to Kukkuk. This was a fishing village built out from the shore of mangrove swamp, on wooden stilts. The huts were wooden, and very shaky, as was the passageway between them, leading to a make-shift restaurant projecting further out over the water. It was extremely primitive, one could see the water between the floor-boards, and we threw our fish-bones and crab shells straight into the sea from our rickety table; but the fish we ate was superb, especially the bowls of chilli crab. It was a two-hour drive to get there, through rubber and palm-oil plantations and some fields of pineapples and pepper, but it was well worth it.

During those holidays, we had planned a major family expedition up the east coast and into the game reserve in Pahang, the Taman Negara. The Hibberts joined us for this; Reg and Ann's three children had also come out, Jane, aged seventeen, George, aged fifteen and William, aged eleven. Hugh and Jean Wilson came down from Hong Kong too, where Hugh was the naval Commodore, and we all met at Jerantut, to embark in a long-boat for the four-hour journey up the Pahang river into the reserve.

However, before that, we had driven slowly up the east coast staying *en route* at Pekan and Kuantan.

Through Charles Letts we had introductions to the family of the Sultan of Pahang, the largest of the Malay states, on the north-east coast. We had met two of the Sultan's sons, the Tungkus Makhota and Abdulla, and had been invited by their mother the Sultana, to stay at one of their guests-houses in the grounds of the Istana (palace).

We set off at 6.00 am, and after crossing the Johore Causeway, turned east on the well metalled coast road through Mersing. Ginny had been well dosed with Dramamine, and remained quite lively: she was a notoriously bad traveller, but was probably helped by the excitement of seeing her first rubber plantations, sago, groundnuts and rice growing, and particularly by her first sight of the jungle.

On arrival at the Istana, we found the house of Tungku Azam (the Sultan's second, and favourite wife) with whom lived Tungku Abdulla, the third son. He and two younger brothers led us to the bungalow we were being lent, passing on the way the Sultan's palace, newly built of white stone, with slender black pillars supporting canopies of yellow concrete, like inverted parasols on the flat roof. The imposing entrance was crowned by a large golden onion-shaped dome.

Our bungalow was of wood, raised on stilts; it had a long veranda, on to which the rooms opened. The four bedrooms were small, each with a double bed; there were no mosquito-nets nor fly-screens at the windows, which were small, and only opened on a swivel-slat principle; there was no air-conditioning, except in the sitting room, where I quickly spotted that the rattan settee had wide foam rubber cushions, of which I made a mental note.

The three Tungkus stayed for tea which a house-boy produced, and conversation was a bit stilted; they then left us to unpack and change.

Each bedroom had a wash-room, with WC, and one cold tap over a high stone jar built into one corner, too high to climb into, so one used the dipper provided to ladle the delicious cool water over oneself as an improvised shower.

At Tungku Azam's house we were greeted by her and the three young men we had already met, as well as a large number of girls, all dressed in colourful Malay costume; they resembled a group of butterflies. The sexes were segregated, so that although James and Michael were able to talk animatedly to the princes, who spoke English, the girls and women did not, so our end of the room was silent, while we repeatedly bowed and smiled at each other. Suddenly Emma gave a resounding hiccup, quickly followed by another, and another; the whole room erupted into laughter, and the ice was broken; after that we all seemed able to communicate with much fun and enjoyment. Dinner was not helpful to poor Emma's hiccups, being a stone-cold curry but very hot indeed chilli-wise!

One of the Tungkus' sisters had been married only a few days previously, and we were taken upstairs to see the bridal bedroom. It was dazzling, being decorated entirely in brilliant salmon-pink: walls, ceiling, carpet, curtains and bed; the last was a tester, and the hangings were of shiny satin; the bed-head was upholstered in satin with a large coronet embroidered in pearls. There was no room for any other furniture in the room, and it was obviously a source of great pride to the whole family.

It was a delightful evening after the slightly sticky start. The three Tungkus took us over to their father's palace after dinner, and then escorted us back to our guest-house.

There are many flying insects in Malaysia, but I had not appreciated quite how big some of them are, nor how noisy they can be. As we were preparing to go to bed, James called from his room that he had a large creature under his bed which was making a noise like a loud frog's croak; I went to investigate, and with my torch I spied a beetle which was certainly quite sizeable.

'Don't make such a fuss, James,' I said, 'it's only a cockchafer or something.'

'Well, I'm not going to bed with that in my room, that's for sure!' cried James flatly.

'Oh really, James, you are feeble! I'll get it out for you,' I said impatiently, with which I bent down and reached under his bed. This was not a wise move, for I was already in my night-dress, and the insect obviously found the sight of my cleavage irresistible, for with a mighty whirring and clatter, it took off, and flew straight down it; its wing-span was seven or eight inches. Michael said the din of my screams and the family's laughter must have been audible in the Istana. The Tungkus certainly enjoyed the story the next morning.

I found sleep impossible in a small double bed with Michael, with no air-conditioning and very little ventilation, so I prudently moved to the cushioned settee in the sitting-room which I had spied earlier.

That day we took a picnic to a nearby beach; on our return the Tungkus came round to join us for tea, and then a swim in their pool, which was a stone tank filled with cooling fresh water.

We left the next day, and drove up the coast to Kuantan, where we were able to stay in a rest-house almost on the beach, which was light and airy, with the cool sea breeze blowing through it.

After an early supper, we drove north to Chendor beach, hoping to see turtles coming up to lay their eggs. There are several species which come to this beach, some up to twelve feet long. They come up each year, usually in August, at high tide. They clamber out of the sea, and up the rising beach, and choose a spot above the high water line, where they dig a hole in the sand about two feet deep, then they squat on the edge, facing inshore, and expel their eggs into the hole. When they finish, they cover the eggs and fill the hole with their flippers, turn and lumber back to the sea.

The eggs are soft-shelled, and a popular delicacy, and so are ruthlessly taken by local people to export by air to Tokyo, New York, London etc. or rather they were so exploited, until the Malaysian government realised that the turtles could soon become extinct, if some form of control was not imposed.

The eggs contain gas, which causes them slowly to rise through the sand during incubation, so that they reach the surface at exactly the right moment to hatch. The baby turtles, little more than an inch long, turn instinctively toward the sea, and have to brave the dangerous journey down the beach and out to their natural feeding-grounds in deep water. Meanwhile predators await them, gulls and other birds and land creatures, and then fish. They come to Chendor because there is a reef not far offshore, and if the little turtles can reach it safely, they can dive deep, avoiding their predators and finding adequate food.

When the government realised that controls were necessary to preserve the species, they imposed concessions on the beach, selling permits to local entrepreneurs (usually Chinese), allowing the eggs to be taken, on condition that a proportion were hatched and reared, and in due course released over the reef. This way, their continued reproduction is assured.

Thus when we saw the Chinese digging up the eggs which we had just watched being laid, we were not surprised and when we were then taken to some sheds along the beach, to a fenced compound, where the eggs were reburied in a marked site, and then shown tanks of baby turtles of varying sizes happily swimming about, we were duly impressed. The turtles only lay at night, so we had taken torches with us, and unlike some less fortunate friends, we didn't have to wait long, as a turtle came out of the sea just after we arrived, and laid between forty and fifty eggs.

From Kuantan we drove on to Jerantut, where we met the Hibberts and Wilsons on the river bank, where our long-boat awaited us. It was shallow draft and narrow, and we sat in pairs on rubber cushions with our legs outstretched in front of us, and boards to lean against. We could trail our hands in the water and there was a metal awning to protect us from the sun. The two Malay boat-boys spoke no English, but were smiling and friendly.

The Sungei Pahang was very wide, with the jungle coming down to the banks on each side. We chugged along at about 6 knots, occasionally slowing through shallow rapids on bends. We saw many kingfishers and other birds, and were watched by the odd monkey as we passed. Family groups of Malays were washing near the river banks, and all waved.

At one point we met another engine-powered long-boat, which passed us at speed. Our boatmen turned across its wake, in a slightly slaphappy way, so that we shipped a large amount of river, which dowsed Ginny and Ann Hibbert in the bows, causing much laughter at their expense from those more comfortably seated aft.

It briefly rained quite hard, but our tin roof kept us dry, and the breeze of our passage was deliciously cool. The light faded, and we had begun to wonder when we would arrive, when after over four hours, a roof was sighted, and lights high above the river; we drew alongside a bamboo jetty, and wearily trundled our heterogeneous pieces of baggage up to the rest-house, 100 feet above, and overlooking the river.

It consisted of two wooden chalets, which our party filled; it was situated south of the centre of the game reserve, and when the season first opens in April each year, tiger, elephant and other animals can be seen from the hides built in the surrounding jungle. However, by August the animals have mostly retreated into the deep forest, and we saw nothing larger than deer, although some members of the group swore they had seen a crocodile. We went off in small parties each day to the different hides, our legs protected by trousers and borrowed army jungle boots against leeches, but the revolting creatures find their way through eyelet holes and the smallest crevices, and Ann found she had nourished one to satiety in her groin during a forest walk.

We went in small boats up narrow tributaries of the river, taking picnics to rocky pools where we could swim. This entailed some exciting negotiations through rapids, when sometimes passengers had to get out and help push or lift the boats between the rocks; returning downstream we'd be swept along at tremendous speed, the boat-boys working hard to avoid projecting hazards.

On our first day, four of us were to go off in the afternoon to spend the night in the high hide, and so they spent the morning pottering in the vicinity of the rest-house. The rest of us set off after breakfast to go up river. We had two small boats, each with three cushioned seats; there was very little free-board, and it was certainly a case of being careful not to rock the boat. The huge jungle trees met overhead, with ferns and orchids hanging from the branches; when the others were asked to disembark to help manoeuvre the boats through some rapids, I was firmly told to remain seated, I imagine as I had shown a degree of incompetence when embarking at the rest-house jetty, and had slipped and fallen partly into the river, to the great amusement of the boat-boys.

Meanwhile the 'High Hiders' had set off, and had a frustrating night seeing no game other than bats, mosquitoes, rats and leeches! They returned the following morning after a disturbed and uncomfortable night, but we greeted them as conquering heroes, which helped to restore their morale.

That afternoon Ginny joined the group who returned to the pool up the Sungei Tahan for another swim; as she lay basking on a boulder in the sun, wearing her bikini, large turquoise butterflies surrounded her, and alighted on her canvas shoes, so that her feet were completely smothered in them; we presumed they were feeding on the salty residue from her last bathe in the sea.

We were surprised by the change in the river in the last twenty-four hours without rain; the water-level had dropped by well over a foot, and had cleared of mud to a lovely peaty brown clarity. The rapids were more fun for being shallower, and we were constantly running aground, so that Hugh Wilson would jump overboard to help lift the

*The Hibberts, Ann, William and Reg, after a night in the high hide, Taman
Negara game reserve, Pahang, 1969.*

boat over the rocks. Our engine kept stalling at the most critical
moments just when most power was needed to get up the narrowest
and fastest running channels, so we then drifted backwards at
increasing speed, which was quite exciting. When we started back, we
prevailed upon the boat-boys to kill the engines, to allow us to drift
downstream; in the silence we could then hear the jungle sounds, and
birds did not take flight until we were close enough to see them
properly. In this way we watched a large rhinoceros hornbill cross the
river just in front of us, uttering its loud raucous cry. He perched right
above us on a clear dead branch giving us a perfect view; he was a
good forty-eight inches long, black, with a white banded tail, and his
enormous beak was yellow, the upper horned mandible curving
upwards, and shaded from orange to bright red at the tip; a truly
magnificent bird.

Our boat-boy spotted some monkeys, but we could only follow
their progress from tree to tree by wildly waving branches. The other
boat-boy saw elephant tracks in the sand of the river bank, clearly
recognisable, said Ginny, but as we didn't see them, we were enviously
sceptical about that! We heard barking deer, and calls from other
animals, birds and frogs which we could not identify. When it became

too dark to see, we used the boats' engines again, and had a hilarious race back to base, which the boat-boys enjoyed as much as we did.

After dinner James produced a length of hollow bamboo, out of which he tapped a live leech on to a leaf. Most of us had by then experienced, if not acting host to one, at least the doubtful satisfaction of removing one or more before satisfying its hunger, but Emma and I, who had a horror of them, were as yet unblooded, so to speak. It was fascinating to see one and watch its agility: James moved his hand to and fro just above it, and the leech stretched up like a piece of black rubber tube, extending from half, to one and a half inches long, as it wove from side to side trying to reach James' hand; when he moved his hand to the side, the leech looped its way across the table, as quick as lightning. When it does find a source of blood, it injects an anti-coagulant before feeding, and will only drop off, sated, when it becomes the size of a golf-ball; its host is then left with a thin trickle of blood from a microscopic pin-prick, which is often the first you know that you have been feeding the creature.

James said he was going to take several back to Bradfield, where they were being studied in his biology classes. I asked him how he would transport them.

'I'll keep them in this hollow bamboo, and make a cork for it, and we'll all take turns to feed them,' he said. He has always had original and entertaining ideas, many of which are useful and constructive, but the family quickly disposed of that suggestion!

There was torrential rain and thunderstorms that night, but we all set off together the next morning in low-lying mist; we went in three boats, each with three boat-boys, as the rivers were full and fast. We travelled up-stream for two hours, and then turned north-west into a narrow stream which was very pretty, with curtains of jasmine in flower, hanging over the water. We moored at a steep bank and had lunch at a little chalet in a nearby clearing, after which most of the party swam. Meanwhile the nine boat-boys had entirely disappeared, and we realised why they had been so keen to take us to this spot, when they reappeared two hours later, bearing on their shoulders sacks of several kinds of fruit, including the much-prized durians, and also a smaller sack of tiny scarlet chillies; they were all beaming with delight, and we had a noisy return journey, with everyone singing, joking and calling from boat to boat.

James and one of the boat-boys had an arm wrestling match while awaiting the return of the last boat-boy. They sat facing each other, plaiting the fingers of their right hands, with their elbows on the table; each had to try to force the other's hand down to touch the table. James fought well, every muscle in use, and sweat pouring off him, being cheered on by both Malays and English alike, but he was defeated in the end midst laughter and congratulations.

Reg Hibbert and Michael decided they wanted more exercise, so they set off on our last day to climb Guling Gendang, a hill of 1,900 ft, in the jungle. They took two guides, and after a short boat-trip they set off into the forest. As usual, it had rained during the night, so the going was both wet and slippery, with many small streams to be forded or crossed on single tree-trunk bridges. After an hour of walking, one of the guides called twice and there was a reply, whereupon they stopped and waited, and after a little while two Negrito aborigines emerged from the deeper jungle, followed by a woman and a boy; all were scantily clad, g-strings for the men, a short skirt and brief upper garment for the woman. The men had blow-pipes and demonstrated them, for photographs to be taken. Reg and Michael then continued along the track, the Negritos accompanying them, and they met and passed eighteen or more in groups and families, all apparently on the move; the track was littered with the peel and shells of various fruits, which had obviously been picked and eaten from the trees in passing. The Negritos turned off into the forest, and Reg and Michael continued to the summit of the hill; they found a triangulation point there, and a metal pyramid. Their descent was quicker, and they returned to base after six hours of walking, feeling weary but pleased with themselves.

Regretfully we all traipsed down to our long-boat early the next morning. Michael was presented with a bamboo walking-stick by 'Fatso', our name for the fat boat-boy who had been one of our six, and whom we had laughed at because his boat was always the slowest, with the most inefficient engine, and also because whenever any fruit had been gathered, he had invariably disappeared alone with a good proportion of it which was never seen again, except for empty husks and pips lying around!

The boat moved at a spanking pace going downstream, and we saw hornbills and monkeys from time to time. After a while Ann and Ginny were loudly demanding a 'comfort stop', and we landed on a grassy bank mid-stream, where there was cover between wild rhododendron bushes, and the grass was close-cropped like a lawn (close-cropped by what, we wondered?).

'Everything except running hot and cold!' said Ginny.

We reached Jerantut by noon, collected our cars from the local police station, and parted company to go off in different directions. We stayed the night at Seramban on our way home, with Major-General and Mrs Pat Patterson and his family at Flagstaff House, where we much appreciated the clear, clean water to drink and wash in. On to home the next day: a lovely drive through Malacca, Ayer Hitam and Johore Bahru.

A Summing-Up

The traveller in wild Malay
Who hopes to see the elephant,
Will have to be content to watch
The antics of the giant ant.
The music of the common frog
Will be his lullaby;
He will not hear the tiger's roar
Nor rhinos thunder by.
Into the hot and noisy night,
High in the hide he peers:
What's that? A tapir? Two-toed sloth?
Or one more rusa deer?
He'll hear the hornbill's crazy laugh,
The gibbons' whooping call,
And sense a million presences
He cannot see at all.
But now upon the river's face,
So chocolatey and fast,
His speeding boat through rapids skim,
And suddenly, at last,
A cry so strange and new
He hears above the jungle din;
Is it a grand discovery?
Ah no, his friend has fallen in!
Sadly he heads for home once more,
Downstream through forest trees,
Bearing no news of larger game
Than butterflies and bees.
But wise is he, who going back
To city desk and villa trim,
Can say, though he has watched in vain,
The jungle has been watching him.

Ann Hibbert

CHAPTER 18

Singapore, 1969

EARLY ONE SUNDAY MORNING, we drove to Petain Road to see and listen to the weekly Sharma birds' singing contest. A rather charming Chinese custom was their care and affection for pet caged song-birds. Many of the older men had these Sharma birds, as large as our blackbirds, of dark plumage, which were strong singers. On Sunday mornings they would take their birds in cages to Petain Road, where they would match them to sing against each other. The cages would be hung in the lower branches of road-side trees, and their owners sat beneath them to enjoy the birdsong and discuss their rival merits. They were cock birds, and would show off and compete against each other in this way. It was a scene of much interest and pleasure.

Living close to the centre of Singapore city gave us easy access to many aspects of multi-national life. Although numerically largely Chinese, there were Malay and Indian communities and other Eastern groups, many having their own temples and religious festivals. We went to watch Katyika, the Buddhist annual ceremony of presentation of new robes to the monks, together with a parcel of toilet articles. It took place in a Buddhist temple which was on a hillock, and we climbed several flights of steps to reach it. At the entrance there was a serving table, from which boiled rice and an egg were being dished out into each bowl, for which people were queuing to pay a dollar; they then moved on round a long table on which were two rows of large bronze pots, into each one of which the devotees spooned a heap of rice, allocating their egg to whichever they preferred; this continued in ever more frenetic haste as the time drew near for the ceremony.

There was a number of rosetted officials (in European dress) who kept the crowd moving, encouraging everyone through loud-speakers.

We were welcomed by several officials in turn, who pressed on us bottles of sticky sweet drinks. Eventually the bowls of rice and eggs on the serving table were exhausted, but the queue remained as long as ever of those wishing to add their contributions. Any European organisation would at that point have closed the gates, but not the Chinese, who merely removed a few of the large bronze pots and tipped the contents back to replenish the serving-bowls, to be re-issued to dollar-paying devotees (presumable the monks got the money as well as the food, anyway).

Eventually even the organisers grew tired of all this, a firm announcement was made, and everyone surged forward into the inner temple, where the monks, clad one imagined in last year's robes, were seated cross-legged on the floor flanking a huge statue of Buddha. My arm was seized, I was thrust forward, and told to take off my shoes and go into the inner sanctum (by this time I had lost Michael). I obeyed, and was pushed to the front of the crowd between the two files of monks, where there was a table piled with cellophane-wrapped orange robes, and another of parcelled soap, toilet-paper etc., also wrapped in coloured cellophane and tied with ribbon, with a flower or two entwined in the bows. The air was thick with the smoke and scent of thousands of joss-sticks standing in jars all round the temple precincts.

By this time I was squatting on my heels with the crowd, in acute discomfort but unable to change my position as I was hemmed in on all sides, with Chinese elbows, knees and feet digging into every part of my anatomy. Having watched one presentation, and joined in the accompanying chanting, led by one of the monks, who cried through a loud-speaker: 'Now, everybody, say after me please ...' I was suddenly afflicted with violent cramp, and *had* to move, and so stood up and, no-one paying the slightest attention to me, I stepped over the heads and bodies of those between me and daylight and fresh air, and emerged. I found both Michael and my shoes in a large bank of them round the temple walls. We decided to leave at that point, and not wait for the vegetarian lunch which was to be served to all the devotees.

It was so nice that we were made so welcome, and that it was tacitly understood that we would join in the ceremony with the hundreds of Asian Buddhists.

The Hindu ceremony of Thaipusam was not one which I attended, but Michael went to watch it. The devotees had their arms, faces, ears, tongues, backs and chests pierced with steel needles up to two feet long. On their chest and back, these formed a supporting framework for a great wire erection like an enormous bird-cage. They walked in procession bearing these great frames, and in some cases they also towed small trolleys secured to the flesh of their backs by hooks.

Another temple event of great devotion was the fire-walking. Those taking part left the temple together in procession and made a short pilgrimage, to return and re-enter the temple by another door. As they came back, with the watching crowd chanting and singing, they walked through a trenched foot-bath of water and milk in their bare feet, and then straight on to a large banked-up bed of burning charcoal about two feet deep and eight feet long; it had been lit and kept burning from the previous day. All the devotees were men or youths, some men carrying small children on their shoulders. After passing over the burning coals, they stepped into a second trench of milky water.

The Singapore government provided a unit of the fire brigade to be present throughout these ceremonies, in case of accident, but we never heard of one, and Michael saw that none of the fire-walkers was burned.

My mother-in-law, Agnes, died suddenly in September 1968, and Michael flew home for her funeral and to spend a few days at Homme with his father. It was a sad time, and poor Kyrle was shocked and confused. Ernle and Bunnie, his second wife, were also there for part of Michael's stay.

From then on the situation at Homme deteriorated, and with it, Kyrle's health, along with his capacity for managing his own affairs.

He came out to spend Christmas with us, and brought papers with him suggesting that he should pass Homme House on to Michael at once. As it would have been the house and garden only, without the 180 acres of woodland and park, Michael pointed out that it would not be viable to run the house without the financial support of the estate. Kyrle understood this and the proposal was dropped.

At this time Kyrle was High Sheriff of Herefordshire, and in February he had many commensurate duties to do with the Judges Assizes etc. He became overtired and ill during the very cold weather, and developed pneumonia; we think he also had a mild stroke. He was never the same again, becoming difficult and fractious, totally unlike the genial and happy man I had known and become so fond of over twenty odd years.

I returned to England in February to help him in his convalescence, and to try to find a resident couple to look after him. James and Emma came to Homme over Easter. It was not an easy or happy time; poor Kyrle varied from one extreme to the other, showing me much affection one day, and opposing my every suggestion for his welfare the next.

A couple was found, the wife to be housekeeper and her husband to help Kyrle, to drive him about and to nurse him when necessary. They only stayed a few weeks.

One day Kyrle asked me to collect together all the family silver that remained (much had already been given to Michael and Ernle); and to pack it up. I was told to put it into Lloyds Bank in my name. Luckily I was able to dissuade him from this, and it was lodged at Lloyds, but under his own name. Later in the year I was thankful I had insisted on this.

Another couple was found to look after him, and installed shortly before I returned to Singapore.

During the summer we corresponded regularly and affectionately with both Kyrle and Ernle. The latter wrote very amusing letters about the situation at Homme, where matters were never static for long, one pair of carers replacing another every few weeks. We knew Michael would be leaving Singapore at the end of the year, and retiring from the Navy early in 1970, and in one of my letters to Ernle, I wrote saying how worried we both were about Kyrle and his confused state of mind and poor health, and how much I feared the future living at Homme after Michael's retirement. Ernle and Bunnie extrapolated that paragraph and showed it to Kyrle.

In November Michael flew to London on a duty visit, which gave him the opportunity to visit his father, and spend a few days at Homme. Ernle and Bunnie were also there.

A few days after his return to Singapore, Michael received a letter from Kyrle to say he had changed his will, and was not going to leave the Homme estate to Michael (as old Uncle Cecil Money-Kyrle had wished and decreed), but was leaving it jointly to him and Ernle, and that they should share it and divide the accommodation between them.

Michael was astonished and bitterly hurt that Kyrle had not mentioned this or discussed it during his recent visit less than a week earlier.

Within another few days I received a curt letter asking me to return

Homme House, Much Marcle.

the silver which I had 'stolen' during the three months I had spent looking after him in the spring. Thankfully I was able to reply that it was lodged in his own bank under his own name. I never received an apology.

I was amazed that Ernle could go to such lengths to discredit me in Kyrle's eyes, but I am sure he was encouraged to do so by Bunnie, who had also succeeded in driving a wedge into the happy relationship I had had with my mother-in-law, Agnes, for many years before she died.

After that it was out of the question for the four of us to live at Homme together, and when Kyrle died, Ernle bought Michael out, at a fraction of the true value of the estate.

I have never been back, nor have I had anything further to do with Ernle and Bunnie, other than exchanging civilities at family weddings and funerals.

The solicitor who supervised the change of will and subsequent split of family and estate was, like Ernle, weak and unworthy. It became apparent later that he had expected that Michael might and could have challenged his father's mental capacity to make such a new will, but Michael had no stomach for such a fight. He went abroad again within a year of his retirement from the Navy, to take up the post of General Manager, Middle East Navigation Aids Service, based at Bahrain, where he remained until 1976.

CHAPTER 19

Borneo, 1969

THE CLOSING OF MICHAEL'S family saga has leap-frogged the months, and now I will revert to Singapore, and my last adventure as a naval wife.

Sadly, Ginny left us to return home early in 1969, and was able to escort Kyrle, and look after him on the journey, after his Christmas visit to us.

Just before the Christmas holidays began, I had taken Ginny up to Hong Kong, where we stayed with Hugh and Jean Wilson in the lovely house which was the official residence of the Commodore, Hong Kong; it was part of the way up the Peak, with views over the harbour, and an ideal stopping off point to show Ginny as much of the colony as possible.

In January 1969, Michael said that if I was going to achieve my other lifelong dream of seeing Borneo before we were due to return to England, I had better do something about it.

Accordingly, I went down to Mansfield's shipping line offices to find out about sailings of their small cargo boats which carry a few passengers on their trading route round Borneo. I also began to approach a few kindred spirits to find one who might like to accompany me.

Marsh Beet, the American wife of Trevor, a naval captain on Michael's staff, was an effervescent character who always saw the funniest side of everything; she was a big woman in every sense, both in stature and in heart; sadly she had not been too well, and had a circulatory condition which caused her much pain in her legs. She and Trevor decided that a cruise would give her a chance to rest and recuperate.

There was a ship sailing on 11th June, which would be away for three weeks, in which two single cabins were available; in this, a friend, Eric Wingate, the head of the Straits Steamship Company, was very helpful. Michael was away in England when the day came for us to embark in *Kimanis*, which lay off-shore in the harbour. She was to sail at night, and Anne and Tom Stocker offered to take me out to the ship. We met Trevor and Marsh for dinner in a floating restaurant in the harbour before embarking. Trevor managed to arrange for his naval launch to do some 'night training' and it came round from the naval base to pick us all up and take us out to find *Kimanis*. She was lying surrounded by a maze of small ships anchored almost nose to tail in the Inner Roads, rather like the Exeter by-pass at Bank Holiday weekend; the *Kimanis*, reassuringly larger than her neighbours, was surrounded by heavily laden lighters, three or four deep along both sides of the ship, which was loading cargo from both port and starboard simultaneously.

We found our cabins, which were large and airy, with comfortable beds, and pleasantly furnished, each with its adjoining shower and WC. The upper deck was spacious, with cushioned rattan chairs and a few small tables, and there were plenty of long reclining chairs for sunbathing; there was a library and, more important, a bar. Marsh and I decided we could survive for twenty days without too much pain.

Loading was still going on when Trevor and the Stockers left us; the noise from the well-deck just outside our cabin windows, where port and starboard derricks were working, was considerable. The ship was lit up with arc lights, and teemed with Chinese cargo-handlers, wielding their vicious hooks in a wildly alarming manner, it seemed to us. We watched the loading for some time from the upper deck, speculating on the contents of rattan-wrapped rolls, large round baskets of split bamboo, of huge hessian-wrapped bales and countless crates. Shouts, clangs, bangs and the whirring of the derrick machinery continued unabated, and still the bottoms of the lighters were covered with more cargo to be loaded. Eventually we went to our cabins, and to bed. It was very hot at anchor, although we each had an efficient electric fan, but I finally slept in spite of the din, till I became dimly aware that the noise had ceased, and we were under weigh, and then of a delicious cool breeze sweeping in through the open windows.

The following account is from my journal of the trip:

Thursday 12th June.
Rose at 7.00 am and went on deck, to claim chairs after much thought, in the strategically best places for a cool breeze, and distance from a small children's paddling pool. Marsh appeared, and a Mr and Mrs B, who are also doing the round trip from Singapore; Mr B is a

cheerful Scot on a recuperative holiday after an operation. There is an Australian family on board too, with two young children, and also two young women travelling together, and three or four Chinese. These, with us, comprise the first class passenger list.

I decided to go up to the boat-deck to sun-bathe during the morning, as our upper deck is almost entirely shaded (for which we were thankful). The Master's permission had to be asked, and he arranged for part of it to be roped in, as there are no side rails up there. I had not realised that the only means of access was by a vertical narrow iron ladder outside the rail from our deck, leading through a small square hole in the deck above; there were no rail nor handholds going up the ladder. After so much trouble had been taken I felt I had to ascend in spite of the stiff breeze, which tore at my book, cushion, hat etc.; once above, and having negotiated hawsers, pulleys, fire-buckets and life-boats, I found two deckchairs in the space forward of the funnel, and I collapsed into one, clutching my possessions to prevent them from being blown overboard, wondering how I would ever get them, and myself down again. An hour later Mrs B clambered up, and we eventually descended together when it seemed time for some liquid refreshment around noon. Marsh had sensibly remained below; the captain, whose name was Davies, joined us for drinks.

After an excellent lunch, at which the pudding was called 'Chipolata pudding with Raspberry sauce', which proved to be a sort of blancmange which only Marsh was brave enough to try, we retired to our cabins to make up for our short night's sleep.

I taught Marsh to play Scrabble after dinner; a young Chinese was obviously longing to join us, so we invited him, and he proved to be charming, from Tele-communications in Kuching. I stayed up late, as the deck passengers who were camped below my cabin windows had several transistor radios among them, all tuned to different oriental stations!

Friday 13th June. Pendeng (for Kuching).
Woken at 6.00 am by the blare of many transistors 12 ft from my head. Went up on deck, where the sky was purple and threatening, but the sea was mirror calm, and no rain fell.

Islands slipped by, green and jungle-covered, hardly a dwelling to be seen nor fishing-boats, nor ships. The clouds passed, and we emerged into brilliant sunshine during the morning. In the afternoon we entered the wide muddy river (Sungei Sarawak) which was the approach to Pendeng, the port for Kuching.

Pendeng consisted of a group of Shell oil tanks, a saw-mill, a rough wooden jetty with a few *attap* (palm-thatch) houses on stilts at the water's edge. We anchored in a wide pool in the river. At once a launch came out, laden with new deck passengers and their heterogeneous luggage, which included plastic and enamel food carriers, and bunches of plantains and pineapples, presumably to be their subsistence for the journey. They poured onboard, and almost as soon as the launch departed, it returned as crowded again, and yet again . . . We wondered where they all would find space, for the well-deck outside my cabin was cluttered with deck cargo, cables and hawsers, and even the seven or eight deck passengers we'd brought from Singapore seemed cramped; however, they all squeezed in, plus umpteen more transistors, all loudly blaring. The upper deck where we had deck accommodation by day was also chaotic, as most of it was roped off and converted into an office area for Customs and Immigration officers. We moved to the other end of the deck, and after dinner settled to our Scrabble, but were somewhat surprised to find ourselves the centre of a milling throng of Malay and Chinese youths, who had boarded at Pendeng, and who are travelling in some form of lower first class accommodation; they were a pleasant lot, but by sheer numbers took up a lot of deck space.

Saturday 14th June.
We were woken by cocks crowing! Presumably today's dinner for some of the deck passengers: perhaps a Dyack family is moving house, and their livestock with them.

I went up on deck early to take our books, sewing etc., and claim chairs; there were already some of the party of youths there, one fat young Chinese was doing press-ups and other fairly strenuous exercises, encouraged by his chums, who stood by with books on Physical Training in their hands, reading from them to Fatty. I teased him and the others, and I learned that the group is undergoing government training in forestry, and they are on their way to Miri, where they are to continue their course in the growing of timber in swamp conditions.

It is the Queen's official birthday, and so Michael's CB has been announced in the honours list. I invited the Captain to a midday drink and in chatting to us, he told us that the morning cock-crow was from Dyack fighting cocks. He also said that he hoped to get Marsh and me ashore tomorrow at Miri, but it would depend on the weather, as it is a very exposed anchorage, and can blow up quickly, making it unpleasant, or even impossible, to return by launch to the ship.

We share a table with the Bs in the dining saloon, and Mr B is already beginning to set Marsh and me a-tooth-agrind! He's a proper Jimmy Know-all, wordy and pompous, added to which he treats his wife and the stewards alike . . . both as slaves, and not deserving the smallest courtesy. Marsh and I let our hair down over Scrabble and liqueurs after dinner, and felt much better for it!

We anchored at Miri at midnight.

Sunday 15th June. Miri.
I decided I couldn't face Mr B at breakfast, and so had fruit in my cabin instead.

It was a hot morning, the sea calm, and so when told the launch would take us ashore at 9.00 am, Marsh and I gathered up our cameras. The run in took half an hour; the shoreline was flat and long, offering no shelter. We pottered out of the Customs house into the little town and went to look round the market, where we bought mangoes, chicus and thin-skinned green oranges, which were sweet and juicy. I saw turtle eggs, so bought some to take back to the ship for dinner. I noticed a few grey clouds gathering.

It was hotter than ever, but we wandered down a long road, bordered by spreading flame-trees in full bloom. In the shade of them there was a gathering of young men, and we went to investigate. They were surrounding a Strong Man advertising some magic patent Body-Building Elixir, by a great demonstration of glistening muscle, and by having his chum lean on the end of a spear, with its point touching Goliath's throat: the spear first bent and then broke, of course!

A taxi took us out of town to the old Rest House, an old colonial type wooden house on stilts, next to the Government Residency, now occupied by the local Chinese governor. It was in an area of what had once been beautiful government houses, set high with distant views out to sea, but now the unfenced gardens with frangipani, bougainvillaea and alamanda are run down, the houses shabby and uncared for, with rubbish drifting everywhere; the Rest House was deserted, so we returned to Miri in our taxi.

It had begun to spot with rain.

We thankfully found the air-conditioned Park Hotel, where we ordered large cool drinks, and stayed until it was time to make tracks for our launch. By this time it was pouring with rain, and our taxi tried to charge an exorbitant sum for driving us the few hundred yards to the Customs House, but the driver soon realised we were not the greenhorns we looked. It was now deluging, and we were soaked to the skin, and the sea was white-capped and choppy. The half-hour run back to the ship was quite exciting, and I watched Marsh a little anxiously, as she'd told me she was not a good sailor, but she remained rosy and cheerful. However, we did wonder if the last laugh would be on us, as the Captain had told us that in a swell, sometimes passengers had be lifted on board from the launch in a basket; we had hardly believed him, but on reaching the ship's side, we realised it was going to be tricky for the launch to pull alongside the gangway, in the limited space left by the lighters moored fore and aft of it, they, and we, all bobbing about in the swell.

Eventually I made a leap round the angle of the unstable gangway rail, carrying our bags and shopping, and then Marsh too safely bridged the gap. It was all great fun, but we decided we'd not bother to go ashore at Miri again.

Our turtle eggs for dinner were not a conspicuous success. The first I ate was undoubtedly bad, and I had to beat a hasty retreat to get rid of it; Mr B took one reluctantly, never having had one before, and voiced guarded appreciation; Marsh gallantly swallowed hers and loudly acclaimed it as delicious, but I think only out of kindness to me! Mrs B chickened out altogether, and there were no takers from the other table to which I had sent some.

We berthed at Labuan during the night.

Monday 16th June. Labuan.
A hot day, humid and steaming after yesterday's pouring rain.

I was ashore early and went to find the market to buy local fruit. There are always apples, oranges and bananas available onboard, but never anything more imaginative, or local. I met the Chief Steward, with whom I've made friends, who said he'd been buying some local fruit for us, but even so, I went on and bought more, delighted to find the first mangosteens of the season.

Wandered back to the Customs gates, where I persuaded a clerk to give me a pass enabling me to take a taxi up the long jetty to the ship, to collect Marsh, who because of her leg trouble, cannot walk far. She was ready, and off we went to see the Second World War cemetery in the centre of the island. This is an area cleared from the jungle, the grass mown like velvet, with flowering shrubs and trees planted among and around the head-stones. It was beautifully kept, and absolutely quiet; like Kranji in Singapore, there was an almost tangible aura of peace and resignation about it.

We then drove across the island to the point on the far shore where the Japanese had surrendered to the Australians in 1945, on a grassy clearing under coconut palms.

The scent of flowers hung over the little island; we drove through padi, market gardens and coconut groves, and we passed the pretty blue and white mosque.

We returned to *Kimanis* for lunch, and sailed at 3.00 pm.

Tuesday 17th June. Kota Kinabalu.
We moored alongside the jetty at Kota Kinabalu at 6.00 am having lain offshore at anchor all night. A cool grey morning, with no rain.

With breakfast of mangosteens and pomelo came a note from Mansfield's agent, saying he would be away, but his deputy, a Mr Mitchell, would call on us at 9.00 am. He was pleasant and friendly, and told us that we were invited to lunch by Mr Duffy, the British High Commissioner. First Mr Mitchell took us to the golf club, which was right on the beach; we paddled but did not swim, for the sea was muddy and dirty after the rain. Later we were told we'd been wise for an English woman on holiday had recently been stung while swimming, by a submerged jellyfish, and had died fifteen minutes later!

Mr Duffy was a bit sticky when we first met him, but soon thawed, and the lunch-party was fun. We met Mr and Mrs Pavet, some New Zealanders from the Education Department, he is the Manager of the Port Authority. Both were easy and friendly.

After lunch Mrs Pavet took us shopping, and I bought a funnel-shaped porter's basket, two feet high, eighteen inches diameter at the top, narrower at the base; the women porters carry them on their backs with straps round their shoulders and foreheads. It is beautifully made and decorated, in split bamboo, and will remind Michael of the charms of his girl porter on his recent climb of Mount Kinabalu with Charles Letts.

The following day we were collected by Victor Lim, a nice-looking young Chinese who is Harrison and Crosfield's agent. He and his wife drove us up to Kota Belud, 53 miles north-east of Kota Kinabalu.

To begin with the country was flat, residential suburbia, giving way to padi and small-holdings, with occasional magnificent views of Mount Kinabalu, 13,455 ft, rearing into the sky in purple and blue peaks. It was revealed, which is unusual, for normally the summit is obscured by cloud by 9.00 or 10.00 am.

In places the road was being mended by gangs of women, who in their vivid batik *kebayas* (blouses), over black trousers, and brightly coloured hats, resembled clusters of butterflies. We saw mango and avocado trees, laden with fruit, and so had to stop to buy some; grey buffaloes in mud pools gazed at us as we passed.

Gradually the road started to rise and we found ourselves looking down on a wide river, across which was a bamboo and wire suspension foot-bridge, which dipped and swayed as women carrying large baskets and bundles on their heads crossed over it. We crossed further along, on a narrow concrete bridge with no parapet nor railing at the side; the car was just the right width to cross, but we were told that many vehicles go over the edge in monsoon periods, when the river and winds are high.

We passed rubber plantations, unkempt with undergrowth rambling uncontrolled between the trees: very different from the immaculate avenues in Western Malaysia, which stretch like the aisles of vaulted cathedrals as far as the eye can see.

The further we drove, the nearer we came to Mt. Kinabalu (the Chinese Widow), and we stopped several times as we rounded a blind corner, and she suddenly loomed ahead, rising blue above the lower foothills.

At the small village of Tamparuli, there was a market under the shade of many trees; we stopped to wander through it, and Marsh bought some crisp golden finger-length flakes of fried and sugared tapioca, which were delicious. In one corner, in an arc on the ground, sat a group of women selling compacted three inch cubes of tobacco, and betel nut prepared like shiny brown sugar cubes. The women were middle-aged and handsome, spotlessly clean in their gay batik, and pleased to have their photographs taken. There was much joking and laughter, and an old man nearby, pointing at my camera, hopped up and down excitedly, shouting with delight:

The market in Tamparuli, Borneo, 1969.

'Cee Nay Ma! Cee Nay Ma!' Sad for them that I was no Hollywood talent scout!

After Tamparuli the road climbed steeply, sometimes entirely shut in by the jungle, wafts of flower scent filling the car; the next moment we glimpsed, far below, a tiny flat valley, its padi and *attap* dwellings like dolls' houses on a draughts board, a river shining like molten tin in the sun, and distant islands on the horizon.

We stopped once more in Kota Belud; the market here was roofed but open-sided, so one could wander in shaded comfort along the rows of stalls. I bought a bamboo gourd flute, but alas! I never learned how to play it.

After lunch at the Rest House above the town, we set off to return to the ship.

We sailed at 6.00 pm and watched the pinks of the setting sun reflected across the sky in the clouds round Mt. Kinabalu, and on her summit which stood out above them. We passed through islands on a calm blue sea; gradually the light faded, darkness wrapped the islands, and the ship was once more enveloped in the cocoon of night.

Thursday 19th June. Kudat.

Having been warned that the call at Kudat would be brief, I was ashore by 0710, the ship having moored alongside an hour earlier. Captain Davies had told us that there was little of interest there, but I don't like to risk missing anything. In fact there was nothing remarkable about the tiny port, and in ten minutes I'd walked up the only street, finding nothing but little shops selling everything from cord to curry-powder, and fly-swats to flip-flops. I walked on, and found a smelly creek with small fishermen's wooden shacks on stilts, roofed with corrugated iron, and many scruffy boats, some being lived in, and filth strewn everywhere; one such boat was being built on a make-shift slip: it was about 30 ft long, with thick ribs of timber and 1½" planks forming the hull.

I was back on board for breakfast, and we enjoyed an inactive day after the excitements of Kota Kinabalu yesterday.

Friday 20th June. Sandakan.

We woke to find the ship at anchor in a large bay a hundred miles wide in which lay many small islands. There being no berth available in the port, *Kimanis* must wait for one, and is unlikely to go alongside until tomorrow.

Marsh and I had been offered an escorted tour of the town in the afternoon by Alan Atkins, of the Malaysia-Australia Road Projects Company, who collected us by launch after lunch, and took us on a shopping tour of the town. Marsh bought some Borneo pearls, large flat blisters, grown artificially by inserting a bead in an oyster-shell, in one of the river-bed farms. I didn't like them, but found some attractive turquoise glazed flower pots, slightly bell-shaped, which will be filled with orchids and put on our veranda in Singapore.

A Mrs Peg Guy had written me a note, suggesting she takes us out to the game reserve eighteen miles out of town, where young orang-utans are reared having been orphaned by poachers. She had been asked by Claude Fenner to look out for our arrival, and said she would pick us up at 0900 the next day.

She arrived in a Land Rover which seemed to be full of children, one of whom was hers. She is Australian, vivacious, talkative and very amusing. She kept up a lively commentary throughout the drive, on Borneo development and way of life, shouting through from where she crouched with the children, most uncomfortably, I thought, in the back, while Marsh and I sat in front with the native driver. (Note: The word 'native' is not in any way derogatory in Borneo; on the contrary, those to whom it applies are proud to be so-called, rather than Chinese, Malay, etc.)

At length we turned off the metalled road, and bounced along a rough laterite track for a few miles, till we came to a clearing in the jungle, with several cages, at present unoccupied but used for sick or newly arrived very young animals in need of full-time care for short spells. As soon as they are strong enough, they are freed into the jungle, from which they return to be fed until they are able to fend for themselves; even then, they often return to visit their erstwhile human caretakers.

There were about twelve red orang-utans when we arrived, some playing high in the trees, some lying in the undergrowth, and three young ones at the top of a pole playing with the ropes and chains fixed to it for their amusement. All eyes switched to us, and several of the animals ambled toward us; one fully grown one ran up to Peg and took a flying leap into her arms, where she cuddled and nursed it, and indeed only disengaged herself with difficulty, so affectionately entwined round her neck was it! This was Stella, one that had become very tame in the reserve from early babyhood, but which now lives entirely free in the forest; Peg has known her for several years, and is thus always warmly greeted.

The children had gone off to find a baby gibbon monkey, which had been found motherless when it was still unweaned; it too was cuddled and stroked, and was a most endearing little creature. One of its older relatives was leaping about in the vines overhead, swinging and springing from one to another, and large orang-utans were crashing about in the tree-tops nearby.

(Orang-utans are only found in Borneo and Indonesia, and were then, in 1969, nearly extinct. The local government had only realised five years earlier that they must be preserved and protected to prevent them from dying out, so this reserve was started, and has been most successful in rearing young motherless animals and rehabilitating them in the wild. The word 'orang-utan' means 'red man'.)

After dinner on board, Marsh fetched some new playing cards, and we decided we'd play bezique. The game went well until it dawned on us that something was not quite right, and on counting the cards, we discovered we were eight short from the two packs! We abandoned our game, and on the spur of the moment we thought we'd go ashore for a drink at the nearby new 'Nak' hotel. There we were received by a gross and leering Sikh, who ushered us up to a first-floor darkened night-club, in which there were only six Chinese men, and a bored sequinned singer, wailing into a mike. Our arrival was greeted with a stunned silence, but we ordered drinks, of which I cautiously verified the brands of spirits, and after a slightly hysterical half-hour we returned to the mundane security of our ship.

Peg Guy collected me the next morning to go swimming at Perhala Island, at the entrance to the harbour, Marsh having chosen to stay onboard. Several families embarked from the Yacht Club in a Harrison Crosfield launch which took us out to the high rocky island, which was wooded on its landward side, and fell sheer to a long sandy beach to seaward. We spent a glorious morning there, but saw a number of purple Portuguese Man-O'-War jellyfish and did not dally long in the water in consequence; someone else had died on this beach recently, within minutes of being stung.

When we sailed that afternoon, there was a large gathering on the jetty of obviously well-to-do natives, seeing off newly embarking passengers. There were some middle-aged women in colourful sarongs and *kebayas*, with necklaces and earrings of gold coins, and with brilliant chiffon scarves gracefully draped over their chignoned hair and shoulders. All were animated and gay, and made an attractive sight; one younger woman stood apart, tall and full of figure, with graceful upright carriage; she wore a sarong of large blue, purple and bright pink checks, with an emerald green chiffon *kebaya* and head drapery; she had three large gold coins hanging between her breasts, and was vivid and elegant.

We took onboard a large pontoon during lunch, when the whole ship lurched as it was lifted inboard; it sits thwart the ship just aft of my cabin windows, and is held there by two derricks and huge hooks and hawsers. I hope nothing slips!

Monday 23rd June. Lahad Datu.

During the night we sailed round the north-east point of Borneo, and down into the Celebes Sea, then turned south into Darvell Bay and anchored off Lahad Datu. No shore leave was allowed, but a large amount of heavy cargo was unloaded, tractors, road-making and timber-clearing equipment, and to get at this from the hold, the pontoon had first to be lifted off the casing and into the sea, moored alongside, and then hoisted back onboard again.

We sailed again mid-morning, and we were invited up to 'monkey island', the small deck above the bridge, to watch the ship pass through the Straits of Semporna, which are between two coral reefs, running through a string of islands; this passage is only navigable in daylight. We had hoped for sunshine and low tide so as to see the reef coral, but the tide was high and the sky overcast. Even so, it was a wonderful half-hour of beautiful scenery and sand-bar with pounding surf below.

We berthed alongside at Tawau at dusk, where work began at once unloading cargo.

Tuesday 24th June. Tawau.

Marsh has a heavy cold, so will remain onboard today.

I went ashore to explore the town, and called on Mr Welsh, the local manager of the Hong Kong and Shanghai Bank, to whom Joe Lever had written from Singapore, introducing me. He is a pleasant young man, who invited us to dinner to meet John Anselmi, who might be able to arrange for us to go up-country tomorrow.

I looked round the busy little town, searching for sea-shells, and visited the fish and fruit markets. Back onboard at lunch-time, I found a swarthy Philippino awaiting me at the top of the gangway, with a sack of shells. He tipped it out on deck, and when he realised it was quality we wanted, and not just quantity, he sent a boy back to his boat on the other side of the wharf (to which he brings small cargoes of Philippino goods to trade here). The buzz quickly got round, for soon we were inundated with small dark men, all bringing bags, baskets and sacks of shells, large and small. We both collect them, and when I brought out my book on shells, the men looked through it, shouting with glee when they spotted an illustration they recognised, and some ran back to their boats to fetch yet more; it took half an hour to choose what we wanted, and half an hour to persuade them we had enough and wanted them to leave! They were charming people, grinning and as excited as us over the hunt for treasure. (It is essential to find shells that have been fished while their occupants are still alive; empty, or dead, shells are tumbled about in the sea, and quickly lose their colour and gloss.)

I was looking in my shell book after the Philippinos had left, when I found that one variety, *Volute aulica*, is rare and only found in the Philippines; I knew there were many more which we had not selected, so after lunch, I set out, with one example held high in one hand, and wandered among the boats. I soon had a crowd round me on the wharf, all of us squatting round mounds of shells, bargaining, laughing and jabbering away; it was the greatest fun, and I eventually returned onboard sweaty but triumphant.

Tom and Brenda Welsh had a drink with us when they came to pick us up that evening to go to dinner with them. Marsh had cried off due to her cold. They had also invited Brenda's sister Heather, and her husband John Anselmi, who owns a large cocoa estate up-country. They were all in their twenties and thirties, John being the eldest; he offered to take us to see his estate the next day. It was a delightful evening, everyone lively and amusing; they were two most attractive couples.

I looked in on Marsh before going to bed, she looked wretched, and is opting out of tomorrow's trip.

Wednesday 25th June.
John rapped on my cabin door at 0700, demanding loudly if I was ready. I shushed him, and we crept down the gangway. Heather had not come, so John and I set off in his comfortable car, and drove out of the town and up into the jungle. Most vehicles are jolted to pieces in a few months by the rough dirt and laterite roads up-country, but after two years, John's car still glides smoothly without a rattle: a good advertisement for Mercedes.

We drove between 100–200 ft high trees, some swathed from crown to ground with a creeper heavy with scarlet flowers. At length we reached the cocoa plantation of small bushy trees ten to twenty feet high, under feathery shade trees (cocoa must have filtered sunlight, and very moist leaf-mould for its shallow roots). The leaves are oval, six to eight inches long, and those at the tip of each sprig are pink; the flowers grow straight from the trunk or thicker branches, and are tiny creamy stars. The developing pods are green, but when ripe turn bright yellow-orange, and are as long as the leaves; they are segmented like a cantaloupe melon.

We watched Ibans (local tribesman) breaking open the ripe pods with their *parangs* (long slightly curved knives) then scooping out the beans, which are surrounded in a sticky opaque mucus; I sucked a bean and found the mucus sweet and fresh, almost citrus. The beans are then fermented by being left in large covered crates for a few days; the mucus heats and ferments and it is this process which gives the bean its chocolate flavour. Before fermentation, cocoa beans taste bitter and are unappetising, but after being dried they are like bitter chocolate; they resemble flattened brazil nuts. After drying, the beans are bagged up for shipping to Cadbury's and Van Houtens, two of the companies which buy John's product.

John told me that he now owns a very large plantation, having bought the land several years ago when there was a slump in cocoa, and planters were forced to sell out or switch to palm oil production; now there is a glut of palm oil, and shortage of cocoa! [This was in 1969.]

I was by then famished and thirsty, having missed breakfast, so we drove to one of the labour lines high in the hills, where there was a shop of sorts, and I was revived with a bottle of some rather suspect 'Orange' drink, and a packet of stale Chinese biscuits; they tasted like manna, and, refreshed, we resumed the tour.

Oil palm next, and after driving through the jungle, we came to the experimental plantation, where John is trying to develop a strain with a heavier oil yield. This is a new venture, with no results as yet.

We stopped to look at an old hemp plantation; there is no demand for it now that it has been superseded by nylon. I was interested to learn that hemp is a variety of the banana plant, and looks exactly the same; the hands of fruit form, but do not mature. John lifted some fibres from the outer glass-smooth sheath of the main stem, stripping one from the top to the ground, about ten feet long; he asked me to break it: it cut my hand and remained intact.

We drove on to the top of the watershed, along tracks a foot deep in mud, caused by the heavy timber-working equipment up there. Colossal trees were being felled by Dyack workers using chain-saws: bilian, which is so hard it will never rot, and so heavy that it has to be transported by road, as it sinks in river or sea; seria, red, yellow or white, beautiful trees soaring 200 ft high, with clean reddish boles, no branches till the crown is reached on the roof of the forest. These trees are searched out and felled by the timber speculators, then dragged out by enormous tractors with powerful fork-lift and hinged jaws, which rip up the floor of the forest: the rape of the jungle, John calls it.

We started back for lunch, but were seduced into stopping again and again by glimpses of hornbills flying through the trees; by a carpet of purple leguminous flowers like lupins, underplanted through a whole plantation of oil palm, to re-nitrogenise the soil; by the many wild orchid plants still clinging to the tops of felled trees awaiting transport out of the forest. We gathered some of these, for me to try to smuggle into Singapore, where orchid fanciers among my Chinese friends always wanted specie varieties from which to hybridise new ones.

Another halt was to observe through field-glasses two swarms of wild bees resting high on the silver bole of a giant *Kayu Rajah* (King of the Forest), rising fifty feet or more above the other tall jungle trees.

At last we rejoined the metalled road, and drove back like Jehu, where we arrived an hour late for lunch, to find Heather smiling and unperturbed.

John took me back to the ship after lunch, and in the evening he and Heather came onboard for a drink and to meet Marsh. They are such a charming couple, and I will always remember with gratitude the wonderful day John gave me, and for giving up so much of his time.

Thursday 26th June. At sea.
We sailed early from Tawau, and after breakfast, Mr and Mrs B, Marsh and I went up on the high deck above the bridge again, for the return passage through the Straits of Semporna. Alas! There was still no sun, as on the outward passage, but at least the tide was low, so the sand bar was exposed, and we could watch hundreds of reef egrets feeding in the shallows. Many small fishing boats were out, with men balancing on high bowsprits, spear fishing; among each group of boats was one small one with only a child in it, standing thrashing the surface of the sea with a long pole, presumably 'beating' for the fishermen.

There followed a quiet day, with no sun and a deliciously cool breeze. In the evening, at our request, the ship's cook served a Chinese dinner, which we all enjoyed as a change from the usual menu, and then Marsh and I played noisy games of Racing Demon on deck.

Friday 27th June. Sandakan.
We berthed alongside early, far too early, we thought, for Peg Guy to
come down to the ship as she had said she would, to take us to a shell-
shop. But Peg is indefatigable, and at 0830 she walked into the dining-
room, calling loudly for coffee; stewards scuttled hither and thither, I
dashed up to find Marsh, who was still not dressed, and who came
exactly as she was in her zip-up short dressing gown! (The ship was to
sail again at 10.00 am, so there was no time to lose.)

Luckily the ship was not far from the shell shop, and when we
reached it, it seemed only to sell baskets of dried fish: squid, sea-slugs,
sharks' fins and sea-horses, the last to go to Japan, to make 'eye
medicine' we were told. The stench was appalling, but ranged on
dusty shelves, behind the sacks and barrels, were hundreds of shells of
every imaginable variety, large and small. I climbed up and over every
obstacle to reach the more inaccessible shelves, while Peg and Marsh
concentrated on boxes pulled out for them by the amazed Chinese
shop-keeper. At first he wanted to give us all we selected, and could
not understand our excitement, but when I spotted an antique native
gong, his business sense revived, and after some hard bargaining, I
bought it and also a handful of sea-horses and some shells. Marsh came
away delighted with her choice, and we then dashed back to the ship,
where almost as soon as we were onboard, the gangway was raised, and
Peg waved us good-bye as the ship moved seaward.

A newly loaded cargo was a consignment of sea-shells for onward
transit to Japan to make mother-of-pearl buttons; they were conical,
about three inches in diameter at the base, and the same in height;
they had recently been fished, and their occupants were still alive. The
large net which contained them was put out on deck just below my
cabin windows; the stench from the slowly dying fish in the hot
sunshine was horrific! Luckily I only had to endure it for one night,
for they were off-loaded at the next port of call.

Saturday 28th June. Kudat and Kota Kinabalu.
We berthed at Kudat in the small hours, but only spent two hours
there.

All day we sailed south-west along the coast, enjoying magnificent
views of Mount Kinabalu, the summit rising clear against the sky
above the clouds enveloping the lower slopes.

There was an exciting race to beat another ship also trying to reach the one available berth at Kota Kinabalu; the loser would have to ride out at anchor overnight, causing a tiresome delay in unloading and loading freight. The *Kimanis* throbbed under full power as we surged toward the harbour, where we berthed successfully just ahead of our rival.

Marsh and I dashed ashore to do some shopping before the guests arrived whom we'd invited to drinks. She bought a batik sarong for Trevor to have made into a shirt, and I found a glorious plant, *Philanopsis grandioso*, the Borneo White Butterfly orchid, for which I had been searching at every port of call.

The friends we had met here on the outward voyage all came onboard, and also Bill Cook, the local head of Harrison Crosfield, who had then been away; he is a delightful and amusing bachelor, strongly resembling Rex Harrison, the film star. Marsh and I agreed he must cause many a maiden's heart to flutter, and perhaps some matrons' too! The Mitchells came, and also Tom Duffy, and we were a gay and noisy gathering until they left at 7.45 pm.

A handsome Malay family embarked this evening, obviously well-to-do. The woman was much ornamented with gold rings and bangles, and a cluster of twenty gold sovereign-sized coins was pinned to her *kebaya*. Her husband was tall, and slim, with refined features that could almost be Spanish; the woman also had the same facial structure, although their teenage son looked more eastern; they all were dark-skinned, and were a distinguished trio. They had a mare and foal with them in two crates, which were hoisted on to the deck near my cabin windows. The family were very concerned about the animals, and fed them handfuls of green fodder from four bulging sacks they had brought with them. Later they bedded down on mats near the horses, the woman covering herself completely with her sarong, but when the wind blew up in the night, they moved below.

Sunday 29th June. Labuan.
As soon as we berthed alongside, the foal became restless in its crate and began to kick and even attempted to shy and buck and rear. I was alarmed lest it should damage itself; the mare never moved. The family with their horses disembarked at 8.00 am. I wonder about them, what their background is, and where they were going.

A number of passengers are disembarking here, so we shall not have to scramble so early in the morning for the more comfortable chairs!

Spoken too soon, for four more joined, a young colourless female missionary, who is very earnest: Marsh and I agree she will be unlikely to convert us! Three 'Gaiety Girls' as we have nicknamed them, rather stringy women in their fifties; they are all tall, very thin, and with the leathery complexions that Western women acquire who have spent too long in the sun or a tropical climate.

We were delayed all day here by unexpected cargo to be loaded. It has been very hot, humid and airless, and we were glad to sail in time for our cabins to cool down from the breeze of our passage before going to bed.

Monday 30th June. Miri.
Another brief visit here, berthing early and sailing again by 0900.

Four Dyacks (men) embarked to join the deck passengers, and I was lucky enough to see them before they put on their shirts, and so was able to see clearly their body tattoos from shoulder to waist, and the painful five or six inch pattern of 'manhood' up the front of their throats; this custom distinguishes Dyacks from all other tribes. One of the four had the torso tattoos, but none on his throat, so he could have been from another tribe, or not willing to undergo the agony of the throat operation. The women of the tribe are not tattooed.

In the evening Mr and Mrs B challenged Marsh and me to a Scrabble battle, which we preceded at dinner with a bottle of champagne to stimulate our brain cells; this, on opening, was found to be flat.

'No bang when cork come out!' said Aschid the bar steward, with a look of misery on his normally cheerful face, so as it was the last bottle onboard, we had to make do with white Chianti. Cabinet pudding was on the menu, and good and solid it looked; we encouraged our adversaries to have some, and it seemed to have the desired effect of stultifying their thought processes, for we beat them soundly, and Marsh and I went smugly to bed!

Tuesday 1st July. Pendeng.
A very hot night indeed; I was reduced to winding a towel around my neck and down my cleavage in a vain attempt to keep the sheets dry.

Pendeng at 8.00 am. Not a breath stirring up the long swampy river, and an overpowering smell of steaming mud and swamp.

We'd dropped, and picked up more deck passengers by 9.00 am, and were off again on the last lap to Singapore. Returning down river, we looked out for crocodile and monitor lizards in the swamp, but saw nothing.

As we left Borneo behind, the usual welcome sea breeze picked up, and we enjoyed a cool day on deck.

Wednesday 2nd July. Singapore.
Our last day at sea. We anchored in the outer roads at 6.45 pm; immigration and Customs came onboard (I had hidden my orchid plants behind my shower curtain, for the import of plants into Singapore was forbidden without a licence).

A stream of sampans came out to the ship, pushing and jostling to get to the gangway, where the deck passengers were clustered with their varied baggage, waiting to get ashore. There was much shouting, swearing and haggling with the boat-boys. The sea was quite choppy, and people were crowding and shoving to get down the unsteady gangway, and then leaping onto the rising and falling bows of the sampans, which were all the time being edged aside by the next one touting for custom. It was chaotic, and great fun to watch from the deck above.

We had dinner, and then saw a naval launch approaching through the darkness. Michael and Trevor came aboard, and Aschid brought forbidden drinks to our cabins (the bar had been closed as soon as we entered territorial waters).

As soon as the gangway had cleared, we finally disembarked, bidding sad farewells to kind Captain Davies and the crew. My orchids remained in my cabin, and were magicked ashore via the naval base the next day.

And so I closed my journal of my memorable Borneo experience.

CHAPTER 20

Last Naval Occasions

In July James and Emma flew out to spend their last school holidays in Singapore, during which we made many 'last time' visits to favourite spots; supper from itinerant food stalls in the open air night markets; launch picnics out to Raffles lighthouse; morning shopping expeditions to China-town, to see once more the Death Houses and the shops beneath them selling scale models in paper of everything a lonely spirit would need in his after-life: his house, his motor car, his furniture were all made of coloured paper glued to frames of split bamboo, in addition to which he would be supplied with packets of pretend paper dollars. All of this would be burned after his death, to rise in the form of smoke, to provide him with all the comforts in his spirit that he had been accustomed to on earth.

The same artisans who made these also made marvellous kites, and it was fun to watch kite-flying contests, when the strings had been coated with gum and powdered glass, to enable the contestants to fly their kites across the strings of their rivals, thus cutting them loose, so that they would fall, defeated, to the ground.

In August we went on a last family expedition up into Malaya; we drove up to the Cameron Highlands, where we rented a small house. It was blissfully cool, and a relief to escape the heavy humidity of Singapore for a few days.

While there we were able to arrange for a local guide to escort us to an Orang Asli (Aborigine) village in the jungle, occupied by the Semai tribe. We drove out of Kuala Lumpur to the north, and then, leaving the car, had a long walk along jungle paths which seemed endless, and were not easy walking. At one point we had to cross a river, and the only means of doing so was by walking the length of a tree-trunk which bridged it; this was round, wet and slippery, and there was no rope nor nearby branches to hold onto. Emma and I looked at it in horror, and she exclaimed:

'I can't walk along that! I won't cross over – I can't! I can't!'

I was in complete agreement with her, but felt that I must set an example with bracing advice (which was as much to myself as to her), so I said briskly:

'Of course you can! It's quite easy; you just run across with your feet turned outwards. Look, like this! If I can do it, so can you!' and I somehow waddled across. Poor Emma was still in a panic, but when her father spoke sharply to her, she did manage to negotiate the nightmare somehow. She and I commiserated with each other, and we remember the incident clearly even today. Funnily enough, it didn't seem so bad on the returning trek; I think we took a deep breath, and just ran for it.

The village was in a clearing, with long-houses on stilts, access to which was up other slim tree-trunks with very inadequate wedged grooves cut up the length as footholds. We were invited inside one, where several families had their sleeping alcoves; in one, a woman was sitting by a cooking-fire in which she was roasting roots of tapioca, which is the aborigine staple diet in that region. We were each given one, which looked like an elongated blackened potato; we bit into them and found the flesh an unappetising opaque grey, but I enjoyed the flavour, which was not unlike sweet chestnut; the rest of the family was not so appreciative.

The aborigines were very friendly, and demonstrated their eight foot long blow-pipes, which they used to kill monkeys and other small animals, their only source of protein. On our return walk, we were met by a small man with long hair to his shoulders, wearing only a G-string, carrying a large stem of wild bananas on his back which was almost as big as he was. He was running through the trees, bowed down by his load, and did not stop to speak to us although our guide called out to him; he looked quite ape-like, a vivid reminder of our origins.

We visited a tea estate in the hills, and saw the women pickers plucking off the green tips and throwing them over their shoulders into large baskets on their backs. These were tipped on to long wire mesh trays to dry, and then would be rolled and packed for export.

On leaving the Cameron Highlands, we drove to the west coast and spent a few glorious days at Lumut, near Pangkor. We swam from long golden beaches and took boats to Emerald Island and other coves, enjoying long lazy days in the tropical paradise setting.

On our way back to Singapore we stayed a night at Kuala Lumpur with Claude and Joan Fenner, breaking us in for our return to civilisation.

The author, Emma, James and two Malay tea workers.

Back in Singapore the social round resumed. We were invited to a reception at Command House for HRH Princess Alexandra. As ever, she charmed everyone; we were presented to her, and afterwards remarked on her grace and dignity. She is truly an example for all Royals, world-wide, to emulate.

Guests came and went, and by far the most enjoyable visitor was Winn Everett, who was staying with her nephew Peter, a naval commander, and Penelope, his wife. They spared her to stay with us for a week, and it was great fun taking her round our haunts, and on a launch picnic. She always enjoyed everything so much and her appreciation and sense of fun was shared by all who met her.

During the monsoon period that winter, there was exceptionally heavy rainfall which persisted for several days, resulting in serious flooding. Singapore lies very low, hardly above sea-level, so that at high tides, the flooded monsoon ditches bordering every road cannot drain into the sea; therefore roads become so deeply flooded as to be impassable.

We had moved to another house by then, on a steep rise above Cluny Road, so our house was not flooded, but the road at the foot of our drive was three feet deep. It was a national holiday, and so everyone was at home from their offices; it was wet and cheerless, and so I suggested to Michael that we telephone Anne and Tom Stocker, who had moved into our old house in Tanglin, and propose going round for a drink.

'Lovely!' said Anne, 'but how will you get here through the floods?'

'We'll walk,' I said, 'suitably clad, of course!'

Michael wore swimming-trunks and a short-sleeved shirt, and carried a Chinese paper umbrella, and I wore an old pair of shorts and a loose shirt, and also a rather dashing blue plastic shower cap resembling a mob cap, with a spray of plastic flowers stitched across the frill in front; we both had on our swimming shoes. We set off down our drive into the swirling water in Cluny Road; it came up to our thighs, but we waded on, causing much amusement to the Chinese we passed. There was no traffic, of course, so we walked on the crown of the road, where the water was slightly less deep. It was about a mile to the Stockers, who were waiting with warm towels and hot toddies to greet us.

As our departure drew nearer, farewell parties for us began, the pace increasing as time grew shorter. The Tan Chin Tuans gave an amazing farewell dinner for us at Raffles hotel; it was a marvellous evening, which ended with Chin Tuan making an affectionate and delightful speech, which was totally unexpected.

Meanwhile the unhappy situation at Homme unfolded, as described in a previous chapter, and the days moved relentlessly on towards our dreaded return home to what awaited us there, and of course Michael was sad at the thought of his imminent retirement.

His naval career ended in mid-December, when we flew home with a forty-eight hour stop-over in Rome to gather our energy and courage. This was not a good idea, for it was cold and wet there, and we both wanted to get back to resolve the situation.

James and Emma joined us at Homme for Christmas, a dreary holiday; Kyrle and Ernle each tried to justify their actions to Michael, but the heart had gone out of the family, and we four decided we must leave Homme as soon as possible.

We found a house at Camberley which we rented briefly while Michael looked for a job. He officially retired from the Navy on 1st April, and we emerged from beneath the umbrella of security in the Services, into civilian life. He was offered the post of Naval Sales Manager in the armaments division of Hawker Siddeley in Hatfield,

Admiral Sir Peter Hill-Norton presents HRH Princess Alexandra to the author and Michael. Ann Hibbert is in the background.

and we began house-hunting in Hertfordshire. It is not an interesting or beautiful part of the country, and I found it more and more depressing. Gradually we extended our search further eastward, and eventually found the house we have lived in happily for over twenty-five years now, in a picturesque small rural village in the north-east corner of the county.

Shortly after joining Hawker Siddeley, Michael was offered the post of General Manager of the Middle East Navigation Aids Service, based in Bahrain. This company is responsible for the lighthouses, lightships and buoys in and around the Arabian Gulf, and was the job Michael always said he'd love to have after he retired from the Navy, so he was delighted; his employers at Hawker Siddeley were tolerant and understanding, and agreed to release him, and so once more he left the shores of England, and its present unhappy associations, and returned to the Middle East. I stayed at home to provide a base for James and Emma, and we all flew to and from Bahrain for holidays from time to time.

And so ended the naval chapters of my life, and a new era began, full of opportunity for travel of a different kind, and many other adventures.

Index

Rank and appointment given are as held at the time.